REVIVAL
IN THE
RUBBLE

REVIVAL
IN THE
RUBBLE

*How God Rebuilds
His Broken People*

JOHN KITCHEN

John Kitchen
Isa. 57:15

CLC
PUBLICATIONS
Fort Washington, PA 19034

Revival in the Rubble

ISBN: 0-87508-873-2

Copyright 2006 John A. Kitchen

Published by CLC Publications

U.S.A.
P.O. Box 1449, Fort Washington, PA 19034

GREAT BRITAIN
51 The Dean, Alresford, Hants. SO24 9BJ

AUSTRALIA
P.O. Box 213, Bungalow, Cairns, QLD 4870

NEW ZEALAND
10 MacArthur Street, Feilding

to

Lou

Thanks for telling me of Jesus

Contents

Foreword.. 9

Preface... 11

PART I — *The Person of Revival*

1   Becoming a Person of Influence... 17

PART II — *The Preparation for Revival*

2   Make It or Break It.. 37

3   Real-World Revival... 51

4   I Don't Even Know Where to Begin!.................................67

5   Big Job, Little Time... 83

6   When Opposition Mounts.. 97

7   Flawed Foundations... 113

8   A Bull's-Eye on Your Back... 131

9   We've Got It All—But Something's Missing.................. 145

PART III — The Profile of Revival

10 The Power of God's Word...................................... 163

11 It's My Fault!... 183

12 I the Undersigned Hereby 197

PART IV — The Perpetuation of Revival

13 To Obscurity—and Beyond!................................ 215

14 Joy in the Lord... 229

15 A Creeping Compromise..................................... 243

Endnotes... 259

Foreword

You must do more than simply read this book. *Why?* Because God wants to do something magnificent in your heart and mine, and in the heart of our struggling nation. He is searching for people who are broken, prayerful, and wholly surrendered to Him, people with whom He can share and satisfy the single greatest passion of His heart—revival. Pastor John Kitchen reminds us that this is what God found in a layman by the name of Nehemiah. And that is why it is critical that those who care about the glory of God, and the destiny of our nation, prayerfully ponder this powerful and passionate plea for spiritual awakening.

It's interesting that exactly one hundred fifty years ago God raised up a "layman" in New York City to become a modern-day Nehemiah. His name was Jeremiah Lanphier. God used this surrendered servant to lead God's people and our nation into what has commonly become known as the Third Great Awakening. Though we haven't seen a nationwide revival since that remarkable outpouring, both Nehemiah and Lanphier engender hope that God will "do it again."

Nehemiah was an unlikely candidate to become a revival leader. He had never been to the homeland of his beloved people, the Jews. He didn't have firsthand knowledge of what was at stake for the people of God. Nor was he in a vocational position to help. He was not a theologian, a priest, or even a prophet. But he had heard about the condition of Jerusalem and the distress of his people. And because he was broken and surrendered, God was able to work through him to restore His people and their city to its prior glory.

Even if we don't envision ourselves being a Nehemiah, each of us can be a Hanani. When this messenger of the Lord arrived in Susa and expressed his concern over the condition of Jerusalem, did anyone expect Nehemiah to drop everything to become the torchbearer of revival? When we spread the truth about the rubble in our land today, God will use it to ignite passion in others and stir them to godly action.

Revival is not just a nice idea or another alternative. It is our *only* option . . . our *only* hope as a nation. As John Kitchen highlights, the book bearing Nehemiah's name is the last historical record we have before 400 years of silence settled over the people of God. God's silence, no matter what form it may take, or in whatever era it is experienced, is truly a fearful form of His judgment. It behooves us to take another look at what was on God's heart before those silent years if we are to comprehend what is on God's heart today.

I pray God will use this book to spark an authentic work of His Spirit in our day . . . that historians once again will be able to record that God visited America in revival! Read it carefully, prayerfully, and with a humble spirit of obedience, asking God to bring revival to your own heart. I don't know about you, but I want the thrill of telling my children and my grandchildren that I was there when God's Glory came. When ashes turned to beauty. When rubble turned to revival.

Byron Paulus
Executive Director,
Life Action Revival Ministries

Preface

We have heard with our ears, O God;
our fathers have told us what you did in their days,
in days long ago. (Psalm 44:1)

Why not here? Why not now? Why not us? These are the questions that I can't shake from my heart. We have heard with our ears what God has done in generations past. Is it all hype? Is it overstated, airbrushed propaganda? Or did it really happen? If it did, why doesn't it again? Why isn't it now? Why isn't it here?

Call it what you want—*revival* is a common term—but I want it. A deeper intimacy with God. A clearer evidence of His presence. A more powerful impact among and through His people. We expect more from our churches. We expect more from ourselves. We expect more from (gulp!) God.

Is it okay to admit that? I submit that it's not only acceptable, it's *required* if we are ever going to experience what God desires for us.

The state of things in our churches is not good. True, in America, eighty-five percent of people identify themselves as Christians and ninety-five percent say they believe in God as an all-powerful, all-knowing, perfect Creator who rules the world. Why then is the influence of such a massive throng so muted? If eighty-five percent are Christians, how can seven out of ten of us have no clue what John 3:16 means? How could only a third of our citizens know what "the gospel" is? How can nine out of ten of us fail to accurately describe Christ's Great Commission? Look within our own camp. How can nearly half of born-

11

again Christians say that Satan is not a personal being, but merely a symbol of evil? How can twenty-eight percent of born-again Christians believe that Jesus sinned while on earth? How can over one-fourth of born-again Christians preach that it doesn't matter what faith you follow because they all teach the same basic lessons? How can one-third of us say there are no moral absolutes? How can two-thirds of all regular church attenders admit to having never (yes, never!) experienced the presence of God in a church service?[1]

Rubble. It's all around us. We walk over it all the time. It's the crumbled superstructure of a previous generation's true spiritual experience with God. Most never notice that on which they trample. But every so often God awakens a heart and injects into it disturbing, unsettling questions: *Is revival really possible? In these days? Inside* my *heart? In the midst of a people like us?*

> *RUBBLE: THE CRUMBLED SUPERSTRUCTURE OF A PREVIOUS GENERATION'S TRUE SPIRITUAL EXPERIENCE WITH GOD.*

Nehemiah was just such an individual. He asked those same kinds of questions. The state of the people of God had never been lower. The condition of the nation of God had never been worse. The prospect of the promises of God being fulfilled had never look more unreasonable. The purposes of God appeared lost amid the rubble of what had once been.

Can God do it again? Will God do it again? Here? In me? In us? Or is this it? Do we need simply to dial back our expectations?

When God wants to do a fresh, reviving work in His people, He finds a person and breaks his heart. He makes that person look upon the state of God's people and work and then imparts to him the great grief that fills His own heart. When God wants to do a new thing, a fresh thing, a God-thing, He starts with one and breaks him. Then God draws out that brokenness in convulsive, compulsive, confessional praying.

That's what He did in Nehemiah's day. That's what He'll do in ours, if He should sovereignly grant us to experience a fresh outpouring of His Spirit.

God starts with one. Then He causes the fire of God to arc from that heart to a few others. They begin to believe . . . again. They begin to dream . . . again. He brings them to the place where they would rather die than live without the fullness of God. And they begin to tell God just that. They can't help it. They can't hold it back. They won't hold it back. They must. They will. They won't be dissuaded.

Is that your heart?

Do you agonize, wondering before God: Why not *here*? Why not *now*? Why not *us*? If so, read on.

Part I
The Person of Revival

Lord, revive the church—beginning with me.
— Samuel M. Shoemaker

Revival is God's finger pointing right at me.
— Wilbert L. McLeod

When God sovereignly determines to revive His people, He usually begins by awakening one person. The history of God's people is studded with the names of solitary souls who refused to let go of God until He blessed them. Their spiritual tenacity was first granted them by God and then used by Him to ignite a field of other parched souls. The result is always a sweeping move of the Spirit in which God is exalted, His people revived, and the lost converted.

In the thronging masses of newly awakened hearts, however, never lose sight of that one solitary figure who became the torch of God to set His people ablaze once again. God is always prior. His first move in revival is always to find one willing heart and break it. Nehemiah stands as a prototype of one so burdened and so blessed.

1

Becoming a Person
of Influence

*I*t's starting to come into focus. No, it's more than simply focus; it's a weight. You don't just *see* the need, you are starting to *feel* it. God is opening your eyes, but it's not simply a cognitive recognition that something is wrong, it's a burden that has come to rest upon your heart. You want to make a difference. You *must* make a difference; God is calling you.

How can *I* make a difference? If God is calling me to do something to influence His people, why am I still in this job? Why has He placed me in a family that seems so disinterested in the things of God? Why this school? This office? This neighborhood? This city?

Do the great dreams, hopes and aspirations that God has injected into your heart seem hopelessly detached from where it is God has set you? Ever wonder how you are going to get from where you are to that place where God is using you in significant, eternal ways?

You are not alone. You might be surprised at just how many people within close proximity of your life feel the same way. But there's another guy not so far from where you are who has felt that weight and wrestled with that frustration. He's only as

17

far away as your Bible.

His name is Nehemiah. In the Biblical book that bears his name, we discover him to be a man like us. The opening sentence ("The words of Nehemiah, son of Hacaliah," 1:1) informs us that what lies before us are basically Nehemiah's memoirs, his personal journal. In fact, peering into these pages we almost feel uneasy, as if we are looking in on intimate revelations of heart and spirit not meant for public consumption. It's like peeking into someone's diary. But our uneasiness is soon matched by a compelling familiarity. Not many lines into the book we catch the sound of a familiar echo. It is the sound of a frustrated man. We meet a man with a divinely given passion for the purposes of God, but one who wrestles with what God is doing in his life. Nehemiah's heart has been invaded with a desire to do something big for God. It's about to explode with a burden to be used by God.

Sound familiar?

Note that it was this kind of man that God chose to close out the historical record of the Old Testament. Malachi gives us the last prophetic word, but Nehemiah is the last historical record we have before 400 years of silence settled over the people God had chosen. Nehemiah served and then it was forty decades before God broke the silence in the person of John the Baptist as he announced the arrival of the Messiah, Jesus.

Nehemiah was like you and me; he simply wanted his life to matter when viewed through the lens of eternity. To understand something about our common struggle, we have to understand something about the times in which Nehemiah lived. You are all too familiar with the vexing conditions in which you live. Take a moment to familiarize yourself with Nehemiah's.

As a faithful Jewish man living four and a half centuries before Christ, Nehemiah found himself in a mess. The nation of God was in disarray. The kingdom of Judah was filled not just with people of common descent, but with a people of common desolation. Their dreams had been destroyed. David had led the nation of Israel to its zenith. They had been dreamy days of

God's blessing. Then Solomon came to the throne and, though blessed for a time, his unfaithfulness began to dissolve the spiritual threads that held the fabric of the kingdom together.

God had promised that discipline would follow unfaithfulness as the night the day (Deut. 28:15*ff*.). He had pledged to divide the nation and scatter its people (Deut. 28:64*ff*.; 1 Kings 11:9–13). No sooner was Solomon gone than ten tribes anointed one king and the other two tribes another (928 B.C.). For over 200 years the people of God lived divided from one another, growing increasingly corrupt and wandering farther from God with each passing decade. God, through His prophets, picked up the ancient warnings of discipline and made them new to each generation. Yet there was no turning back, at least not in a lasting and permanent way. God eventually brought the promised judgment. The northern kingdom of Israel was led off into captivity by the pagan kingdom of Assyria (722 B.C.). Then, in a series of failures the southern kingdom of Judah first saw their nobles led away by the Babylonians into captivity (605 B.C.), then the city of Jerusalem captured and their king led away (597 B.C.), and finally the walls reduced to rubble, the city burned, the temple destroyed and its holy articles for worship taken away to a land of idols (587 B.C.).

*I*N THE WORST OF TIMES, WE SHOULD BE ALERT TO A FRESH MOVE OF GOD. *H*E DELIGHTS TO BRING REVIVAL OUT OF RUBBLE.

The Jewish nation, as it had been known, ceased to exist, except in the heart and mind of God and in the heart and mind of a faithful remnant.

Nothing could have been worse. It was as bad as it could get for a believer. It was the end of everything that mattered.

It is in just such times that we should be most alert to a fresh work of God. He delights to bring revival out of the rubble. There, in the rubble, God unearths one of His promises and begins again.

In Nehemiah's day God went back to His Word (Jer. 25:11). God began to do a new thing, just as He had guaranteed. God began restoring His people. He began to restore His temple and the worship He desired from there. And He began to restore His holy city, Jerusalem.

Through the fall of the kingdom of Babylon and the rise of the Persian and Median kingdoms, God began this new work. He shaped the heart of a pagan king so that a man named Zerubbabel was able to lead approximately 50,000 of the Jews back to the city of Jerusalem (538 B.C.; Ezra 1–2). Then Ezra was able to lead approximately 1,500 more back to Jerusalem (458 B.C.; Ezra 7–10).

Zerubbabel's call had been to rebuild the temple in Jerusalem (Ezra 3–6). Ezra was called to reestablish the worship of God in that temple. Ezra came with the Word of God and said, "Now that we have a temple we ought to worship God according to His Word" (Ezra 7–10). But a partially repopulated city with a temple and regular services did not fully fulfill the plan and purposes of God.

God sent back our man, Nehemiah, to finish the job. His job was to restore the city of God. He was to rebuild the walls that had been destroyed. His calling was to bring revival in the rubble. And in the process, Nehemiah became a pattern for us as we seek a similar revival in our day.

What God did through Nehemiah was not merely to raise a physical wall, but also to become a pattern for how God would rebuild His broken people throughout the ages. Here we discover how God restores His church when we've blown it and, through our own doing, we are missing out on all God intended.

How does God rebuild His people in the midst of corporate failure? Every page of Nehemiah has something significant to say in answer to that. For now, however, let's stand back and discern a pattern that emerges when we observe Nehemiah's life in its entirety.

Nehemiah's own memoirs reveal that he held three positions or fulfilled three roles during his ministry. He was a cupbearer to the king (Neh. 1:1–2:10), a builder of the walls of Jerusalem (Neh. 2:11–6:19), and the governor of the city (Neh. 7:1–13:31). These three roles were tangible realities for Nehemiah, but they also paralleled a process that God was working out through his life in order to achieve God's purposes. That process is a repeated pattern wherever God uses a life to rebuild His broken people.

Begin to discern this pattern with me. *First, God grants you a position.*

We each come to that day when we take stock and we realize God has granted us a position somewhere, doing something. It isn't the same as what God grants the next guy or the big guy or the famous guy. But it's our position and it's given by God. It is, therefore, a divine assignment with a divine purpose behind it.

For Nehemiah, his position was cupbearer to the king of the Persian Empire. Over time, Nehemiah began to realize that this position had been granted him by God. He began to put two and two together and discovered a simple equation for figuring out what God is doing in a person's life and how He plans to use that for the good of His people and the glory of His name. The equation is simply stated as: *My position is granted that God might use me in His providence for His purpose.*

God has given you a position somewhere, in connection with some particular people, so that in His providence He might use you for His purposes.

Take the equation apart and examine its parts.

God has given you a *position.* Nehemiah confessed, "I was cupbearer to the king" (Neh. 1:11). Big deal. Compared to what Nehemiah knew God wanted to do for the glory of His name, what was being a cupbearer?

Perspective is everything, for in the eyes of the unbelieving Nehemiah had it made, simply because he was cupbearer. As cupbearer he tasted all wine and food before it reached the lips of the king. In a world of intrigue, someone was likely to poison the king. The cupbearer made certain all was well in the royal kitchen. You obviously want a trusted person in such a position. Simply putting the cup to your mouth without swallowing wouldn't suffice. No insincere "Mmmm" after sampling the buffet. The cupbearer had to be trustworthy.

Thus the cupbearer was not a mere lab rat employed to lessen assassination attempts. He was also a close advisor to the throne. The cupbearer wielded significant clout in the king's corner.

And there was Nehemiah! Ponder that for a moment. Just a couple of generations before, Nehemiah's ancestors had been lead off in captivity as defeated slaves. And now, in a providential turn of events, God had moved a Jewish slave's son into one of the most influential political positions in the kingdom.

It would be easy for us to think, "Way to go, Nehemiah! You've gotten yourself a cushy government job! Good for you!"

There's only one problem, Nehemiah's heart wasn't in his job. And his mind was forever wandering outside the royal courts. Nehemiah's dream was 800 miles away in a city called Jerusalem.

Have you ever found yourself saying something like, "If I really look at my life honestly, I've got it pretty good. I've got a lot more than many people do in this world. But I've got to admit, my heart's not in it anymore"?

That was Nehemiah's problem. Anyone else in that empire would have jumped at the chance to be cupbearer to the king. Nehemiah had a position. God had given him that position. But his heart was owned by another dream. He was consumed with a different, bigger vision.

Nehemiah had heard about those 50,000 of his brothers going back to Jerusalem with Zerubbabel. Perhaps he had listened to the pleas for others to join the 1,500 more who went back with Ezra. He wanted desperately to go, to throw caution to the wind, to move in faith, to join God in what He was doing. He longed to be a part of *God's* city, *God's* worship, and *God's* people. It's difficult to be faithful in places like that, isn't it? It's easy to begin to grumble, "Why doesn't God let *me* . . . ?"

It's not easy to be faithful in your current position when your dream is somewhere else. Yet faithfulness is what God required of Nehemiah. That was precisely the sacrifice Nehemiah offered up to God. Nehemiah served faithfully in that position and in the end it positioned him perfectly for what God wanted to do next in His great purposes.

In God's own good time He revealed to Nehemiah His intention to providentially use that position for His purpose.

We often reason, "Someday I'm going to do _____ for the Lord," or "Someday I'll make a difference. I'll get a different job. I'll live in a different place. I'll work with different people. I'll live for a different purpose, something more eternal, something more important, something more meaningful." We all must ask the question that surely came to Nehemiah's mind: Is it possible that God has placed me exactly where He wants me?

> *F*AITHFULNESS POSITIONS US PERFECTLY FOR WHAT *G*OD WANTS TO DO IN *H*IS GREAT PURPOSES.

It may not be where *your* heart and mind and dream are, but it's exactly where *He* wants you in His providence. The dream, vision, desire, and burden may be preparatory, rather than immediate permission to make a move. It doesn't mean the dream isn't correct; it just means that the way you may be thinking about the dream might not be correct.

It turned out that Nehemiah was exactly where God wanted him to be in order to make maximum impact for the kingdom of God. As we shall see, Nehemiah was granted a leave of absence from his position as cupbearer. He was appointed by the king of Persia to rebuild the walls of Jerusalem, and funded with monies from the pagan treasury of Persia! The sovereign hand of God is breathtaking as it sweeps through your life! But don't lose sight of the fact that it was because Nehemiah was faithful in his position that he was available and, in the providence of God, could fulfill the purposes of God.

The difficulty of being faithful in a position that appears disconnected from the purposes of God is overcome by focusing yourself on those purposes, not on your position. Nehemiah could discern the providential move of God in his life because he was focused in on God's purposes.

How do I know what God's purposes are so that I can be aware when He moves providentially to use me in the position I'm in for the fulfillment of those purposes? How do I discover the purposes of God? The same way Nehemiah did, through the Word of God.

Nehemiah was a man immersed in Scripture. He knew, for example, that Jeremiah 25:11 was still on the books: "This whole country will become a desolate wasteland, and these nations will serve the king of Babylon seventy years." Nehemiah was where he was because God had said it would happen! It was part of the purpose of God that the people of God would be disciplined. The Bible said so.

Nehemiah likely knew what Daniel, one of his contemporaries, had discovered: "In the first year of his reign, I, Daniel, understood from the Scriptures, according to the word of the LORD given to Jeremiah the prophet, that the desolation of Jerusalem would last seventy years" (Dan. 9:2).

How did Daniel discover that? He too was in captivity. His heart was also in Jerusalem. He desired to do something big for God. How did he know the purposes of God? He went to the Word of God and he found the prophet Jeremiah. As he read he put his finger on a specific text and began to calculate, "It says that we're only going to be in captivity seventy years." Daniel began to count and suddenly stopped short, "You know what? It's getting close!"

So Daniel began calling out to God, "God, You said it! Here it is. These are Your words. Help us! The time is approaching. Move on behalf of Your people."

God did.

Nehemiah, I'm confident, clung to the same scriptural promise. He knew the Word of God, so that he was cognizant of the purposes of God, that he might have eyes to see the providence of God and how He wanted to use his position for those purposes.

The purposes of God are discovered, not only through the Word of God, but also through the *acts* of God.

Nehemiah knew what God was up to in the present because he knew what God had done in the past. He had studied the things God had performed.

So, we naturally ask, what did Nehemiah perceive that God had done? If you turn to the left in your Bible, leaving Nehemiah and passing through Ezra, you will come to the end of Second Chronicles and the answer to your question. In the Hebrew compilation of the Scriptures this was all one continuous narrative, and thus we do well to connect the dots historically.

Here we encounter the historical description of the nation's departure out into captivity. In outline form, what happened? Nebuchadnezzar stole the articles of the temple used in the worship of God, along with the wealth of the nation (36:18). Second, he burned the temple (v. 19a). Third, he broke down the protective wall around the city (v. 19b). Fourth, he destroyed every building of any consequence in the city (v. 19c).

Why? Because he was a greedy, power-mongering pagan. But what Nebuchadnezzar didn't know was that it was so that "The land enjoyed its sabbath rests; all the time of its desolation it rested, until the seventy years were completed in fulfillment of the word of the LORD spoken by Jeremiah" (v. 21).

Gone—both the temple and the wall!

The chronicler then took a big, bold marker and arched over that seventy years and pointed to the decision of Cyrus, king of Persia. "The LORD, the God of heaven, has given me all the kingdoms of the earth and has appointed me to build a temple for him at Jerusalem in Judah. Anyone of his people among you— may the LORD his God be with him, and let him go up" (v. 23).

Tally things up. Gone: temple, temple articles for worship, populace of the city, protective walls of the city.

Seventy years later, what had God restored? Through Zerubbabel, part of the population and a rebuilt temple had been restored. Then, almost sixty years later through Ezra, God restored more people and the worship of God in that temple.

A dozen years after Ezra's arrival, Nehemiah went down the checklist in prayer. "People: partially restored—check. Temple: restored—check. Worship: imperfect, but restored—check." Then Nehemiah came to the last item on the list of things destroyed by Nebuchadnezzar. "City walls: um, er, well, God, we need walls to secure Your city!"

Grabbing the first visitor from Jerusalem he could find, Nehemiah asked, "What about Jerusalem?" (Neh. 1:2). The answer he got disturbed him: "Those who survived the exile and are back in the province are in great trouble and disgrace. *The wall of Jerusalem is broken down*, and its gates have been burned with fire" (v. 3).

I believe Nehemiah prayed something like this: "O God, Your acts based on Your word are not yet complete. The house has been restored. Ezra is there preaching the Word of God to restore the worship of God. But, Lord, the city is not secure. It has no wall. There's still one more item on Your divine checklist to be done!"

Nehemiah began to realize that in the providence of God he had been put in his position so that he might help complete what remained to be done for the establishment of God's people.

You want to know what God is up to. You want to know why God has you where He has you. You need to look at what God has said and at what God has done. Then ask Him, "What is yet undone? What must happen for all of this to be true among all of us?" Then be still and listen.

Wait on God. Cry out to God. Beg God, "How have You so positioned me—in terms of who I am, where I live, the job I hold, the gifts You've given me, the temperament You've fashioned me with, and the people I know—so that I might be a strategic part of what is yet unfulfilled of Your promises to us?" Ask, "Why have You given me this position and how is it that You want to use that in Your providence to fulfill all of these purposes among all of these people?"

The equation still holds true: *Your position is granted that God might use you in His providence to achieve His purpose.*

As we continue to sweep across the whole of Nehemiah's memories we realize that God did not *leave* Nehemiah as a cupbearer (1:1–2:10). He made him also to be a *builder*, the builder of the walls of Jerusalem (2:11–6:19).

God grants you a position. You discover that your position is part of a bigger, divine plan. Nehemiah was discovering that God was moving him into that plan, by transitioning him from a cupbearer to a builder. He became a construction contractor to rebuild *the one missing part in God's grand restoration project* —the walls of Jerusalem.

The words "wall" or "walls" appear thirty-three times in the book of Nehemiah. The casual reader might ask, "What's the big deal about walls? The Babylonian bullies knocked them down—so what? We'll get around to painting the fence soon enough."

The walls were not for mere decoration, however. What residents of the ancient Middle East knew was that city walls were significant for three reasons.

One was *security*. A wall around a city meant it was secure. "All these cities were fortified with high walls and with gates and bars" (Deut. 3:5). Walls secure things from two directions. They serve to keep some things from coming in and to keep other things from gong out.

Walls were also about *perspective*. Sentries stood guard and watched over the surrounding plain from the walls of a city. They detected approaching armies. They observed life outside the city as well as inside. A city's walls were the highest point around. The walls were a place of perspective from which they could oversee what God had given to them.

Finally, a city's walls were a place of *witness*. When king Saul and his sons were murdered, their bodies were taken and were fastened to the wall of a certain city (1 Sam. 31:10). Picture it—headless corpses hanging from the city wall. (On second thought, don't picture it.) It sends a message, doesn't it? It's a witness. Foreign armies hired as mercenaries would come to a city and hang their shields on the outside of the walls so that approaching armies would realize, "Oh, we're not just dealing with amateurs; we're dealing with the armies of the nations" (Ezek. 27:10). The walls thus became a community billboard.

City walls obviously served a physical purpose, but they also served a symbolic purpose. They were a picture of God for His people. Seventy-five years before Nehemiah ever walked into Jerusalem another man stood in the rubble of those walls. He was a Jewish man with a heart like Nehemiah's. His name was Zechariah and you can read his prophecy in the Old Testament.

He stood upon the scattered stone refuse of what had been the center of the glorious kingdom of Israel. He walked the perimeter of the city and examined the fallen walls; he saw the vulnerability and desolation of God's people. Then he cleared his voice and, in God's name, described a coming day when a perfectly restored Jerusalem "will be a city without walls" because "*I myself will be a wall of fire around it* . . . and I will be its glory within" (Zech. 2:4–5).

God is a wall to His people. This prophecy refers to the future reign of Christ from Jerusalem, but the truth is for us even now. The lesson we learn from Nehemiah is not to go home and build a big wall around your yard. It is to find God to be a wall about us and a glory within us. That sounds like revival—revival in the rubble.

How is that going to happen? By trusting God to be our security. By thinking His thoughts (by the Spirit through the Scriptures) and thus seeing with His perspective. By allowing Christ to become our defense witness (1 John 2:1), for whom we then bear witness (Acts 1:8). God is to become all that, not only for us individually, but also for us as a whole people.

God has put you where you are to be a part of restoring God's people, individually and collectively, to all He wants them to be. You have some part to play in that grand purpose and it relates to your God-given position. That's why God the Spirit moved Nehemiah to pick up pen and ink to write these things down—that you might come to discover that your position is a part of a larger plan. It is a plan about you individually and us corporately becoming the people of God.

As grand as that is, it is not the end. Many would settle to see that their position in life is part of God's great plan, but God does not. Add this to the mix: your position and God's plan relate to God's *passion*.

> *Y*OU HAVE A PART TO PLAY IN GOD'S GRAND PURPOSE, AND IT RELATES TO YOUR GOD-GIVEN POSITION.

God has a plan. He has granted you a position of significance in the unfolding of that plan. That plan relates to the things God is most passionate about.

To bring that plan to fulfillment and to satisfy God's great passion, He moved Nehemiah out of the role of builder and into a third role. No longer is Nehemiah a cupbearer, nor even a builder. The position Nehemiah holds throughout the latter part of the book is that of governor of Jerusalem (7:1–13:31). He had served. Then he built. Where once he built, now he rules, leads, and administrates.

Nehemiah's mission was about more than bricks and mortar, though that was a very necessary part of what he was called to do. His purpose was to share and satisfy the passion of God's heart.

What are *you* passionate about? Passion taps into energy reserves you didn't know you had. Passion creates vision where there was myopia. Passion transforms duty into joy.

What is *God* passionate about? God has, according to the latter chapters of Nehemiah, three great passions that He wants you to share with Him as He reveals to you His perspective on your position and His plan. God's goal is to impart these passions from His heart to yours.

Nehemiah discovered God's passion for His people. "So my God," said Nehemiah, "put it into my heart" (7:5). Put what into his heart? The people of God. Look carefully at chapter 7 and you will see a long list of names. To us they appear as strange collections of letters with odd pronunciations, but to God they each had a face, a family, and a future.

Eugene Peterson says, "At our birth we are named, not numbered."[1] Your parents don't call out, "Offspring #2! It's time for dinner!" We don't do that to our children; we *name* them. We name them because they are people—individuals created in the image of God, for the purposes of God, to share in the glory of God. Peterson continues,

> The name is that part of speech by which we are recognized as a person. We are not classified as a species of animal. We are not labeled as a compound of chemicals. We are not assessed for our economic potential and given a cash value. We are named.[2]

This list of names in chapter 7 is about Nehemiah being moved by God to discover who was there among the people of God. It's true—it is easy to love humanity, but hard to love people. Yet God loves us all, and also loves each one of us. You are the passion of God's heart. The world doesn't orbit around you or me or any other single individual, but God has a passion, a love for people, and He wants us to share that passion.

Nehemiah also came to discover that God is passionate about His Word. Thus we read in the next chapter "all the people [the folks designated in chapter 7] assembled as one man. . . . They told Ezra the scribe to bring out the Book of the Law of Moses" (8:1).

Do you notice? "*They* told Ezra" to get that book of God and teach them. They ordered their leaders, "You get the Bible and get back here!"

> So on the first day of the seventh month Ezra the priest brought the Law before the assembly, which was made up of men and women and all who were able to understand. He read it aloud from daybreak till noon as he faced the square before the Water Gate in the presence of the men, women and others who could understand. And all the people listened attentively to the Book of the Law. (8:2–3)

"Bring out that book of God, we want to hear it!" There they stood, absorbing the words of God. No padded pews. No seats of any kind. They stood and listened attentively for hours as the Word of God was read and explained. Sounds like revival to me!

Throughout the rest of the book we find Ezra and Nehemiah taking that word of the LORD and helping the people, teaching the people, counseling the people to bring their lives in line with that word.

It's about people. It's about the Word of God. It's about the lives of people being transformed by that Word. That's *God's* passion. That is central to God's heart because He is also passionate about people's fellowship with Him.

GOD IS PASSIONATE ABOUT PEOPLE— ABOUT SEEING THEM TRANSFORMED BY HIS WORD AND COMING INTO FELLOWSHIP WITH HIM.

The last five chapters of Nehemiah's diary find him laying one hand on the shoulder of people while in the other hand holding the Word of God. He bridges from the words of God to the people of God in order to bring their lives in line with all God wants them to be so that they might live in fellowship with Him.

Meander through those chapters. You'll find repentance, re-dedication, and reformation. It's all about fellowship, vertically and horizontally.

God asks us to be faithful in the position in which He has placed us so that we might see that this position and our very lives are part of a bigger plan. Part of seeing and accepting our place in that plan is coming to share a whole new passion with God for what's really important. God's great desire is to impart His heart to us—to make what is passionate in *His* heart passionate in *our* hearts.

As we've already noted, Nehemiah is the last historical word we have before the coming of Jesus Christ. After 400 years of silence, John the Baptist came declaring, "Prepare the way of the Lord!" What a privileged position Nehemiah held. What an incredible part he played in God's plan. God has a part for you to play in the same plan. Take note of the pattern that has emerged from a survey of Nehemiah's life: *Faithfulness in my God-given position results in discovering God's purpose for my life and ultimately in my sharing God's passion with Him.*

Two truths resonate in my heart as we prepare to enter Nehemiah's life. I am reminded that a change of position without an increased understanding of God's purpose won't cure what's ailing me. Change for change's sake doesn't really change anything. I'm also coming to realize that faithfulness where I am is required before I get to go where God ultimately wants me to be. Faithfulness now means fruitfulness later.

Now, I hear weeping. Let's go see what has Nehemiah so upset.

Reaching Toward Revival

1. Study your life—how has God positioned you in your family, workplace, community, church or school? What roles do you fill in each setting?

   _____

   _____

2. How do those positions facilitate or frustrate your dreams?

   _____

   _____

3. What dreams has God put in your heart? How might they relate to your God-given positions? To His purposes?

   _____

   _____

4. How does focusing on God's purposes change the way you see the positions you hold in life? How do your positions in life seem to distract you from God's purposes?

   _____

   _____

5. What does faithfulness in your current God-given positions look like?

   _____

   _____

6. How do your positions in life relate to God's passion for His people and His Word?

   _____

   _____

7. If you are faithful where God has placed you, how will it help you discern God's ultimate purpose for your life? Or help you share in God's passion with Him?

   _____

   _____

Part II

The Preparation for Revival

In almost every case the beginning of new blessing
is a new revelation of the character of God—
more beautiful, more wonderful, more precious.
—J. Elder Cumming

There is an idea in regard to revival that
the thing is done suddenly, by a magic pill.
—Oswald Chambers

Revival cannot be organized, but we can set our sails
to catch the wind from heaven when God chooses
to blow upon His people once again.
—G. Campbell Morgan

Revival is a process; it does not just happen. From the human vantage point it may appear to descend suddenly from heaven without prior notice. Yet behind these surprising encounters with God there lies a runway He has been building in order to launch this new move of His Spirit. History reveals that where God has visited His people with genuine revival there are discernible preparations He has made. Nehemiah and the people of Israel in his day reveal these basic preparations God undertakes before He stirs up His people afresh.

2

Make It or Break It

T here are some things that you cannot bring into being by making them, but only by breaking them. An omelet would be one. You don't technically *make* an omelet, you *break* an omelet into being.

An oak tree is another. You don't make an oak tree. An oak tree is broken into existence. As an acorn falls to the ground, it dies, is destroyed and only then does life come. An oak is broken into being.

Jesus pointed out the pattern of death before life when He said, "Unless a grain of wheat falls into the earth and dies, it remains alone; but if it dies [i.e., is broken], it bears much fruit" (John 12:24, NASB). This is a spiritual pattern that holds true in all Christian experience. As British naturalist Charles Raven said, "We must be broken into life."

There's something else that you can't technically make come into being but that must be broken into existence. It's revival. No person can make revival happen, it has to be broken into existence. We must be broken into wholeness. That's the Biblical pattern. In God's economy, wholeness only comes through brokenness.

Not surprisingly, then, Nehemiah begins with brokenness. The book of Nehemiah is about how God brings revival out of the rubble of His people's lives. This is about how God intends to rebuild His people after failure. When God begins to rebuild

He starts with that which is broken, but He does so for a reason we might not suspect.

Suppose you are shopping for a new house. The real estate dealer exclaims, "I've got a great little fixer-upper for you!" You skeptically tour the house, looking for what's wrong with it. You're hunting for what is broken. You take inventory of the things you will immediately fill a dumpster with. If you purchase the house you will want to get rid of whatever is broken so that you will be able to see what you've got left to work with.

That's human, but it's not how God works. God looks through the rubble of His people and their experiences not to see what He should get rid of but what He's got to work with. Broken people are God's most cherished resource in revival. God *looks* for brokenness, and He begins the revival there.

In God's eyes the broken are not trash to be discarded but a treasure to be held onto. The rebuilding begins on the strength of the broken.

As Nehemiah's journal opens, the trophy inside the case is broken. Nehemiah himself is the trophy of this book. His heart, passion, longing and leadership are on display. But the trophy inside the case is broken. As the diary opens, our hero is bawling his eyes out. He's come unglued. He can't eat. He can't focus. He can't do his work well. He is broken! It's not the way we would like to start a book or a revival. It's not the way you'd choose to develop the main character of your story, but it's where God always begins when He revives His people.

> WHEN GOD WANTS TO DO A NEW THING, HE SEARCHES FOR ONE TRULY BROKEN PERSON.

When God wants to do a new thing, He searches for one truly broken person. But what exactly does it mean to be broken?

With Nehemiah as Exhibit A, we discover that a broken person is a bereaved person. There's been a death. Something has been lost. There is grief, pain, emptiness. This is where the book opens and where revival is birthed.

The words of Nehemiah son of Hacaliah:

In the month of Kislev in the twentieth year, while I was in the citadel of Susa, Hanani, one of my brothers, came from Judah with some other men, and I questioned them about the Jewish remnant that survived the exile, and also about Jerusalem.

They said to me, "Those who survived the exile and are back in the province are in great trouble and disgrace. The wall of Jerusalem is broken down, and its gates have been burned with fire."

When I heard these things, I sat down and wept. For some days I mourned and fasted and prayed before the God of heaven. (Neh. 1:1–4)

It's obvious that Nehemiah had lost something precious in his eyes and that he was undone. He was bereaved.

It is true that broken people are bereaved people, but don't assume that the equation works in reverse—that bereaved people are necessarily broken people. Loss can be embraced in a number of different ways, many of which have nothing to do with brokenness. When you lose something or someone precious, you may become bitter rather than bereaved. In such cases bitterness only reveals that you've never really been broken by the loss. The blow may have shattered your dreams. There may be many shards of your life scattered down the trail. Yet there may still be a core intact that believes that you have a right to something better. That hard core that rolls your hands into fists is bitterness, not brokenness.

Loss can make us self-reliant. But renewed self-reliance in calamity only reveals that we've never really been broken at all. That self-reliance proves that we think that we can still make it on our own. There remains some self-sufficiency that we need to declare and vindicate. We feel the need to justify our existence and demonstrate our ability to rise above life's hardships. That is not brokenness.

Loss can make us self-pitying, but self-pity reveals we've never really been broken at all. There is a great deal of pain in self-pity, but our eyes are still on self. Down deep somewhere among the rubble of life there is a pulsating, beating "self" that remains unbroken. In such a state we are not yet a candidate for revival because although we may be suffering, we're not yet broken before God. Not all who experience loss are broken by it.

God begins to rebuild His people where someone is broken over the right things. People get worked up over all sorts of things. God is looking for those whose hearts break over the things that break *His* heart.

It's a curiosity to me to see the things people become passionate about. It's interesting, for example, to watch "Celebrity Week" on one of the TV game shows. At some point in every show the host turns to the celebrity guest and makes note of the charity they are playing on behalf of. Some of the strangest causes are chosen. The host, with broad smile and a tone of worked up sincerity, turns to the celebrity and says something like, "Today you're playing for the International Society for the Prevention of Cruelty to Morel Mushrooms."

What?!

Then the guest star becomes teary eyed; his voice cracks as he describes in a couple of sentences his deep commitment to the cause. I find myself thinking, "Of all the things to be broken over, you choose *that*?"

People get broken over all kinds of things, but we need to be broken over the right things. We must learn to pray as Dr. Bob Pierce, founder of World Vision, prayed, "Oh Lord, let my heart be broken by the things that break the heart of God."

Nehemiah was broken over two things. There were two areas where he felt he'd suffered a tragic loss. The first was *the people of God.*

What was Nehemiah's first question to the visitors from Jerusalem? "I questioned them about the Jewish remnant that survived the exile" (Neh. 1:2). Nehemiah was concerned for the people of God. You notice he calls them "the Jewish remnant." The title "Jews" was one not used until they had been taken away in exile. Only when the nation was disciplined through exile at the hands of the Babylonians were they referred to in this way. Exile in a foreign, pagan land is precisely where Nehemiah and most of the rest of the Jewish people found themselves. There they were given the name "Jew." It was a term in those days that arose out of defeat. It was a designation that signified, "We are broken. God has disciplined us. We have sinned."

Nehemiah also refers to them as those "that survived the exile." Virtually all of the Jewish people had been removed from their land by the Babylonians. Only the poorest of the poor, who appeared to be no threat to rebuild or rebel, were left in the land. But God had begun to restore His exiled people to their land. Some seventy years before Nehemiah's return, God sent some of the exiles back under Zerubbabel's leadership (538 B.C.). Again, about twelve years before Nehemiah himself returned, God sent another group back under Ezra's leadership (458 B.C.).

It was these people that Nehemiah grieved over. He was thinking, not so much about the poorest of the poor people and their descendants who had remained, but about those who had returned with the hope and promise on their hearts that God was going to use them to rebuild the temple, restore the worship of God, and rebuild the city walls.

Note the answer Nehemiah received as to their welfare: they "are in great trouble and disgrace" (v. 3). Nehemiah's response? He mourned and wept for days; he fasted and prayed. He was broken over the people of God and the state in which they lived.

What is it that breaks your heart? Has it anything to do with the state of the people of God?

In America, if you call yourself a born-again Christian, statistics tell us that you are more likely to get a divorce than if you call yourself an atheist.[1] Those

> *WHAT IS IT THAT BREAKS YOUR HEART? HAS IT ANYTHING TO DO WITH THE STATE OF THE PEOPLE OF GOD?*

who deny the existence of "the God of heaven" (v. 4) have a more permanent home life than those who claim to be born again. There is something wrong with that!

Among those who identify themselves as born-again Christians, seven out of ten don't believe there is such a thing as absolute truth.[2] If pushed to the logical limits of their position, these "born-again" folk admit that they do not even believe Jesus is absolutely the only way to heaven. They'd regurgitate the popular mantra: "Oh, He works for me and I look to Him for my comfort, but I couldn't really say He's absolutely the only Savior of the world."

Do you realize that in the decade preceding 1996, not one county in this country saw an increase in the percentage of born-again believers?[3] And more recent statistics indicate no significant change in that trend.[4] Is there not something wrong with that?

Some estimates say that more than half of the men who will gather for worship in our churches this next Sunday are currently entangled in Internet pornography.

There is something wrong with these things and they should break us. But what's our response? Quite often we excuse it: *"Yes, but you see . . ."* Or perhaps we fight for redefinition: *"How do they define a born-again Christian?"* Or we point fingers: *"That group over there skewed the results for the rest of us."* Anything but brokenness.

Nehemiah was broken over the people of God, but it was because He was also broken over *the promises of God.* Nehemiah's question for the visitors from Jerusalem was not only about the condition of the people living there, but "also about Jerusalem" itself (v. 2). Jerusalem, the City of Peace, was the place where God had chosen to make His presence dwell. He staked the reputation of His Name on that city. It was the focus of the promises of God.

The answer? "The wall of Jerusalem is broken down, and its gates have been burned with fire" (v. 3b).

Nehemiah had prayed diligently for the prosperity of God's purposes in the land of promise and its capital city. But nothing was any better than it used to be. The returnees were no closer to seeing the fulfillment of the promises of God.

I'm convinced Nehemiah knew the promises of God. As noted in the previous chapter, Nehemiah knew that Jeremiah the prophet had declared the people of God would be led off into captivity as discipline for their sin, but that God would restore them after seventy years (Jer. 25:11). He knew that the people had been taken captive and exiled from Israel, the temple destroyed, its articles of worship stolen, and the city and its walls destroyed (2 Chron. 36:17–20). Nehemiah had prayerfully and carefully monitored the progress of the restoration begun through Zerubbabel and Ezra. The temple had been rebuilt, worship restored, and the populace was beginning to return. But the city was in ruins! As Nehemiah held the people of God up against the promises of God, he saw a vast difference between their experience and what God had promised them. That distance broke Nehemiah's heart.

Broken People Are Better People

It is when the lives of the people of God are held up against the promises of God that the kind of brokenness God is looking for takes place.

But brokenness hurts. Why should we embrace brokenness instead of run from it? Quite simply because, in God's estimation, broken people are better people.

It's true that broken people are bereaved. They have lost something. But they've come to face that loss. They freely acknowledge something is amiss. There's no excuse-making, no finger-pointing—just honest brokenness.

Why is that better? It's because broken people are better soil for the life God wants to plant within them. They are better candidates for the revival God wants to send. Nehemiah exemplifies that for us in the remainder of his first chapter.

Better at Praying

He shows us that broken people pray better. What was the response of Nehemiah's broken heart? "When I heard these things, I sat down and wept. For some days I mourned and fasted and prayed before the God of heaven" (v. 4).

The vast majority of us pray. Yet among Americans who claim to pray, the average length of the prayer is less than five minutes long.[5] Think of that. There is nothing wrong with praying for five minutes, but there is something decidedly unhealthy about routinely stopping after five minutes. If a five-minute prayer is the sum of one's prayer life, something is wrong. Does this betray something about the condition of our hearts?

I assert again, broken people pray better. Linger for a moment over Nehemiah's prayer. Does this sound like our praying?

> O LORD, God of heaven, the great and awesome God, who keeps his covenant of love with those who love him and obey his commands, let your ear be attentive and your eyes open to hear the prayer your servant is praying before you day and night for your servants, the people of Israel. I confess the sins we Israelites, including myself and my father's house, have committed against you. We have acted very wickedly toward you. We have not obeyed the commands, decrees and laws you gave your servant Moses.
>
> Remember the instruction you gave your servant Moses, saying, "If you are unfaithful, I will scatter you among the nations, but if you return to me and obey my commands, then even if your exiled people are at the farthest horizon, I will gather them from there and bring them to the place I have chosen as a dwelling for my Name."
>
> They are your servants and your people, whom you redeemed by your great strength and your mighty hand. O Lord, let your ear be attentive to the prayer of this your servant and to the prayer of your servants who delight in revering your name. Give your servant success today by granting him favor in the presence of this man. (Neh. 1:5–11)

Notice the fervency of his prayer. He was knocked off his feet. He sobbed. His heart was turned inside out with grief. He lost track of time, even missing meals as he lingered before God (v. 4). All of this over something going on 800 miles from where he lived. This was his response to conditions in a place he'd never even visited. Nehemiah was likely three generations removed from anyone who'd even lived in Jerusalem. His father had never seen Jerusalem, but here he is broken by its desolation.

Nehemiah lived in a palace, had a prestigious government job, and had personal security, but he was broken over something he had never seen in a place he had never been. He had one of the highest positions in the land, so he's got all the ego strokes he'd ever need, yet he was broken. He had access to the royal kitchen, yet he fasted for days. He was the cupbearer, tasting the best wine and food the land could offer before it was brought to the king, yet he refused to partake of any of it for himself because he was so broken before God that he had to pray.

Mark also the content of his prayer. If you look beyond the surface, you discover that this prayer is filled with Scripture, especially passages from the book of Deuteronomy—for example, verse 8 (see Deut. 28:64), verse 9 (see Deut. 30:1–4 and 12:5) and verse 10 (see Deut. 9:29).

Nehemiah was praying, as it were, with his Bible open. "God, this is what *You* said!" He prays thus because he's broken. Derek Kidder has well said, "He is empty-handed, but not uninvited. He knows the threats and promises of Scripture well enough to make a strong, not a tentative, plea."[6]

Better at Worshiping

Broken people also worship better. Notice how Nehemiah addressed God. He cried out, "O LORD, *God of heaven*," pointing to His sovereignty over all things. He calls Him "LORD, God of heaven." He took up the holy, covenant name of God, that name which particularly exemplifies that He is the God who keeps His promises. He saw God as "the great and *awesome* God." The word translated "awesome" is a form of the word for fear. Nehemiah had come to see God for who He is and to see himself in light of who God is. The fear of the Lord had gripped his heart. And God was to Nehemiah the One "who *keeps his covenant* of love."

Brokenness runs you aground upon the rock of God's character. Worship is the result. No more illusions of self-sufficiency. Only God is great. And Nehemiah's got the order correct

—praise before petition. He doesn't ask for a thing until verse 11. He is simply broken. He is genuinely worshiping.

Better at Repenting

In addition, broken people repent better. That's an odd statement, I realize, but it is justified. Notice Nehemiah's pronouns: "*I* confess the sins *we* Israelites, including *myself* and *my* father's house, have committed against you. *We* have acted very wickedly toward you. *We* have not obeyed . . ." (vv. 6–7).

What's notable about the pronouns? They're plural! "*We* sinned, therefore You took *us* into captivity." Nehemiah had never even been to Jerusalem. He was several generations removed from the downfall and destruction of the city. He hadn't committed the sins that led to the removal from the land. Yet he made himself as culpable as those who had.

*I*N THE FACE OF DISCIPLINE FOR SIN, UNBROKEN PEOPLE POINT FINGERS. B*UT* BROKEN PEOPLE FREELY TAKE RESPONSIBILITY.

Nehemiah had a refreshing understanding of the corporateness of God's people. You won't find that much in today's self-justifying, blame-shifting, finger-pointing Christian culture. In the face of discipline for sin, unbroken people point fingers. But faced with similar chastening, broken people say "me," "I," "my," "we" and "our."

Better at Seeing

Broken people also see better.

See what?

Themselves, for one thing. One word is repeated over and over in Nehemiah's opening chapter: *servant*. Eight times in the span of six verses! To the unbroken, the title "servant" is demeaning. To the broken it's a badge of honor.

Broken people also see their faults more clearly. Broken people are willing to face, unveil, and admit the wrongs they've committed.

The broken also see the promises of God better. Verses 8 and 9 are largely in quotation marks. Nehemiah has put his finger on the open text of Scripture (Deut. 28:64; 30:4) and is praying, "God, keep this word You've spoken!" Tears of remorse and repentance wash the eyes of our hearts to see God's Word more clearly.

The broken also see their circumstances more accurately. The only thing Nehemiah added to his prayer was the simple notation, "I was cupbearer to the king" (v. 11). The unbroken view their position in life as something they've earned. It's theirs by right. Yet to the broken their position in this world is a gift from God. It is, therefore, something that fits His purposes and which they are responsible to Him for.

Better at Waiting

One last thing: Broken people wait better than unbroken people do. Nehemiah *"for some days* . . . mourned and fasted and prayed" (v. 4).

How many days is "some days"? Our curiosity causes us to ask, "How many days did he actually go without food?" We wonder, "How long did the tears actually flow?" The answer is not immediately obvious, but we do notice that it came to a head one day. The reservoir of petition was filled patiently until in one climactic request Nehemiah prayed, "Give your servant success *today* by granting him favor in the presence of this man" (v. 11).

When was that day and how long was it from the time he had heard the news and was initially broken by it? Notice chapter 2:1, because it designates the day referred to in 1:11. By comparing the two dates (1:1; 2:1) we discover that for four months Nehemiah has been broken, praying, weeping, worshiping, confessing, repenting, and calling on God. Four months! Sixteen weeks could not dissipate his urgency, fervency, passion, commitment, expectation and faith before God. The passing days only stoked the fires of God's work in his heart.

Nehemiah saw that he was providentially positioned by God to do something more than just pray, but he didn't move forward for four months. Interestingly, his father's name (Hacaliah, v.1) means "wait for Yahweh."[7] Had he learned how to wait on God from a father whose heart similarly longed for the restoration of God's people in God's city? At any rate, Nehemiah waited until God said "Go!" Broken people know that ill-timed efforts result only in earthly results. They want more than that which can be accomplished in the flesh. Broken people have had their fill of human efforts, answers, and results. They are hungry for something more and they are willing to wait on God to have it.

Broken people are bereaved people; they've lost something precious to God. They can't live without recovering it.

It's not that unbroken people are satisfied. It's just that unbroken people see problems. Broken people see God. Unbroken people see those who created problems. Broken people see the promises of God and long to taste of them. Unbroken people try to break something to fix the problems. Broken people already know they're broken and that there is no blaming to be done.

God wants to bring revival out of the rubble of our lives, marriages, and churches. He doesn't start by discarding the broken but by seeking them out. He is sifting through the rubble of broken relationships, addictive habits, hidden sins, and divided churches, looking for people who are broken. They are the foundation stones of the altar upon which He will kindle a blaze of revival. Broken people are God's most cherished resource in revival.

Arthur Wallis said it well: "Brokenness is not revival; it is a vital and indispensable step toward it."[8]

Reaching Toward Revival

1. Why do you think true revival must begin with brokenness?

   _____

   _____

2. What breaks the hearts of the people you know?

   _____

   _____

3. What breaks your heart about your own life? What breaks your heart about your church?

   _____

   _____

4. What promises of God's Word appear to be going unfulfilled among the people of your fellowship? Who, if anyone, seems to care?

   _____

   _____

5. What is different about the prayers of people with broken hearts?

   _____

   _____

6. Describe what next Sunday would look like if you and those you worship with came with broken hearts?

   _____

   _____

7. If we sense we are not broken before God, what should be our next move?

   _____

   _____

3

Real-World Revival

How am I to live a godly life when under the leadership of an ungodly person? What is a Christian wife to do with a contrary husband? How is an employee bent on exalting Christ to live out his faith before an ungodly employer? How is a teen new in her faith to honor both her unbelieving parents and her Savior?

How is this revival God wishes to send going to happen in the real world? *Your* world? When the strains of the closing hymn are over, the sanctuary barren, and the pulpit empty, how is it God actually gets His work done in this world?

Take Madge for instance. She's a believing woman married to an unbelieving man. She admits that there was a time in her life when she had walked away from her commitment to Christ. She made choices unworthy of Christ. Somewhere in the midst of that time she made a stupid decision and she married a man who was not committed to Christ. Now that she's returned to her Lord she's suffering the effects of being unequally yoked with this man. He ridicules her faith. He belittles her "religion" in front of the kids. There's scoffing and mocking as she goes out the door on Sunday morning. Sometimes he puts his foot down and forbids her to go.

What does revival look like at this address?

Think about Ernie, a man who loves Christ and wants to

51

honor God with his whole life, including in his work. But Ernie works for an ungodly man. The atmosphere of his workplace is a direct representation of the inner life of his boss. Foul language fills the air. Calendar-girl pinups wallpaper the rooms. Dirty jokes abound in the lunchroom. Policies, if there are any in the business, are generally reduced to one: "make money." Little else matters. Procedures are underhanded, unethical and, Ernie fears, at times maybe even illegal.

How does Ernie live out the life of God before such a man and in such a place? How will God's kingdom ever come to the place where he spends most of his waking hours?

Then there is Heather, a teen who has recently come to Christ. She has put her faith in Jesus Christ and been born again. She is changed. Yet Heather's parents don't share her faith. It's a "phase" she's going through. They debate with her over every meal. Because of their years they are able to manipulate the conversation and back her into a corner. When she doesn't know what to say, she feels stupid, unfaithful, unworthy. Her parents suddenly start scheduling family outings during worship services or youth group. Though they don't realize it, she hears them on the phone to family and friends telling about their daughter who is caught up in this "cult."

What will the life of God poured into Heather look like?

Nehemiah understood the problem. He lived in the real world. Nehemiah had little time for ivory-tower philosophizing. The harsh realities of life in a pagan culture slapped him in the face every morning and pried at his mind every night as he tried to sleep.

Nehemiah was in exile, a stranger from the start. His body had been birthed in Babylon, but his heart had been birthed in another, very far-off city. He had never seen Jerusalem. But Nehemiah loved God. He loved God's people. He loved God's promises. Nehemiah stoutly believed in what God had promised to do in His people as they were in their homeland and especially as they were in the city of Jerusalem.

Nehemiah was also a high-level official in the most powerful government in the world. His boss ruled from India to Libya, from the Black Sea to the Persian Gulf. His employer possessed more clout, more raw authority and power, than any other man on the face of the earth. His name was Artaxerxes I. He had personally put a stop to all rebuilding projects in Jerusalem, which was the burden on God's heart and now on Nehemiah's heart as well (Ezra 4). The irrevocable nature of the law of the Medes and the Persians etched his decision in stone.

How, then, did Nehemiah maintain complete submission to God and yet render honorable service to a powerful pagan king? How did God send revival in such a tangible, real-world setting? As Nehemiah's journey begins to unfold before us we discover that heavenly success in our earthly sphere requires a combination of prayer, planning, and the providence of God.

If God's life is to be infused again into His people, it will begin with prayer. That is precisely where Nehemiah had been for four months. Having received devastating news about the condition of the city and people of Jerusalem, Nehemiah was sent to his knees and left there. The events of both chapters 1 and 2 took place in the twentieth year of Artaxerxes (1:1; 2:1). The months, however, were different. The time from Kislev (1:1) to Nisan (2:1) was four months. For four months Nehemiah had been praying in brokenness!

What did Nehemiah get out of such an extended time before God? We assume that prayer produces answers. It is true, it does. But prayer may produce other results as well. Prayer may, for example, produce pain. Pain is exactly what Nehemiah got from his praying.

> WE MAY ASSUME THAT PRAYER PRODUCES ANSWERS, AND IT DOES. BUT PRAYER MAY ALSO PRODUCE PAIN.

By the time the events of chapter 2 took place Nehemiah had been weeping, fasting, mourning, and praying for weeks on end. The sum of his intense praying was not relief, but an increase in his burden. After fasting, praying, mourning, weeping, and falling down before God for four months, Nehemiah tells us,

"When wine was brought for him, I took the wine and gave it to the king." And then he added this interesting note: "I had not been sad in his presence before" (v. 1b).

Chew on that last line for a moment. The most personally devastating news that Nehemiah could have possibly received came four months before and yet he hadn't missed one day of work. He hadn't worn a hang-dog expression. He didn't mope, complain, whimper, whine, or gripe. He was personally shattered, but he did not bring that to his workplace. For four months!

Employees take note. But just because he didn't let on doesn't mean that he wasn't in pain. Indeed he was. And eventually it showed. What is unresolved on the inside eventually shows on the outside. "So the king asked me, 'Why does your face look so sad when you are not ill?' " (v. 2).

Did Nehemiah's brokenness simply become too much to conceal? Or did he reveal it on purpose? Nehemiah's devotion over those multiplying months did lead up to one climatic prayer in which he begged, "Give your servant success *today* by granting him favor in the presence of this man" (1:11). Did he plan, after four months of praying, to go to the king and let it be known how he was feeling?

We don't know for sure, but what we do know is that four months of non-stop, intense, fervent, heart-searching prayer yielded Nehemiah one grand thing: continued and increased pain.

To such news most people will reply, "Thanks, but no thanks. I don't need more pain." Why would anyone pray if what they get out of it is pain? People tell me, "I tried praying, and it didn't work." I want to ask, "What do you mean it didn't work?" What they usually mean is "It didn't make me feel better."

We have come upon a mistaken notion that prayer is some kind of heavenly therapy intended to make me feel warm and wonderful inside. Is it possible that prayer's primary purpose is not that we share our burdens with God, but that He shares the burden of His heart with us? Is prayer possibly more about changing my heart than changing my circumstances? If it is, then it may mean the more I pray the more I'm likely to experience pain, the pain that is on God's own heart.

Does God ever feel pain over His people? Of course He does. "Do not grieve the Holy Spirit of God" (Eph. 4:30). In Nehemiah's day God was grieved over the condition of the people and city of God and over the promises that He longed to fulfill through them. God found a man that was willing to stay before Him in prayer until He could impart to him the burden that was on His own heart.

Ravi Zacharias concisely summarizes Nehemiah 2: "You will never lighten any load until you feel the pressure in your own soul." Nehemiah would never be in a position to lighten the load of the people of God until He felt the full weight of their devastation. God was imparting to Nehemiah the load, the heaviness, the pain that was on His heart for the people and city of God.

Prayer is an integral part of seeing God's will worked out in the sphere of our earthly existence, but in the birthing of God's purposes in your locale you are likely to experience many a pang.

Prayer also may put us in places of panic. Having prayed for months and having been overcome finally by his grief, Nehemiah found himself standing eye-to-eye with the most powerful man in the world, who inquired as to his problem. The result? "I was very much afraid" (v. 2b).

Why the fear? Because the very thing Nehemiah wanted most was happening; he got exactly what he prayed for. He had the personal attention of the king—the one man on the face of the earth who had the resources to do something about the burden upon his heart. Nehemiah had prayed, "Give your servant success today by granting him favor in the presence of this man" (1:11). Now God was answering Nehemiah's prayer right before his eyes—and it scared him to death! There wasn't a sense of settled peace, contentment and joy. Just panic. "I was very much afraid." The word *terrified* would capture the idea.

Comfort prayers, when answered, produce comfort. Self-centered praying probes the heavens for soft, cuddly responses from God. But faith prayers, courageous prayers, God-pleasing prayers, may very well produce a touch of panic when God begins to answer, because we've been asking for something bigger than we can handle by ourselves.

GOD-PLEASING PRAYERS MAY PRODUCE A TOUCH OF PANIC WHEN GOD BEGINS TO ANSWER, BECAUSE WE'VE BEEN ASKING FOR SOMETHING BIGGER THAN WE CAN HANDLE BY OURSELVES.

I want to know exactly why Nehemiah was frightened. Perhaps he was simply afraid of the anger of Artaxerxes. Persian law forbade anyone from appearing in the presence of the king with anything other than a pleasant, reverent countenance. One's personal and emotional life were irrelevant. The only one permitted a bad day in the Persian court was the king. To appear in the king's presence with a long face could mean dismissal from one's duties, banishment, or even death. Persian law put all those options in Artaxerxes' hand. Esther, not long before this, recounted for Mordecai the Persian law which forbade appearing in the king's presence uninvited, on penalty of death (Esther 4:11). This is what Nehemiah faced and perhaps that is what frightened him.

I think, however, there is another explanation for Nehemiah's fear. Yes, I'm certain Nehemiah understood the gravity of standing before King Artaxerxes, but he was even more fearful of the King of kings.

Consider this: Sixteen times in nine verses (2:1–9) the Hebrew word for "king" is used, always in reference to Artaxerxes. It is used so many times in such a brief span that it leads you to believe someone is trying to make a point. Yet planted in the midst of those sixteen references to the earthly king is one ominous reference to "the God of heaven" (v. 4). Nehemiah doesn't just designate Him as God, but as "the God of heaven." He is the One who sits enthroned above all things in absolute sovereignty.

There exists a divinely planted tension between an earthly king with whom Nehemiah must deal, and the heavenly King who oversees it all. There is a dynamic tension of relationship and submission to both.

Nehemiah's moment of truth had come. The entire future of God's plan, of God's people, of His promises to those people, of the redemptive work of God throughout history to reconcile man to Himself, would hinge on what happened in the next few moments. And the gate of God's will was going to either swing wide open or be locked shut, on the hinge of Nehemiah's next words.

More than even panic before an earthly king, I believe Nehemiah was receiving the gift of the fear of the Lord before his heavenly King.

When you live before an earthly authority figure that doesn't share your commitment to Christ and has earthly power to make your life miserable, there is certain trepidation. Yet ultimately we have to choose our fears, and Nehemiah chose the fear of the Lord. He discovered that praying, while very much a part of seeing God's will worked out in our physical circumstances, also often yields things we don't bank on, like pain and panic.

Strangely, prayer also often produces more prayer. Nehemiah prayed and it yielded him one thing, the need to pray more.

Standing before the searching eyes of the king and the wide-eyed attention of the entire royal court, Nehemiah answered the king's question. In a gush of pent-up emotion he replied, "May the king live forever! Why should my face not look sad when the city where my fathers are buried lies in ruins, and its gates have been destroyed by fire?" (v. 3).

Was there a hot rush in Nehemiah's cheeks as he drew another breath? Did he feel the danger of his revelation before the king? Would it be interpreted as criticism of the palace's foreign policy?

Nehemiah's dissatisfaction was now a matter of public record. Before you continue, let the tension that must have filled that royal court at that moment squeeze you. Like the hourglass turned upside down, suddenly everything has funneled to this one point. Everything in God's redemptive work for humanity had funneled down to this one moment, in one room, in one city, with one man standing before an earthly king. What he said next was going to have huge implications for the redemptive work of God among mankind.

What are you going to say to this earthly king, who possesses all the raw power and resources and authority to grant your desire, but who doesn't share your commitment to God? Will it open up the way for God's will to be done and His salvation to come? That is what Nehemiah was feeling the weight of! His prayer was being answered. He got what he was asking for. Yet it pushed him back to prayer again. The king inquired, "What is it you want?" What did Nehemiah do? "Then I prayed to the God of heaven" (v. 4b).

Don't you love that? It is perhaps the best illustration of what some people call "arrow prayers"—those which are shot off toward heaven while on the run, and usually when in trouble. No matter what you face, no matter how limited your opportunity to pray, you can cry out to God with perhaps nothing more than the words "Help me, Jesus!" and He will hear and honor that prayer.

In the comfort of that thought, however, don't miss what often goes unnoticed: Nehemiah's arrow prayer, sent heavenward in a fleeting moment of need, grew out of four months (indeed, an entire lifetime) of regular, consistent, fervent prayer. Don't let yourself think, "Oh, I don't need to pray now. I'm too busy. But if I get into trouble, I'll just cry out to God and He'll help me." Worse yet, don't reason that "If I pray hard now and I get what I ask for, then I'll get to the place where I won't have to pray so much." Prayer is not intended as a means by which we can eventually become independent of God, but as the regular channel through which we are able to reaffirm and express our utter dependence upon Him. For that reason, often the very answers to our prayers are given in such a way that they push us back to God in prayer again.

Was it only prayer that got Nehemiah to where God was ready to unleash His will in and through him? Not at all. Remember, it is a combination of prayer, planning and providence that sees God's life unleashed anew in His people. Nehemiah had been praying for four months, but we soon discover he had been doing more than just praying during that time. He had been doing some planning as well.

A COMBINATION OF PRAYER, PLANNING AND PROVIDENCE SEES GOD'S LIFE UNLEASHED ANEW IN HIS PEOPLE.

I answered the king, "If it pleases the king and if your servant has found favor in his sight, let him send me to the city in Judah where my fathers are buried so that I can rebuild it."

Then the king, with the queen sitting beside him, asked me, "How long will your journey take, and when will you get back?" It pleased the king to send me; so I set a time.

I also said to him, "If it pleases the king, may I have letters to the governors of Trans-Euphrates, so that they will provide me safe-conduct until I arrive in Judah? And may I have a letter to Asaph, keeper of the king's forest, so he will give me timber to make beams for the gates of the citadel by the temple and for the city wall and for the residence I will occupy?" And because the gracious hand of my God was upon me, the king granted my requests. (vv. 5–8)

How do I know Nehemiah had been doing more than just praying? How do I know he had been planning also? How else did he come up with a wise estimate of how long it would take him to rebuild the walls of Jerusalem and when the king could expect him back (v. 6)? How else did he know to prearrange for letters of passage so the governors of the provinces he would pass through would not encumber him (v. 7)? How else did he know the name of the keeper of the king's lumberyard near Jerusalem (v. 8)? How else did he come up with a plan to rebuild—

not just the walls, but also the fortress by the temple and a personal residence (v. 8)?

The fact is, Nehemiah had been praying for a miracle, and planning on getting one. For four months he prepared for the day God would answer his prayers.

And that kind of faith-filled planning produces several things within us. It produces diplomacy, for one thing.

What reason did Nehemiah give for his sadness? He was smarter than to boast, "I'll tell you what's eatin' me! I'm from Jerusalem, King, and you've been messing with my people. You've been messing with the God of the universe. You've been messing with God's city. You've been messing with God's promised land. You've been standing in the way of God's promises. You'd better stand back!"

Nehemiah may have felt like saying something like that, but much time in God's presence had leeched that venom off his heart. There is a lot done and said in the name of the Lord that passes itself off as faith. Too much of it is nothing more than brash arrogance. Generally, it is counterproductive to God's purposes. Weeks of praying and planning produced a wise diplomacy within Nehemiah that allowed him to be God's man for the moment.

Note Nehemiah's diplomatic response to the king's question. The problem, he said, was "the city where my fathers are buried" (vv. 3, 5). Why didn't he just call it Jerusalem?

The reason is simple. The king had passed a law several years before that said no one could rebuild Jerusalem (Ezra 4:21). The laws of the Medes and Persians were irrevocable. So, rather than say, "King, you made a poor choice a few years ago," Nehemiah generically referred to "the city" and then designated it as the one "where my fathers are buried." He wisely appealed to the king on the basis of a Near Eastern cultural reverence of one's ancestors. Artaxerxes didn't share Nehemiah's faith in God, but he did share something culturally about the basic way that Nehemiah thought. It was to that common respect for one's ancestors that Nehemiah appealed. Thus Nehemiah's request bypassed the hot button of the king's authority and went straight to the king's sympathies. Rather than setting up unnecessary barriers, Nehemiah opened a door.

That is wise diplomacy. I believe Nehemiah had planned for the day he could speak to the king.

There's another subtle, but powerful note of Nehemiah's diplomacy here. Notice that he calls himself "your servant" (v. 5). We might sweep right by that notation without thinking much about it if we're not careful to mark the connection of chapters 1 and 2. He said to a man of earthly authority, "I am your servant." But remember what the most often repeated phrase of chapter 1 was? It was the phrase "your servant(s)," used eight times in the span of six verses, and always in the context of being a servant of God.

Yet now Nehemiah speaks the same phrase to an earthly king. He is saying, "King Artaxerxes, I understand your authority, and I want to acknowledge before you and all the royal court that I understand my place." He was not pushy or arrogant, but diplomatic and respectful. Note his speech, "If it pleases the king" (v. 5) and "May the king live forever!" (v. 3). This was not schmoozing, "working the angles" or salesmanship. It was heaven-sent tact, courtesy and diplomacy.

If God has placed a person in authority over you, you are to show respect and submission to that office. Such respect is a sign of spiritual maturity, not weakness.

Nehemiah's diplomacy was matched by an equally weighty daring. Nehemiah stepped forward in bold faith.

His burden had been revealed (v. 3). The king asked, "What is it you want?" (v. 4). So Nehemiah placed his request on the table (v. 5). The king asked a follow-up question about how long it would take, and Nehemiah answered him. Just that quickly, Nehemiah had his leave of absence (v. 6). Months of prayer, and it was all over just like that! He got what he had prayed for. His burden of prayer was over, right? Not quite.

Perhaps the king had turned back to the queen or maybe they both had turned toward the third course of their meal when Nehemiah cleared his throat and said, "Ahem, dear King, there is just one more thing . . . " He stepped forward, "If it pleases the king, may I have letters to the governors of Trans-Euphrates, so that they will provide me safe conduct until I arrive in Judah?" (v. 7).

No one interrupted the king of Persia—ever. But Nehemiah just had. "Just one more thing, if I may. You see, I've drawn up this little paper here. Could you just sign right here on the bottom line? Just so those guys across the river who don't like us very much won't give us a hard time? Just sign right here."

That's bold! To say to the king of the greatest nation on earth, "Your word's good enough for me, but there are some people that really won't believe this when I tell them, so if you could sign right there . . ." That's daring faith.

Nehemiah dared to ask for a *certified* answer to prayer. He also asked for a *generous* answer to his prayers. "By the way, king, could you also please pay for this whole project out of the government coffers?" That's nervy! But know what? He got it. "Because the gracious hand of my God was upon me, the king granted my requests" (v. 8).

Try that sort of thing off-the-cuff, and it will go nowhere. Fire off that request without the launch pad of much time with God and some wise planning, and it will blow up in your face. But if you have waited before God, pouring your heart out to Him, and if you have consistently, patiently, planned for the day when He answers your requests, then when He does, take up all the promises of God and move forward boldly.

> WE MUST BOTH REST IN THE SOVEREIGNTY OF GOD AND ASSUME OUR OWN RESPONSIBILITY. WE DON'T MAKE GOD'S WILL HAPPEN; GOD MAKES HIS WILL HAPPEN THROUGH OUR OBEDIENCE.

God demands both praying and planning. We must both rest in the sovereignty of Almighty God and take up our human responsibility. Our human responsibility doesn't make God's will happen, but usually God chooses to make His will happen through our obedience. He does so in His good time and in His own way. Thus revival is not brought about merely by praying and planning; it also comes through the providence of God.

After Nehemiah had spent four months praying and planning, God moved in His providence to change the heart of the king. "The king's heart is in the hand of the LORD; he directs it like a watercourse wherever he pleases" (Prov. 21:1). God reached down into time and space and changed the heart of a pagan, unbelieving, contrary, power-hungry king to grant the will of God for Nehemiah. And when God in His providence began to turn Artaxerxes' heart, it produced three things for Nehemiah.

Success

For one thing, it produced success. "Because the gracious hand of my God was upon me, the king granted my requests" (v. 8). God did it. Nehemiah's success did not come because of superior skills at either praying or planning. It's true, God used these in the process, but in the end it was the providence of Almighty God moving in the specific events of an individual's life that brought success.

Nehemiah got his leave of absence, letters of permission, and government funding. All that from a king who didn't worship his God, didn't believe in the divine promises about his people, didn't care about the city of his ancestors (except that he didn't want any trouble out of it), and who had passed an irrevocable law forbidding the very thing Nehemiah asked!

That is success! Yet the success God granted Nehemiah was far more amazing than that. Ninety-five years before Nehemiah stood in Artaxerxes' court, Daniel prophesied,

> Know and understand this: From the issuing of the decree to restore and rebuild Jerusalem until the Anointed One, the ruler, comes, there will be seven "sevens," and sixty-two "sevens." It will be rebuilt with streets and a trench, but in times of trouble. (Dan. 9:25)

Nearly 100 years before Nehemiah's encounter with the king, Daniel foretold of the "issuing of the decree to restore and rebuild Jerusalem" (Dan. 9:25). That decree came to fruition as Nehemiah dared ask Artaxerxes for permission to return and rebuild the walls of Jerusalem. Daniel said that the issuing of that decree would set in motion sixty-nine weeks ("seven 'sevens,' and sixty-two 'sevens' ") which would culminate in the arrival of "the Anointed One" (Messiah).

A few calculations will reveal that a clock began ticking the very moment (March 5, 444 B.C.) Artaxerxes told Nehemiah "Go!" and that this clock counted down consistently until the very moment and day Jesus Christ was formally presented as the Messiah of Israel at His Triumphal Entry into Jerusalem. Daniel had added, "After the sixty-two 'sevens,' the Anointed One will be cut off" (9:26a). That very week Jesus Christ was crucified for our sins.

Think of it! In one particular room, in a palace in the Persian capital of Susa, 800 miles away from the land and city of promise, 450 years before Christ ever walked this earth, a man named Nehemiah dared ask, "King, could you grant me a little time off so I can rebuild my ancestral city?" What happened in that room set in motion a series of events that would culminate in the arrival of the Messiah, Jesus Christ, as the King of Israel.

That overarching purpose of God may have been far from Nehemiah's conscious thoughts, but it was being worked out at that very moment as he stood before the king. Because one man prayed and waited, because he planned and watched, and because God providentially moved in that one man's life, the redemptive plan of God, that we benefit from, was set in motion. That's success.

Security

Providence not only produces success, it may also produce security. As Nehemiah's account proceeds, he races past all the preparations and packing, and rather mechanically records, "So I went to the governors of the Trans-Euphrates and gave them the king's letters" (v. 9a). Those fifteen words summarize travel through 800 miles of the most dangerous territory on earth. Those whose territory he traveled through would not have been happy to hear of his mission.

Surprisingly, Nehemiah reports, "The king had also sent army officers and cavalry with me" (v. 9b). Nehemiah hadn't asked for an escort. But the king threw them in as part of the deal! It must have added a bit of clout to Nehemiah's mission and a little flair to his entrance.

Mark it down: when God moves providentially to answer the prayers of His patient, prepared people, it results in security. God cares for those who walk by faith. The safest place to be is in the will of God.

Strife

Don't let all this talk about success and security make real-world revival sound easy. Success and security are only note-worthy because they occur in a world of strife. A portentous note is sounded as our account closes out, "When Sanballat the Horonite and Tobiah the Ammonite official heard about this, they were very much disturbed that someone had come to promote the welfare of the Israelites" (v. 10).

Thus we are introduced to two of Nehemiah's main thorns. We will meet Sanballat and Tobiah often in the pages to come. Every action Nehemiah took in his mission to rebuild Jerusalem and revive the people of God was met by an equal and opposite reaction from these enemies of God. Prayer, planning, and the providence of God will produce the will of God in your life, but this side of heaven it will never eliminate opposition and strife.

No amount of prayer (even answered prayer!) ever eliminates the need for a continuing life of prayer. No amount of planning alone can produce heavenly success in my earthly sphere. No amount of providential intervention by God will eliminate all opposition this side of heaven.

That's the real world, isn't it? And it's in this very real world that God wishes to make us as His people channels of His own divine life. As the stage was set for revival in Nehemiah's day, we have been reminded that heavenly success in our earthly sphere similarly requires a combination of prayer, planning, and the providence of God.

Reaching Toward Revival

1. If God got His way in your workplace, what would it look like? How about in your home or school?

   _____

   _____

2. Why would God use prayer to increase the burden on our hearts? Why would anyone pray if it yielded an increase in burden?

   _____

   _____

3. What is the fear of the Lord? What effect would it have upon your life if you experienced it at new depths?

   _____

   _____

4. What relationship should exist between prayer and planning?

   _____

   _____

5. What would God-given diplomacy and tact look like where you work?

   _____

   _____

6. In the real world, how do you find the right balance between resting in the sovereignty of God and taking up your human responsibility?

   _____

   _____

7. Why will God continue to allow opposition and difficulty even as He grants you success?

   _____

   _____

4

I Don't Even Know
Where to Begin!

I don't even know where to begin! Ever had to admit that? Have you stood before some daunting assignment and felt that helpless ache in your gut? It's the result of a head-on collision between responsibility and impossibility.

That feeling and the exclamation are one thing when you're staring through the garage door at the chaos you are charged with bringing to some sense of order. It is, however, an entirely different matter if the task before you is rebuilding a failing marriage. It's altogether different if you are taking on a new position at work that has plunged you in over your head. It is something else entirely when it's the desire to rescue a wayward child from a destructive course he's chosen.

It comes in a variety of ways and in an assortment of circumstances, but it happens in all of our lives. God throws us in over our heads and we cry, "Where do I even begin?"

Nehemiah found himself in that very spot (2:11*ff.*). Having ridden the boney spine of a camel for at least three months, he finally arrived in the city that possessed his heart. As his dream came into view, his heart both soared and sank. It took flight because he finally beheld the city of God. It fell because of the deplorable condition of Jerusalem and its people. The worshipful exhilaration of living a divinely-given dream was matched only by the desperate cry of his overwhelmed heart.

Nehemiah had known no home but Susa, the capital of the Persian Empire. He had been, however, a stranger in the land of his birth, for God had burdened his heart for the people of God and the city of God, Jerusalem. Every time he read the promises of Scripture, his heart broke because he saw what God had intended for His people and His city, and it didn't mesh with the report he heard of the desolations and the reproach heaped upon them.

After God's miraculous intervention, royal permission to return to Jerusalem, government funding for the project, and an official leave of absence from his position as cupbearer to the king, Nehemiah bobbed on camel-back for weeks on end making pilgrimage to his dream. With a heart ready to burst, he drew near Jerusalem.

As the city came into view, he saw for the first time, with his own eyes, the desolate walls, idols of strange gods, and the deplorable state of what had once been the great kingdom of Israel. Nehemiah asked himself, "Where do I even begin in rebuilding this city?"

God reminded Nehemiah then, as He does us now, that *God-sized assignments come with God-given instructions*. God wants us to undertake God-given ministries in a God-ordained way. Nehemiah 2:11–20 describes where to begin in the overwhelming, God-sized assignment He's given you in leading God's people to revival.

Look and Listen

First, look and listen. Such an approach runs contrary to every human inclination within us. We want to *do* something. The first thing we want to do is change something, quickly. What God calls us to do, however, is look and listen.

God's approach requires patience. Nehemiah dispassionately records his arrival: "So I came to Jerusalem" (v. 11a, NASB). The words appear bland, mechanical, indifferent. But you will make a mistake if you rush past the emotion in them.

Think for a moment what arrival in Jerusalem meant to Nehemiah. Nehemiah had never seen Jerusalem with his eyes. With his heart, many times; with his eyes, never. In fact, his *father* had never seen Jerusalem! A distant, long-dead ancestor had been one of those taken into exile and brought to the pagan land of Babylon. From that time on, Nehemiah's people had viewed Jerusalem only through the eyes of hope.

Did Nehemiah recall sitting around the fire as a child and hearing his grandfather relate stories about Jerusalem and the people of God, the great victories that had been won there, the desolations he had seen and the shame and the reproach of being taken captive and put in exile in that foreign land? Had he heard his father recount the promises of God about that city? Somewhere along the line those stories stoked a fire in Nehemiah's heart. Jerusalem became his passion.

What passed through Nehemiah's mind when he crested the final hill and caught his first glimpse of Jerusalem? What emotions welled up within? He reports simply, "So I came to Jerusalem," but this was his life-long obsession and dream! There is power in those few, simple words. It is this passion and purpose that make his next words so amazing: ". . . and was there three days" (NASB).

Nehemiah didn't wave a banner. He didn't stand on a high spot and wave the nation's flag, declaring, "We're going to take this city for God!" No hype, no fanfare, no press conferences—he just showed up and sat around for the first three days. That's patience.

Because of the enormity of the task God calls us to, we sometimes believe the only way to accomplish it is to attack it in haste. What we lack in faith we make up for in a flurry of activity. When we are not certain what to do nor where to do it, we believe it is best to just begin doing *something* . . . fast!

Not Nehemiah. He reminds us that the wisest course is usu-

> *T*HE ENORMITY OF THE TASK GOD CALLS US TO MAY LEAD US TO BE HASTY. NEHEMIAH'S EXAMPLE TEACHES US THE VALUE OF PATIENCE.

ally to stop, draw in a deep breath and survey the situation. We are reminded that patience is a virtue even when the pathway seems obvious. Nehemiah was just looking and listening.

Nehemiah was practicing patience, but he was doing more than just sitting around. He was studying the situation.

> I set out during the night with a few men. I had not told anyone what my God had put in my heart to do for Jerusalem. There were no mounts with me except the one I was riding.
>
> By night I went out through the Valley Gate [on the southwest corner of the city] toward the Jackal Well [south] and the Dung Gate [at the southernmost point of the city, where the city's garbage was dumped into the Hinnom Valley below], examining the walls of Jerusalem, which had been broken down, and its gates, which had been destroyed by fire. Then I moved on toward the Fountain Gate [north, along the side of the city with the steepest cliffs] and the King's Pool, but there was not enough room for my mount to get through [the walls were likely so damaged that even the terraces had given way and there was no firm footing for his donkey]; so I went up the valley by night, examining the wall. Finally, I turned back and re-entered through the Valley Gate. (vv. 12–15)

Nehemiah moved in stealth. He quietly studied the conditions of his divine commission. "What do I have to work with? What exactly is the situation? What's the truth about this place? I've heard it with my ear, but I need to see it with my eyes." By nothing more than moonlight, Nehemiah was asking and answering, "How bad is this *really*?"

Why all these details? He doesn't share his travel diary. He keeps cloaked the emotion he felt. So why reveal this stuff?

It is to remind us that the wise person studies the water before he dives in. How many people are paralyzed because they dove in before studying what was beneath the surface?

Nehemiah was careful to study the water. He had every intention of diving in, but he was willing to be patient and study the situation first.

When I candidated in the church where I presently pastor, I was asked, "What is your vision for this church?" When I replied, "Wouldn't it be a bit presumptuous for me to say what God's vision for this church is?" I was met with astonished expressions. But I thought, "How can I know that? I have never lived here. I don't know the people who fill this community. I don't know what makes this place unique. I don't know the history of this church. I don't know how God has worked in the past, so how can I know what He wants to do in the future?"

When eventually I was called to be the pastor of this church, I began simply by asking questions. In fact I did virtually nothing else in my first twelve months than ask questions—to the elders, to the staff, to the people.

Who are we? What makes this church *this* church? What has God called us here to be and to do? What will we look like when we succeed? What will we not sacrifice on the way to achieving this? How is God calling us to become this, to do this? What specific steps is God calling us to pursue?

I did this in an attempt to be like Nehemiah. As we shall soon see, Nehemiah was a man of action, but he was a man who knew enough to look and listen first. It is easier to give way to the pressure to cast a vision before you even know what's going on than it is to be patient, to look, listen, and study the situation. The wise person, when presented with a God-sized task, looks and listens, practicing patience and studying the situation.

Patience and study yield a wise sense of timing. Sometimes timing is nearly everything. Nehemiah understood this. "The officials did not know where I had gone or what I was doing, because as yet I had said nothing to the Jews or the priests or nobles or officials or any others who would be doing the work" (v. 16).

Nehemiah came to town and didn't say a word about his divine calling. He didn't mention his plans to anyone, except, as verse 12 informs us, to a few men that were already with him. Otherwise he didn't tell a soul what God had laid on his heart about Jerusalem.

Just because you can see it in your heart and mind doesn't mean everyone is ready to receive it. Even if God has shown you

> *J*UST BECAUSE G*OD* HAS SHOWN YOU H*IS* COURSE DOESN'T MEAN IT IS TIME TO TELL EVERYONE ELSE.

His course, it doesn't necessarily mean it is time to disclose it to everyone else. God has a time for everything. We must cue in, not only to His agenda, but also His timing.

How does an existing group respond when a newcomer rides into town, declaring, "You know what your problem around here is, don't you? What you need to do is . . ."? The response is less than enthusiastic.

Suppose you are on a committee at work, and suddenly a new person comes into the group and blurts out, "What are you guys doing? All you've got to do is . . ." What happens to the relationships in the room? Warm fuzzies? Not exactly.

Nehemiah knew that timing is important. He knew that a newcomer has a great advantage and a great disadvantage. A newcomer's advantage is that he sees things differently than those who have been embroiled in the situation for a long time. He sees with fresh eyes.

When a friend visits my church, I like to ask, "What did you see?" I ask that because I walk through the same doors every day; I worship there every Sunday. I see it all the time, and familiarity can blind us. Time makes us see what we once saw, what we want to see, what we want to believe is true.

The newcomer also possesses a major disadvantage: he has no grounds for suggesting change. He says, "We need to change this." They reply, "Y'all not from around here, huh?"

Can you imagine the Jews' response if Nehemiah had come riding into town waving a banner and declaring, "We're going to take this city for God and here's what we're gonna do!"

They could have said, "Nehemiah, where were you when we were starving to death? Oh, you were tasting the king's food in Susa, weren't you? Where were you all these years while we were insecure, without walls around this city? Oh, that's right, you had a cushy government job in Persia, didn't you? Where were you, Nehemiah, when we tried before to rebuild these walls, and the king sent his military, and forced us to stop? Oh, that's right! You were sipping that king's wine to make sure he didn't get poisoned."

Are you rebuilding a marriage? Stopping to look at and listen to the truth about your relationship is not only worth your time, it's absolutely essential. Are you taking on a new job that's over your head? You'll win the support of your coworkers faster by looking and listening than in any other way. Are you burdened for revival in your church? You will save time, energy and resources if you start with looking and listening. If you don't start with looking and listening, you'll *restart* with looking and listening.

Challenge and Inspire

But simply looking and listening won't get God's work done. Patience, study and a concern for timing must eventually give way to doing something about the problem. That is why we must not only look and listen, but also challenge and inspire.

Observation, listening, study and patience, if they never give way to action, can be nothing but a cover for fear or laziness. There has to be movement at some point. There must be a move to challenge and inspire the people of God to take up the call of God.

A leader must challenge his followers to take up the will of God. Nehemiah reported, "Then I said to them, 'You see the trouble we are in: Jerusalem lies in ruins, and its gates have been burned with fire" (v. 17).

Look at us, we're a mess! That was Nehemiah's basic message. If he hadn't taken the time to look and listen, such a challenge could have gotten him in a lot of trouble. It was still a risk; he really hadn't been there long. One of the first duties of any leader is to define reality and work to make his people see it.

And look what fresh eyes saw! "We're pathetic!" Nehemiah said. Someone likely objected, "I don't know, I don't think we're all that bad." Nehemiah dared to say, "We are a reproach to God. Look at us! God has made promises about us, but look at how we live! God has committed Himself to the welfare of this city and look at its condition! This is a blot on God's reputation. This cannot continue."

Rather challenging, don't you think? Yet that is what a leader has to do. At some point someone has to speak the truth or the misperceptions, rationalizations and lies win the day. We become so used to our situation that we don't see our shame. We don't know, because we can't see. We are blinded to what the situation is by our obsession with what we think it is.

It's like cooked cabbage. You prepare the meal, consume it, and clean up after it. Then you go out for the evening. When you arrive back home and open the door—*Whew!* You didn't notice the odor before, did you? But if you step out for a while and come back in, you realize something reeks.

Nehemiah said, "Folks, I hate to tell you this, but something reeks around here! We're the people of God and things ought not to be like this!"

Nehemiah led them to see the disgrace that had become "home." But then he told them that things could change. "Come, let us rebuild the wall of Jerusalem, and we will no longer be in disgrace" (v. 17b). Do you notice the "us" and "we" in the challenge? He took ownership of the problem.

I always listen carefully when I hear people talking about the church I serve. Some folks say, "You know what the problem here for *you guys* is?" Or "You know what *you* need to do?" But there are others who say, "You know if only *we* could . . ." or "One of *our* greatest challenges is . . ." I've discovered that the difference between *you* and *your* and *we* and *our* is not a matter of how long somebody's been around the church but a matter of attitude.

Nehemiah had the right attitude. He was saying *we* and *our*. Though a newcomer, he freely admitted, "I'm a part of this mess. I haven't lived here long, but I've been here in heart and mind for years. I am one of you. We've got a problem and we need to deal with it." You don't challenge people by pointing a finger in their face. You challenge them by getting next to them and saying, "I think God would be pleased to bless us and to enable us to do His will."

Challenging people can be frightening. More often than not, people react against a challenge. Maybe it's with offense: "Who

74

do you think you are?" Maybe it's with a defeatist attitude: "We've tried this before." Maybe it's with self-pity: "We can't do it." It's not often that people accept a challenge. They don't like a reproof. They don't take a rebuke humbly, admit the truth and accept the challenge to look again at themselves and confess, "I think God would be pleased to do better in me." It doesn't happen often, but when it does, you can bet that it's revival beginning to emerge out of the rubble.

The need to challenge God's people is always followed by the need to inspire them. Nehemiah knew that. "I also told them about the gracious hand of my God upon me and what the king had said to me" (v. 18). He gave them proof that the God of heaven remembered them, cared about them, and was ready to reward their prayers and faith-filled obedience.

Nehemiah was testifying! "I can give you evidence because I've been there and God came through for me. I put my life on the line in the royal palace in Susa. I put myself in harm's way for this city and God answered my prayers. I have the decree from the king himself right here to prove it!"

He showed them that God was moving already. He nudged their reluctant faith forward by revealing what they could not have seen on their own: they could move out in obedience because God had already moved in providence.

And the result of a challenge and a little inspiration? "They replied, 'Let us start rebuilding' " (v. 18b).

Amazing! That is simply miraculous. These people had been in Jerusalem a long time. They'd tried to rebuild the city. Ezra had incited them to believe the promises and pursue the dream. They had dared to forge ahead, only to be stopped by the king's own army. Now some guy rides into town and, after three days, says, "I think we can do this. God will help us." And they say, "Ok, let's try!" That is a miracle. Derek Kidner is correct when he says that "so total a response from such a group was as miraculous" as was the favorable response of Artaxerxes to Nehemiah's request to return and rebuild.[1]

To what did Nehemiah attribute the king's willingness to let him return and rebuild? It was simply that "the gracious hand of my God was upon me" (v. 8). This historical fact became his testimony to the people (v. 18).

The "hand of the Lord" was an expression used in Nehemiah's day to describe the power and the presence of God in a person's life (see Ezra 7:6, 9, 28; 8:18, 22, 31). When God put His hand on a person's life, that meant He was pouring out His resources of power, wisdom, love and mercy through that person. Encountering such a person means encountering God in some way. This is not the result of any inherent goodness in the person, but because God's hand rests upon him.

> YOU DON'T REALIZE YOU NEED GOD'S HAND WHEN YOU ARE IN THE WADING POOL, BUT ONLY WHEN YOU'RE IN THE DEEP END.

It is exhilarating when you realize God's hand is resting upon your life. You realize it most profoundly, however, only when you get in over your head. You don't realize you need His hand when you are in the wading pool, but only when you're in the deep end.

My first experience with the deep end of a swimming pool came when I was just a small child taking swimming lessons. Our instructor, thinking we'd mastered enough of the basics in the shallow end, led our class to the deep end where the shimmering surface of the water only half-cloaked an ominous sign reading "13 FEET." He sat each student on the edge of the pool and then jumped in. He explained our assignment: at his signal, jump feet first into the water, sink to the bottom, push off the bottom, resurface and exit the water. Simple, right? One after another the timid children performed their routine to near perfection, each resurfacing with a sputtering grin to have conquered so great a fear.

Then came my turn. I obediently jumped in. My body weight carried me downward. Soon I felt the bottom of the pool under my feet. Then, I panicked. What was step two? I couldn't think; I could only feel—fear! I remembered a ladder next to where I had jumped off. I frantically groped for it with my hands, not realizing it only extended a couple of feet below the surface of the water.

As my fear exploded within me, a strong, firm hand suddenly clasped mine and yanked me to the surface. Gasping for air, I was greeted with embarrassing giggles and my teacher's puzzled question: "What were you doing down there?"

Nehemiah admitted, "I'm in over my head on this one!" How did he get there? Not by foolishness, stupidity or sin, but by obeying God. God purposely calls us out of the kiddie pool of comfortable Christian experience into the deep waters of fuller obedience and trust. It's a frightening step to take personally, and it's even more difficult to invite others to join you there. But the hand of the Lord is not just for apostles, prophets, or an elite corps of Christians. God extends His hand to every ordinary Christian who dares to obey God and take on the things that only God can do. It is the thrill of obedience. It is God's hand resting upon you and moving through you.

Don't miss what happens next. "So they put their hands [there's that word again!] to the good work" (v. 18b, NASB). This is the essence of revival: God's hand moving through your hands. God's work done through your life. His mercy poured through your presence. His patience poured through your love. His power displayed in your weakness. His voice heard through your words. His life mediated to the world through you. That is the hand of the Lord. That is revival.

Define and Defend

Do you want God to do a God-thing in and through you? Look and listen—with patience, study and timing. Challenge and inspire—trust God to extend His hand. There is, however, one more thing that is often required of us in God-sized assignments: define and defend.

Any true work of God will meet with opposition. Not *may*, but *will*. Probably sooner rather than later. Right on cue we read, "But when Sanballat the Horonite, Tobiah the Ammonite official and Geshem the Arab heard about it, they mocked and ridi-

culed us. 'What is this you are doing?' they asked. 'Are you re-
belling against the king?' " (v. 19).

Is God calling you to a God-sized assignment? Are you
tempted to take it on, trusting that "the hand of the Lord" will be
extended to you? Go for it! But do so with your eyes wide open.
Count the cost. You will meet opposition. Often the resistance
will come from the most unexpected places. It will hurt. It will
be frightening. You will likely second-guess your decision, but
it doesn't mean you were wrong.

Nehemiah's opponents had him squeezed. Sanballat was the
governor of Samaria, to the north of Jerusalem. Tobiah was the
governor of Ammon, to the east. Geshem was likely the Persian
designate over the Arab tribes to Jerusalem's south. The Medi-
terranean lay on the west. Pressure from the north, east and
south, with a yawning body of water on the west—Nehemiah
was caught between three devils and the deep blue sea!

You've likely been there, too—or will be at some point, if
you accept God's assignment to become an agent of revival.

At such times we need to make our declaration of dependence. This was Nehemiah's: "I answered them by saying, 'The
God of heaven will give us success'" (v. 20a). Just as amazing as
his appeal to God's enabling was Nehemiah's refusal to assert his
earthly enabling. Geshem, Tobiah, and Sanballat did business
regularly with earthly authorities, in the currency of manipulation,
power plays, and political posturing. Nehemiah could have waved
the letters from the king and said, "I've been authorized by Artaxerxes. I've got the sealed copy right here. See the raised letters
on the seal? I've got genuine, certified permission from the king."
He could have pointed out his military escort.

Instead, Nehemiah declared his dependence on the God of
heaven! Even when standing before the earthly king, Nehemiah
had known he was ultimately standing before the heavenly King.
So now too, he knew his power source and affirmed it. Perhaps his
declaration was as much for himself and the people around him as
it was for those three characters. But either way, Nehemiah knew
that God would show up and prove Himself in the arena of his life

—or else he was in trouble! But he was banking on God.

Nehemiah also made a pledge of allegiance. He went on to say, "We his servants will start rebuilding" (v. 20b). Note the pronoun: "We *his* servants"! That was Nehemiah's pledge of allegiance. Eight times Nehemiah has declared his submission to God alone (1:6, 7, 8, 10, 11). Only once has he said to Artaxerxes, the earthly king, "I am your servant" (2:5). Now again, he pledges his allegiance to the King of kings.

Ultimately, Nehemiah was a servant of God. In measured, respectful commitment, he also recognized his submission to earthly authority. But in the face of opposition, when pushed back to ultimate allegiances, he made abundantly clear whose servant he was.

The day may come when opposition and pressure forces you to state or restate your ultimate devotion to God. We possess a loyalty that makes no sense to those whose worldview is shaped only by the tangible and the touchable.

Opposition also required Nehemiah to establish his bill of rights. "We his servants will start rebuilding, but as for you, you have no share in Jerusalem or any claim or historic right to it" (v. 20c).

"You've got no business here!" Those were strong words, because Sanballat, who was over Samaria, had probably governed the region of Judea prior to Nehemiah's arrival. When Nehemiah showed up with letters proving the king had taken away some of his territory and given it to Nehemiah, Sanballat was probably not thrilled. Perhaps the official rewriting of district lines also trimmed Tobiah's territory, so Nehemiah's appointment and arrival were seen as a threat by him as well. Geshem also likely had a vested interest, due to a lucrative trade route he ran through the area.

> *T*O FOREIGNERS WITH VESTED INTERESTS IN JERUSALEM, NEHEMIAH DARED TO SAY, *"YOU'VE GOT NO BUSINESS HERE!"*

We know from other writings that Tobiah and Sanballat gave their children names related to the Hebrew God Yahweh—

probably motivated by political and financial expediency, rather than religious commitment. But now this guy Nehemiah shows up, saying that it takes more than religious labels and ceremony to make a person a part of the purposes of God.

In the face of such vested interest in Jerusalem, Nehemiah dared to say to these three, "The way this nation, these people, and this city are now defined, you have no part in it. You do not have Jewish lineage. You have no authority in this realm. You have no privileges of worship at the altar in this temple."

What was Nehemiah thinking? Talk about politically incorrect! What exactly was he trying to accomplish?

Nehemiah was a man on a mission. What had he been called to Jerusalem to do? He was to rebuild the city. Remember, Zerubbabel had rebuilt the temple of God, Ezra had restored the worship of God in that temple, and now Nehemiah had come back to restore the city and people of God to their former strength. He was to rebuild the walls around the city. Nehemiah had come to erect walls. Had he picked up a trowel yet? Had any mortar been mixed? Was his plumb line in hand?

Nehemiah hadn't even touched the walls yet. But he had already begun the construction process. He already started building those walls in the minds of the Jewish people. Before those folks ever laid a single stone, Nehemiah had started erecting the walls.

Walls, as we have said previously, were for security, perspective and witness. But a city's walls not only kept outsiders out, they also served to define the residents within.

Your neighbor buys a dog; you put up a fence. In so doing you are saying, "I live here. You live there. Your dog does his business there, not here." The fence defines the boundaries.

Walls define. Nehemiah knew that as much as the residents of Jerusalem needed the walls for security, they needed them so that they could say, "We are the people of God! This is the city of God! This is where God's presence dwells! This is where His temple is! From this place God has promised to bless the nations!"

In that day, God was committed to a localized expression of His presence in the chosen city of Jerusalem among a chosen people, the Jews. If you wanted to meet God you needed to go to Jerusalem. If you wanted to be among the people of God, you had to convert to Judaism. Since the death and resurrection of Christ, the arrangement has changed (John 4:19–24). But in the time in which he served God, Nehemiah needed to define where the city of God was and who the people of God were.

Unfortunately, the walls were broken down and everyone was "in"—there were no standards, no membership requirements, no commitment necessary. Whatever you decided would meet your personal needs was fine, as long as you felt comfortable with it. Truth was not the issue; tolerance was. Sound familiar?

Such a worldview had to be toppled before a better one could replace it. Nehemiah was going after their hearts and minds, where that false worldview existed. The people hadn't touched the physical walls but Nehemiah's work had already begun. He was casting vision. He was defining what it meant to be the people of God before he ever started rebuilding the city of God.

Every mission that was humanly impossible but later shown to be divinely possible, was accomplished in the heart and mind of an individual before it ever became physical reality. The vision was mingled with faith before a single stone was layered with mortar. That person's inner faith was the "substance of things hoped for" and "the evidence" of an as-yet-unseen certainty (Heb. 11:1, NKJV).

John Maxwell once visited Disney World—not to enjoy the park, but to study the corporation's leadership and management style. As he walked through the park, observing the magnificence of Disney's creativity, he said to his guide, "It's just too bad Walt Disney didn't live to see all this!" The fellow quickly replied, "Oh, Walt Disney did see this—up here," and he pointed to his head. "And that's why it's here."

Do you see it? That overwhelming, God-sized thing God is calling you to? The revival God longs to send? Is it built, accomplished, achieved and done in your mind's eye? If it is, that's the seed of faith. It will grow, blossom and bear fruit . . . as you look and listen, challenge and inspire, define and defend.

Reaching Toward Revival

1. What price do we pay for failing to look and listen before we move ahead in God's work?

   _____

   _____

2. Why is patience often the most direct route to revival?

   _____

   _____

3. What risks do we run when we challenge people to higher living?

   _____

   _____

4. What evidences are there of "the hand of the Lord" moving for His people where you live? How can these accounts be used to inspire them to obedience?

   _____

   _____

5. Take the time to write out a fresh "declaration of dependence" upon God.

   _____

   _____

6. How has opposition given you the opportunity to state or restate your ultimate allegiance to God?

   _____

   _____

7. What are the primary forces of opposition to revival where you live?

   _____

   _____

5

Big Job, Little Time

What *if?* It's often a painful game to play, but let's try it, just for a moment. What if a flood wiped out your home? What if it not only ruined the contents, but destroyed the structure as well?

Let's also suppose that you've been given a window of opportunity to rebuild. Since we're playing make-believe, let's also assume that, for that limited span of time, you are guaranteed that all bills for rebuilding will be covered and you will experience nothing but green lights from local and state authorities. There are just two conditions: you and your family must do *all* the rebuilding and you must be done within *one month*.

Could you do it?

What would you need most to see your home completed? Certainty that all supply lines are open and the needed resources are available? Good weather? A guarantee of good health?

All good, but not essential!

To see such a gargantuan task completed in such a limited amount of time, the most crucial thing you and your family would need would be the right attitude. More than lumber, tools, weather, health, knowledge, and skill . . . attitude is irreplaceable!

Am I wrong? Not if Nehemiah chapter 3 is right.

Change a couple of details in our "What if?" game and you have exactly what Nehemiah and the people of Jerusalem faced in Nehemiah 3. The protective walls of Jerusalem had been destroyed. The populace had long been vulnerable to attack. The city had been overrun and its people defeated. The place where God had made His presence to dwell had now been desolate for decades. But a miraculous window of opportunity was now opening to Nehemiah and his people.

Providentially, the Persian king had granted permission to rebuild the walls and the city. Nehemiah was given a leave of absence to lead the reconstruction. Letters were signed and sealed on official letterhead, guaranteeing acceptance of the project by the locals. The promise of free and open access to the kingdom's own lumberyards gave the assurance that supplies would be no problem. And to top it all off, a military escort backed the endeavor with royal clout.

Apparently everything Nehemiah would need for completion of the city's walls was granted him. There was one simple condition pressed upon him by local conditions: complete the project quickly!

Why? Because the enemies of God buzzed about Jerusalem like hornets whose nest had just been pulverized by a baseball bat. They were scrambling. They were angry. They were reorganizing. The job had better be completed *pronto*, because they would try to stop it by any possible means.

Nehemiah's greatest task was to organize an utterly defeated people. He had to enable people who had lived among the rubble their entire lives to see those walls with new eyes. They had to look at *themselves* with new eyes. They had to look at *God* with new eyes! They needed a change of attitude. Revival requires new eyes, a new outlook, a new attitude.

*R*EVIVAL REQUIRES PEOPLE WHO HAVE LIVED AMONG THE RUBBLE THEIR ENTIRE LIVES TO HAVE NEW EYES, A NEW OUTLOOK, A NEW ATTITUDE.

Nehemiah organized the people and rebuilt the wall of Jerusalem in only fifty-two days. To put this in perspective, consider this: Scholars estimate the wall was at least two miles long, enclosing about ninety acres of land.[1] From her excavations, one archeologist estimates they rebuilt the wall to a width of eight feet.[2] This they did in a mere fifty-two days. It required not only rebuilding, but a thorough assessment of the condition of the existing ruins, removal of the rubble, and determining what was salvageable for reuse. They not only rebuilt the wall in that time, they also completely restored ten city gates. Only one word accurately describes the results: miraculous!

Chapter 3 of Nehemiah views the entire undertaking in the rearview mirror. Nehemiah and all the people are, if you will, sitting around at the pot-luck supper after they've consecrated the wall and are savoring the victory. It's almost as if Nehemiah took paper and pen in hand and said to himself, "I had better write this down while I can remember it." We have before us a detailed record of how this all got done so quickly. At first glance, Nehemiah 3 may appear a bit boring. It is full of obscure archeological identifications and bizarre names that are difficult to pronounce. You're tempted say, "Let's move on and see what chapter 4 is like."

If you rush to the next chapter you will miss an indispensable leg of the journey toward revival in the rubble. Here we are reminded that the miracle of completing a God-sized assignment begins with the miracle of a God-given change of attitude.

The remarkable change of heart that God worked through Nehemiah into the Jewish people of his day is revealed in Nehemiah's review of the rebuilding in this chapter. It shows the cooperative spirit of the workers—a change so amazing that only God deserves credit for it.

Nehemiah begins his review of the work at the northwest corner of the city, at a place known as the Sheep Gate. He then moves in a counterclockwise direction around the city, describing how and where and who rebuilt this city wall.

Given their history and the conditions in which they'd lived for so long, it is truly amazing that these people listened to Nehemiah's challenge to rebuild the wall and that they concluded this was God's work. They didn't hear Nehemiah out and then say, "This is fine for you. Just don't count on us." They listened, heard God's voice speaking through Nehemiah's words, and collectively decided, "This is God work." As they put their hands to the work, they realized they weren't merely "doing their fair share"— pitching in, paying their dues, lending a hand or helping out. Because this was God's work, it was also worship.

How do I know this was their attitude? Where did Nehemiah begin his description of the rebuilding process? At the Sheep Gate (v. 1). By the way, he also ended there (v. 32). Why did he start and stop there?

The Sheep Gate was near the temple. Animals destined for sacrifice in the temple likely passed through this gate, thus the name. More than any other gate in the city, it was associated with the worship of God. Nehemiah began here because it expressed the essence of what the undertaking was all about. This is God's work!

Twice we are told this gate was "dedicated" (v. 1). From the very beginning this rebuilding project was consecrated or set apart to God. This was God's wall, for this was God's city, housing God's people where God's purposes were to be fulfilled. And it was the spiritual leaders ("the high priest and his fellow priests") who led the way.

We will discover in Nehemiah 12 that a huge celebration of consecration took place once the wall was completed. But what we discover here is that from the beginning the priests and people were to understand the nature of this work. Through the "dedication" of the work to God it became clear that this wasn't primarily about stone, mortar, tools, and plumb lines. This was about worship. Those things became physical expressions of an inward celebration of worship.

God had called them to the work, so they understood that this was His work.

They were building a physical wall for God. At that stage of redemptive history God had chosen to localize the manifestation of His presence in one place, the temple of God in Jerusalem. God is, of course, omnipresent, but when He was manifesting

Himself among mankind He chose to localize His presence—in a temple, in one city, among one people, through whom He intended to reach all peoples. Thus, when they rebuilt that wall, they were a part of the very expression of God in this world and the mission of God to take His loving salvation to all people.

In our time, post-Calvary, God does not restrict the manifestation of His presence to just one place. When Jesus encountered the Samaritan woman she tried to deflect His searching spiritual inquires by engaging Him in a contemporary debate: "Our fathers worshiped on this mountain, but you Jews claim that the place where we must worship is in Jerusalem" (John 4:20). "We say, 'God is here.' You say, 'God is there.' How can we even discuss spiritual things seriously?"

Jesus' answer was Copernican-like in its revolutionary breadth: "Believe me, woman, a time is coming when you will worship the Father neither on this mountain nor in Jerusalem. . . . A time is coming and has now come when the true worshipers will worship the Father in spirit and truth, for they are the kind of worshipers the Father seeks" (John 4:21, 23).

Worship is not a matter of location but of heart relationship. Though God had once localized the manifestation of His presence in the temple in Jerusalem, now, after the cross, God has chosen another temple to dwell in—His people, the church. "Don't you know that you yourselves [plural—not just individually, but corporately] are God's temple and that God's Spirit lives in you?" (1 Cor. 3:16).

God has called us to a building project in this, our day. The dwelling place we have been charged with building is not made of wood, brick, mortar or cement. It is composed of "living stones" (1 Pet. 2:5)—those who have placed their faith in Jesus Christ.

If we rightly hear God through Nehemiah, we will undertake our own building project. We will not apply it to physical structures but to people. It is in, among, and through His people that God wants to manifest His presence.

Good enough; but they built a physical wall. How are we to build a given people into a dwelling place for God?

Look again at the purpose served by walls around an ancient city. Walls were for *security*. We are to build up people in the Word so that they are steady, sure and secure from the surging tides of a contrary and constantly changing culture (Eph. 4:14–16). Walls were for *witness*. We are to equip one another to bear a winsome and compelling witness for Christ to an unbelieving world (Col. 4:6). Walls were for *perspective*. We are to build the people of God up so that we are able to look at life from God's perspective, not just a human perspective (Heb. 5:14). Walls were for *distinctiveness*, setting some things apart from other things. We need to build up the people of God as holy people, living to the glory of God and not for personal whim or comfort (1 Pet. 2:9).

> *E*VERY CONTACT WITH ANOTHER BELIEVER IS A DIVINELY GIVEN MOMENT OF MINISTRY. *Y*OU ARE TO LEAVE THEM STRONGER, MORE STEADY, MORE ABLE IN THE THINGS OF *G*OD THAN WHEN YOU FOUND THEM.

Every time you encounter another believer you are charged by God to build them up in faith. Every conversation and contact is a divinely given moment of ministry. You are, in that moment, under commission from God to build that person—to leave them stronger, more steady, more able in the things of God than when you found them. It is not a chance encounter. It is no accident. It is God's work!

It would take an attitude adjustment to begin to really live like that, wouldn't it? Revival's fire finds its dry tinder in our attitudes. The big lumber of miraculous impact never catches fire until the small stuff of attitudes has been ignited.

The attitude changes don't stop there, however. This is not only *God's* work, but it is *my* work as well.

If we see things only as God's work, we may conclude, "God is all-powerful; He doesn't need me. He can get His work done any way He likes. I'll just sit over here and see how God chooses to do it." Without an attitude adjustment life becomes a spectator sport, not a walk of faith, fellowship, and worship with the living God.

God imparted a sense of personal responsibility for the work to the people of Nehemiah's day. Significantly, Nehemiah often assigned people to work on the section of wall near their home. "Beyond them, Benjamin and Hasshub made repairs *in front of their house*; and next to them, Azariah son of Maaseiah, the son of Ananiah, made repairs *beside his house*" (v. 23; see also vv. 28–30). The word "house" is mentioned nine times in just twelve verses.

Why was this so ingenious? People likely felt more was personally at stake if they rebuilt the wall directly in front of the yard their children played in. It certainly saved travel time to and from work each day. If their enemies did attack them while at work, they were less likely to abandon the fight and flee if it took place near their home. It also enabled the entire family to get involved.

That was, in fact, one of Nehemiah's strategies—whole family involvement. "Shallum son of Hallohesh, ruler of a half-district of Jerusalem, repaired the next section with the help of his daughters" (v. 12). The sign outside didn't read "Shallum and Sons." It read, "Shallum and Daughters"! Why?

The Law made provision for a man's daughters to inherit his land if he had no sons (Num. 36:7–8). These daughters reasoned, "If the section of the wall by our home isn't secure and this city is overrun by enemies, we'll have nothing for the future." They had a vested interest in the security of the wall near their address.

Some folks were so transformed in heart that they completed work on the section of wall in front of their homes, then asked, "Is there anything else we can do?" You'll notice, for instance, that Meremoth took on two separate sections of the wall (vv. 4, 21). And Meshullam not only rebuilt the section in front of his personal residence (v. 30), he also reconstructed an additional section (v. 4).

A whole new attitude began to sweep through the previously defeated people. "This is my work. I've got to get this done. It is God's work, but God has laid it on me and I'm responsible."

People who didn't even live in Jerusalem came to shoulder the load together with those who did. Residents of Tekoa rebuilt a section of wall and then asked for another (vv. 5, 27). What a transformation in thinking!

One man stood out for his sense of personal responsibility. "Next to him, Baruch son of Zabbai zealously repaired another section" (v. 20a). Over forty different people are listed as having worked on the wall; only Baruch is mentioned for *how* he worked on the wall. Note the word "zealously." The word means to glow or burn. Normally it describes anger, but here it is used in a positive sense. What was it that marked Baruch out from the others? Did he work through water breaks? When everyone else had retired to their homes and were eating their meals, did they hear the sound of trowel on mortar and stone, look out the window and see Baruch still putting his back into the work? Whatever it was, this entire wall thing became personal to Baruch.

But there can be no lone rangers in this kind of work.

At 12:45 p.m. on May 10, 1869, the final spike was driven in the transcontinental railway at Promontory, Utah. Finally, east and west were merged as one! It was a magnificent feat of engineering. Thousands of miles of railway, completed by two competing sides, coming from two opposite directions, somehow met perfectly in one spot. That's teamwork!

We see the same thing in the building of the Jerusalem wall. Depending upon how you count them, there are between forty-two and forty-five sections of wall listed. Though each section differed in length, they would have averaged about 250 feet in length. If everyone owned their section, did the work themselves, and ignored what everyone else was doing, the sections would never meet end to end! Jerusalem would have had a giant circular statuary park surrounding the city, but they would not have had a wall.

There are over forty different people and fourteen groupings of people mentioned by Nehemiah in chapter 3. The miracle is not just that they all began to say, "This is *God's* work." Nor that they started to realize, "This is *my* work." The miracle began to come full circle when they realized, "This is *our* work!"

Entire groups of people began realizing they had to work together if God's work was going to be done.

The civic leaders started working together as never before. Repeatedly we discover rulers "of a half-district of Jerusalem" (vv. 9,

12, 16–18) or an entire "district" of the city (vv. 14, 15) working together. These were administrative districts established by the Persian government to organize the people. They were overcoming political differences and working side by side in God's work.

Some tradesmen began to get involved. The goldsmiths started saying, "Stone and mortar aren't exactly our area of expertise, but let's give it a try" (vv. 8, 31, 32). One of the city's perfume-makers—not exactly your rugged construction type—took responsibility for a section of wall (v. 8).

The local ministerial groups—the priests, Levites and temple servants—worked together on the wall (vv. 1, 17, 26).

The local chamber of commerce even dove in! The "merchants" did their fair share of the work (v. 32).

Perhaps most amazing of all is that out-of-towners started saying, "We want to be part of this." People from the towns of Jericho (v. 2), Tekoa (vv. 5, 27), Gibeon (v. 7), and Mizpah (vv. 7, 15, 19) all organized and sent work teams to Jerusalem. While others were securing the sections near their homes, these men either packed up their families or left them behind. They left homes, fields, and businesses to come and secure God's city. The wall didn't guard their homes. It didn't secure their fields or financial interests. For all they knew, their enemies might be ransacking their property even as they camped out in Jerusalem in order to assist.

The Jews experienced a seismic shift in thinking. They moved from understanding it as "God's work," to seeing it as "my work," to perceiving it as "our work." That is a miracle. That is a sure sign of approaching revival.

We live in a consumer culture. We are confronted with 52,000 options the moment we walk in our local grocery store. Millions of dollars are spent to convince us we deserve every one of them.

I am convinced that we have no idea how deeply this has affected our understanding of Christianity. Probably the biggest impact of the consumer mentality has been upon our understanding of the church. Before we ever arrive at the building for worship we've already been trained to ask, "What's in this for me?" We do so without even a hint of blush on our cheeks.

At some point God's Spirit must free us from the bondage of self-centeredness and make us the people of God.

The late W. A. Criswell, renowned former pastor of First Baptist Church of Dallas, stated our struggle and our need as eloquently as anyone. He wrote,

> The population of this country is 200 million. Eighty-four million are over 65 years of age, which leaves 116 million to do the work. People under 20 years of age total 75 million, which leaves 41 million to do the work. There are 22 million who are employed by the government, which leaves 19 million people to do the work. Four million are in the Armed Forces, which leaves 15 million to do the work. Deduct 14,800,000, the number of state and city office employees, leaving 200,000 to do the work. There are 188,000 in the hospitals and insane asylums, so that leaves 12,000 people to do the work. Now it may interest you to know there are 11,998 people in jail, so that leaves two people to carry the load. That's you and me—and brother, I'm getting tired of doing everything myself.[3]

REVIVAL TAKES A MASSIVE CHANGE OF ATTITUDE, SO THAT WE LOOK AT THE CHURCH AND ITS MINISTRY AND SAY, "THIS IS GOD'S WORK. THIS IS MY WORK. THIS IS OUR WORK! THIS IS TEAMWORK!"

The numbers may not be exact and the results a bit overstated, but you get the picture. If God is going to do something that will say to the world "I live!" it will take a massive change of attitude among His people. Should that happen, we will look at the church and its ministry and begin to say, "This is *God's* work. This is *my* work. This is *our* work!" But it will require even more than this. It will mean we begin to look at God's call and declare, "This is teamwork!"

That's not just a rehash of the platitude "Many hands make light work." It's an admission that an authentic miracle of spiritual oneness is required—many hands working as one.

When gasoline is brought into proximity with fire, one of two things happen—it's either something destructive or something productive. Through Nehemiah's leadership the fire of the Holy Spirit's enabling met with the fuel of many ready hands and the result was miraculously constructive!

Note the many indicators of teamwork in Nehemiah's retrospective on the building project. For example, twenty-eight times we encounter phrases like "next to him," "next to them," "next to that," "the next section," "beside him," and "beyond them."[4] Every occurrence describes a string of miracles as God enabled people to work side by side with folks they didn't necessarily like, appreciate or understand. They were people just like us. Some of them talked too much and worked too little. Others showed up late and went home early. There were those who took an inordinately long lunch break. Still others did shoddy work that had to be redone by others.

It's one thing to get a group of individuals involved in the same job; it's an entirely different thing to get them to work together.

Compare where our guided tour begins and ends (vv. 1, 31–32) and you note that there were priests working next to merchants. The ministerial association worked hand in hand with the chamber of commerce. You discover suppliers ("goldsmiths," vv. 8, 31, 32) and retailers ("merchants," vv. 31, 32) working arm in arm. There was a guy with a sordid past like Malkijah (v. 11; note his compromise in Ezra 10:31), but who now lived in repentance. There was a person like Meshullam (v. 4) who would later fail spiritually (see Neh. 6:18 where he allowed his daughter to marry the son of the man who plotted Nehemiah's death). These worked as one with ordinary citizens.

Nehemiah lists between forty-two and forty-five individual sections of the wall, over forty individuals and fourteen groups of people, and yet they managed to work in such harmony that the ends all met up and were securely connected, so that the wall was completed with no gaps. As mentioned earlier, the average length of each wall segment calculates out to approximately 250 feet. Yet not all sections were of the same length. In fact, one guy and his friends repaired a section 500 yards long (v. 13), while some others did a section the length of one house (vv. 21–23). The work wasn't always equitable, but somehow the diversity of individuals was harnessed and made to work together as one. The result was that the wall was completed in a mere fifty-two days.

Mark it down for what it is. Put it in large letters and italicize it so we don't miss it: *MIRACLE!*

We hear no word about griping, grumbling or complaining. How can that be? Only through a work of God that begins in a major attitude shift for all involved.

This is God's work. This is my work. This is our work. And this is *teamwork!*

The same attitude shift is required to see God's work accomplished in us today. Nehemiah sought to restore not just physical walls around Jerusalem but God's presence in His people as they dwelt there. In the same way, we are called to make God's people the place of His dwelling. Today, on this side of Christ's redemptive work, God makes clear how His people will be built into a place for His glorious dwelling. Paul said the process happens when God gifts His church for the building process (Eph. 4:7–11). Then Spirit-gifted leaders guide the church in building itself into a temple for the Lord (vv. 12–13). The entire church, made of a mosaic of unique individuals, then generates the work of edification (vv. 14–16).

The process is parallel and the application is binding, but Nehemiah had one great advantage. His building project had dimensions—a prescribed height and width. Certain things went here, others went there. There was a prescribed course the wall was to run. It was tangible, touchable, measurable.

Our building is appraised only by "the whole measure of the fullness of Christ" (Eph. 4:13). We keep building until we "grasp how wide and long and high and deep is the love of Christ" (3:18). Our only time restraint is to keep building until

Jesus returns. We are everlastingly to build one another up until God freely dwells in us and moves through us.

The building of the wall is a great success story, isn't it? But it was not without its problems. It never is. "The next section was repaired by the men of Tekoa, *but their nobles would not put their shoulders to the work* under their supervisors" (v. 5).

Not everyone will catch the vision. Some will cling to safety, old bitternesses, or lame agendas. You will not get cooperation from everyone. Rarely is there a unanimous vote. In fact, if you get a string of unanimous votes, it may be a symptom of apathy. Or it may be a sign that the vision is too small—everyone agrees because it won't cost them anything.

The next chapter of Nehemiah begins fifty-two days earlier, walking us carefully through the blood, sweat and tears of the building process. It will be glorious. It will be bloody. It will be jubilant. It will be ugly.

As we rejoice in Nehemiah's triumphs and tremble at the death-threats directed at him, as we marvel at the faith and unity of the people and shake our heads at the bile and intrigue of their enemies, we get to see the biggest miracle of all—a seismic shift in attitude that allowed the people of God to experience a certifiable miracle from God.

1. Why is attitude all-important in doing God's work and walking by faith?

   _____

   _____

2. Is it harder to get God's people to see their *circumstances* with new eyes or to see *themselves* with new eyes? Why?

   _____

   _____

3. Is God manifesting Himself among His people in your local church? How can you tell?

   _____

   _____

4. How can you be used of God to help His people see His work as their responsibility?

   _____

   _____

5. What will be the outcome if God's people don't work as one with a common vision? How can you assure they do?

   _____

   _____

6. What practical steps can your church take to move from seeing things simply as *God's* work to seeing them as *my* work, as *our* work and, ultimately, as *teamwork*?

   _____

   _____

7. What should be our response to Christians who refuse to get involved in God's work?

   _____

   _____

6

When Opposition Mounts

*I*t is a nearly inviolable law of revival: For every divine action there is an unequal (but highly motivated) and opposite reaction. When God moves, evil forces muster. Do something for God's glory and you will experience opposition.

Consider what happened in the community of Cassadaga, Florida. That city had not one Christian church within its boundaries. Not one. It is not, however, an unspiritual place—the city is filled with spiritualists, New Age devotees, and dabblers in the occult. It has been dubbed the metaphysical mecca of Florida. Local mediums even claim that Cassadaga is some sort of portal to the spiritual world.

Seeing a need in the community, a Christian ministry targeted the city for a new church plant. However, when the group attempted to initiate ministry, the Volusia County Council voted to ban them from the city. Tortured logic and twisting of existing zoning ordinances produced a four-to-three decision to prohibit the Christians from setting up shop.

In a federal lawsuit filed by the ministry, attorney Matthew Staver said, "There is no Christian church in Cassadaga. It is certainly a violation of federal and constitutional law to prohibit a church from locating in a secular area of town, and it is even more egregious to prohibit a church solely because of its Christian viewpoint."

If we didn't already have enough evidence, this story reminds us again that obedience to God brings resistance from the world. Speaking the truth elicits a gag rule from proponents of error. Plant your feet for righteousness and you will meet opposition. It is true on the national or international scene, and it will prove true in the theater of your life as well.

*I*F YOU WANT TO SEE *G*OD WORK THROUGH YOU TO BRING REVIVAL, COUNT THE COST. *T*HOSE WHO ARE COMFORTABLE WITH THE STATUS QUO WILL RESIST YOU.

Do you want God to do something through you that only He can do—something God-sized, something that will make the world take note of God's power and presence? Count the cost: there will be opposition. Those who are comfortable with the status quo will resist you.

God called Nehemiah to do something beyond his ability. Nehemiah believed God and stepped forward in faith. Those with a vested interest in the status quo reacted the moment God began to bless Nehemiah's step of faith. Chapter 4 of Nehemiah introduces us to their strategic efforts to end the rebuilding of God's city. Their efforts to silence and still Nehemiah and his irritating dream of a restored Jerusalem are recounted here. But this fourth chapter is also about how Nehemiah and the people of God faced that opposition and saw the will of God done.

Strategies of Discouragement

Note, first, the world's strategies of discouragement. I find six of them.

Strategy #1: Ridicule

One is ridicule. Do God's will and the world will disparage you. Nehemiah's enemies were skilled in mockery.

"When Sanballat [one of Nehemiah's top three enemies] heard that we were rebuilding the wall, he became angry and was greatly incensed. He ridiculed the Jews . . ." (v. 1). Ridicule grows out of anger—anger over encroaching on *my* space, *my* comforts, and *my* agenda. When God does a God-thing, it encroaches on our comfort. Some don't like it and, in anger, they spew forth ridicule.

Notice the specifics of Sanballat's ridicule: ". . . in the presence of his associates and the army of Samaria, he said, 'What are those feeble Jews doing? Will they restore their wall? Will they offer sacrifices? Will they finish in a day? Can they bring the stones back to life from those heaps of rubble—burned as they are?'" (v. 2).

Interestingly, Sanballat didn't speak *to* the Jewish people. He spoke in their presence as they were rebuilding the city wall, but he spoke *to* his friends. He gathered his caustic comrades in a staged scene in which he put five questions to his friends, but made certain he said them loud enough so the Jewish wall-builders could hear each one clearly. The entire episode was staged to produce the desired dramatic effect.

"What are those feeble Jews doing?" Sanballat wasn't just calling them names. There was a half-truth in his question, because the word translated "feeble" means to be weak, withered, frail, or powerless. That is, in fact, what they were. The Jews were powerless in themselves to see God's work completed. That half-truth, thrown in with a dig, got under their skin. That's what ridicule does.

"Will they restore their wall?" He was casting doubt. He was putting into audible words what the Jews may have been secretly wondering in their hearts. "They can't do this! Who do they think they are?"

"Will they offer sacrifices?" Sanballat was mocking their trust in God. He may have been asking, "What are you going to do, *pray* the walls up?"[1] Then an orchestrated belly laugh by the whole bunch underscored their derision.

"Will they finish in a day?" These sissy perfume-makers (3:8), jewelry-makers (3:8, 32), and women (3:12) had no idea what they had undertaken, nor how to complete the job. "I hope you packed a lunch! Are you expecting to finish by nightfall?"

"Can they bring the stones back to life from those heaps of rubble—burned as they are?" When Babylon conquered Jerusalem they not only knocked the wall around Jerusalem down, they also burned much of the city. In the flames much of the limestone would have become weak. Were some of the rocks in the existing wall crumbling in the worker's hands as they cleared the site for reconstruction, even as Sanballat satirized their efforts? Of course, not every stone was worthless; some could be reused in the new wall. But Sanballat wasn't a stickler for accuracy. Ridicule doesn't have to be entirely true in order to be effective. It achieves its purpose if it moves its victim to see more negatives than positives.

Strategy #2: Taunts

Ridicule is powerfully effective, but it's not the only weapon in the world's arsenal of discouragement. Ridicule morphs into taunts. "Tobiah the Ammonite, who was at his side, said, 'What they are building—if even a fox climbed up on it, he would break down their wall of stones!' " (v. 3).

Tobiah was heckling them! The taunt was that their work was so inferior, their workmanship so flimsy, that even if a light-footed fox walked across it the whole thing would crumble. "It's a house of cards in a high wind!"

It was a gross exaggeration, if not a blatant lie. Excavations by Katherine Kenyon reveal that Nehemiah's wall was rebuilt to a thickness of some eight feet. Taunts don't have to be true to the facts, they need only sell one's view of the facts. To be effective, they need only suggest that their illusion is closer to reality than the truth.

Strategy #3: Intimidation

A third strategy of discouragement is intimidation. "But when Sanballat, Tobiah, the Arabs, the Ammonites and the men of Ashdod heard that the repairs to Jerusalem's walls had gone ahead and that the gaps were being closed, they were very angry. They all plotted together to come and fight against Jerusalem and stir up trouble against it." (vv. 7–8).

That is nothing but intimidation. Sanballat was governor of Samaria to the north of Judah. Tobiah was over the Ammonites, to the east. The Arabs were headed by Geshem and were to the south. Then there were the men of Ashdod, the leading city of the Philistines, which was on the west.

Nehemiah and his followers were completely surrounded. "They all plotted together to come and fight against Jerusalem and stir up trouble against it" (v. 8).

It was the international equivalent of what happened to me at prom time during my senior year in high school. Then, as now, the prom was devoted to one great purpose: getting drunk. I chose not to do that, which was a fairly well-known fact in my small class in a small town in central Iowa. In such a small school it was difficult to find another group to hang with. If you were not in "the group," you weren't in *any* group. One day, as the prom drew nearer, I was surrounded by a number of my classmates in the hall. They said, "We know about you. We know you don't. But you will, because we'll find you. We're going to get you. We're going to make you."

Fortunately, they didn't find me that night, but their intimidation worked—on the emotional level, at least. You've likely felt that from the world yourself.

Strategy #4: Propaganda

There's a fourth strategy here. It is propaganda.

"Meanwhile, the people in Judah said, 'The strength of the laborers is giving out, and there is so much rubble that we cannot rebuild the wall' " (v. 10).

The propaganda machine was operating at full capacity! Some translations set verse ten off in a different format, suggesting that this is a bit of poetry. The words have Hebrew rhythm to it.[2] In fact, it is likely that it had been taken up by the workers as a song. They raised these depressing words in song even as they labored with their hands to rebuild.

It was a song of defeat. It reminds me of gloomy ol' Eeyore, of Winnie the Pooh fame. "Everything is horrible. Nothing goes my way. Life is a drag." Let your voice fall off at the end of each sentence to capture the desired effect. So they sang, "The strength of the laborers is giving out, and there is so much rubble that we cannot rebuild the wall."

Where did they get their song? I believe it came from their enemies. Their opponents began to plant the idea, "You can't do this!" Whether they wrote the lyrics themselves or only planted the seed, these words later became the lyrics of the people as they became increasingly discouraged in their work for God. It was the equivalent of enemy broadcasts over allied airwaves, spouting defeatist messages of gloom and doom.

> *OUR HOMES ARE INFILTRATED BY POWERFUL MESSAGES DESIGNED TO DEFEAT US, AND WE DANCE TO THEIR TUNE. IT'S PROPAGANDA.*

It is an example of the enemy stealing the arts and crafting powerful, culturally relevant messages designed to promote defeat among the people of God. Does it still happen today? Are there examples in our society where the media or the arts are taken over by the enemy to sell their messages? It infiltrates our homes, and we dance to its tune. It's propaganda. Someone once wisely noted, "Give me the music of a nation and I care not what its laws may be." You can have the judicial system; take both the executive and legislative branches of government; write the laws to say what you will—but seize the media, and you'll rule the people.

Strategy #5: Paranoia

Paranoia was the fifth strategy employed. "Also our enemies said, 'Before they know it or see us, we will be right there among them and will kill them and put an end to the work' " (v. 11).

Things were serious. Murder was not out of the question—at least that's what the Jews' opponents wanted them to believe. The believers began to jump at the rustle of wind-blown leaves. The snap of a twig brought their hearts to a stop. Every breath came rapid and shallow. Night watchmen spent the dark hours of their duty on pins and needles. The message had been clearly conveyed: "We will move by stealth, under cover of night, grab you and kill you. We will take you away in body bags if we must, but you will not rebuild this wall!"

It was paranoia, and it doesn't automatically disappear when you come to faith in Christ. Sometimes Christians are the most paranoid of all people. We are quick to conclude that everything is a conspiracy, an organized effort by a secret society that is out to get us. Paranoia seldom delivers from danger. More often it seizes our faith and stops our obedience. It makes us feel like Robert Orden: "Sometimes I get the feeling the whole world is against me. But deep down inside I know that's not true; some of the smaller nations are neutral."

Strategy #6: Rumor

Note, then, the final strategy of the enemy—rumor. "Then the Jews who lived near them came and told us ten times over, 'Wherever you turn, they will attack us' " (v. 12).

Who was saying this? The Jewish people who lived outside the city of Jerusalem, among the pagans who had repopulated the land of Judah and were opposed to rebuilding Jerusalem. The Jews living in Samaria, Ashdod, Ammon and among the Arabs came to the rebuilders of Jerusalem and said, "No matter what you do, no matter how you try to defend yourself, they're going to launch a surprise attack on us."

Note the pronouns: "Wherever *you* turn, they will attack *us*." Can you hear it? "You may be passionate about this rebuilding effort. Who knows, you may even be right about it. But you are putting my family in harm's way! And all the defense plans I've heard so far aren't adequate to deal with the rumored attacks we're hearing about."

The pagans living among dispersed Jews outside Jerusalem started planting thoughts in their heads. A whisper campaign began. The rumor mill was cranked up and well fed, and its cross hairs were centered on the resolve of the Jewish people.

The people clamored to Nehemiah at least "ten times"! This is a Hebrew euphemism for "over and over."[3] If at first a lie does not succeed, let it fly, fly again. Sufficient air time can make almost anything sound convincing.

Strategies of Faith

Ridicule, taunts, intimidation, propaganda, paranoia and rumor —these are strategies of discouragement, designed to keep the people of God from doing the will of God. How can we meet and defeat these? The chapter, fortunately, provides a believer's strategy of faith in the face of discouragement. It is a fourfold strategy.

Strategy #1: Prayer

First, there is prayer. Verses four and five recount a prayer uttered by Nehemiah. A couple of things shock us about his prayer. For one, there is no introduction to the prayer. He never said, "Let's pray" or "Shall we bow our heads." But there is something refreshing about that; it reveals that prayer was as natural to Nehemiah as breathing. I had a professor who used begin each class with, "Shall we have a breath of prayer?" That is precisely what praying is—spiritual breathing. Prayer is the soul's involuntary response to the presence of God. Prayer is taking in God's life-giving company.

Hear, then, Nehemiah's spiritual breathing: "Hear us, O our God, for we are despised. Turn their insults back on their own heads. Give them over as plunder in a land of captivity. Do not cover up their guilt or blot out their sins from your sight, for they have thrown insults in the face of the builders" (vv. 4–5).

It's a little unnerving, isn't it? What are we to do with that? It's certainly not a typical Sunday-school prayer. It is embarrassingly and beautifully authentic. Embarrassing because we seldom are so authentic. Beautiful because we've all felt the same way and have been afraid to admit it.

In essence Nehemiah was saying, "God, let them experience all the hardship we've experienced as captives. Give them what we've experienced and let's see how they do with it!" He went on to pray, "God, damn them! Damn them all!"

Before you slam this book shut in horror, reread the passage. You'll discover that is precisely what Nehemiah prayed. He asked God not to forgive the sins of his enemies.

That's uncomfortable, isn't it? What do we do with that? And what do we do with similar statements throughout the book of Psalms? What are we to make of intercessions such as "May no one . . . take pity on his fatherless children" (Ps. 109:12), "May they be blotted out of the book of life" (Ps. 69:28), and "Break the teeth in their mouths, O God" (Ps. 58:6)? God honored such prayer by including it in Scripture. But what are we to do with such passages, with such feelings?

We must begin by realizing that this is authentic. Far too many of us wait to pray until we've got the plastic smile affixed properly. Only when the mask has been adjusted, do we dare go to God. That is hypocrisy. Nehemiah is being genuine. He was simply admitting, "Right now, here's where my heart is." No hiding. No falsehood. No hypocrisy. No masks. Simply, "Here is the reality of my heart."

I am not recommending prayer as some kind of therapy, as a spiritual way to vent pent-up frustrations. That is secular reasoning. I am suggesting, however, that our God is big enough to handle what is on our hearts. He invites us to wring the bile from our hearts in honest prayer. We may be thankful that He doesn't always give us what we ask, and we should be glad that He accepts us only when we come as we truly are.

Prayer begins with authenticity and honesty to God. We must also realize that prayer is not the end of the matter. Prayer is not simply something we only dare utter audibly when we can show we've arrived at the place God wants us to be. Prayer is the designated way of getting from where we are to where He wants us to be. Prayer is as much about transforming our hearts as it is changing our circumstances.

Prayer is not pulled out and waved before the world to say, "See how spiritual I am!" It is the authentic, honest cry of a person who wants God's will in all of its fullness and is struggling in his journey to the heart of God.

Such was Nehemiah's prayer. But I believe the best part of his prayer came after the "Amen." After he poured out the pain, fear, and anger of his heart, Nehemiah matter-of-factly reported, "So we rebuilt the wall" (v. 6a).

NEHEMIAH PRAYED WITH PASSIONATE, GENUINE HONESTY, THEN WENT AHEAD AND DID GOD'S WILL DESPITE HIS FEELINGS. HE JUST GOT UP OFF HIS KNEES AND DID HIS JOB.

What happened to all the emotion? Where did the anger go? What became of all the bile belched up from the bottom of his heart?

What I like most about Nehemiah is that after he had just prayed with passionate, genuine honesty, he had the audacity to believe that God would work with him as he went ahead and did God's will despite his feelings. He just got up off his knees and did his job. He prayed to God, making note of the opposition and his feelings toward them. Then he got busy.

How refreshing! Nehemiah didn't just pray, he got up from prayer and got back to work. He didn't say, "God, get rid of those dirty, rotten pagans, then knock on the door and I'll peek out. If I think it's safe, I'll come out and talk about doing something for You!" No—he prayed and then went right ahead with what he knew to be the will of God.

In the face of intimidation and conspiracy, Nehemiah prayed once again. "But we prayed to our God and posted a guard day and night to meet this threat" (v. 9).

Prayer, yes—and a little planning as well. He dared to believe that he might be a part of God's answer to his own prayer. "We prayed . . . and posted a guard." That's the right balance of the sovereignty of God and the responsibility of man.

It's like the old story of the little girl whose brother had built a trap in which he planned to capture sparrows. The sister felt sorry for the birds. Every day she prayed her brother's trap would fail. One day her mother noticed a new confidence in her intercessions. After three days of the new attitude in prayer, her mother had to inquire about how she could be so positive God would answer her prayer and her brother's trap would fail. The little girl smiled, "Because, Mama, I went out three days ago and kicked the trap to pieces!"

S. D. Gordon once said, "You can do *more* than pray *after* you have prayed. But you can*not* do more than pray *until* you have prayed."[4] Pray first. Pray always. But realize you may be the avenue through which God wants to answer that prayer.

Strategy #2: Protection

Nehemiah knew that he couldn't do more than pray until he had prayed, but once he prayed (and continued praying!) he knew there was something more he could do. For that reason the second part of the believer's strategy of faith involves protection.

"Then the Jews who lived near them came and told us ten times over, 'Wherever you turn, they will attack us.' Therefore I stationed some of the people behind the lowest points of the wall at the exposed places, posting them by families, with their swords, spears and bows" (vv. 12–13).

It was simple, practical, earthly, but not unspiritual. You'll notice that Nehemiah pulled some of the people off the construction crew and put them on guard duty. No doubt he hesitated to do so, for they were on a tight schedule. Yet the reality of the opposition was such that they not only needed to pray about protection, they needed to do something practical and physical to assure their protection. Thus Nehemiah took some of the people off the work line and armed them. He stationed them directly in front of the place they'd be least likely to run from if battle came—in front of their wives, their children and their homes. That's motivation. He made it personal to them. Nehemiah encouraged them to pray, but got them involved in some practical expressions of protection as well.

There are times in our lives that, when we have prayed thoroughly over a matter, the most spiritual thing we can do is to continue to pray and do something practical to protect ourselves. Some people decry insurance as "unspiritual." They demand that we must "trust God" instead of "waste" God's resources on insurance. Frankly, if a person is able and yet does not have certain reasonable kinds and levels of insurance in this day and age, it is likely a sign, not of faith, but of foolishness. Of course we ought to pray for safety, health, and protection. Our trust is in God. Yet the fact remains that those who do not have insurance often expect the body of Christ to help them should hardship come their way. They end up impoverishing the people of God because they wanted to "live by faith."

Strategy #3: Preaching

To prayer and protection, preaching is added to the believer's strategy of faith. A steady diet of Biblical preaching is part of the minimum weekly requirements for spiritual health.

"After I looked things over, I stood up and said to the nobles, the officials and the rest of the people, 'Don't be afraid of them. Remember the Lord, who is great and awesome, and fight for your brothers, your sons and your daughters, your wives and your homes.' When our enemies heard that we were aware of their plot and that God had frustrated it, we all returned to the wall, each to his own work" (vv. 14–15).

Nehemiah was preaching! In essence he simply said, "Remember what the Scriptures say!" His first words were "Don't be afraid . . ." Throughout their history God had repeatedly sent His messengers to issue that command. At least thirty times in the Hebrew Scriptures the command "Do not be afraid" had been repeated. Nehemiah was simply reminding them of what God had said. The command was calculated to recall to their minds those who had faced opposition fearlessly because God had commanded them.

He was also telling them, "Remember who the Lord is!" Nehemiah insisted that God was still "great and awesome."

Everything about everything hinges on what we think about God. Tozer was correct when he wrote,

> What comes into our minds when we think about God is the most important thing about us. . . . Were we able to extract from any man a complete answer to the question, 'What comes into your mind when you think about God?' we might predict with certainty the spiritual future of that man.[5]

Nehemiah forced the people to answer two questions: "Who is God right now, right here?" and "What has this God said to us?" He knew there could be no more vital pursuit than answering those two questions. But there was a third charge issued as well: "Remember who you are!" Nehemiah exhorted them to "fight for your brothers, your sons and your daughters, your wives and your homes." We are a people who exist as God's people *in community*. When we defect from our responsibility to God's people, we cease to exist as God's people. That is not a matter of salvation, but of identification.

Nehemiah reminded them that they had people to defend. They were husbands, fathers, brothers, sons, neighbors. "In view of who God is, in view of what God has said, in view of who He has made you to be, keep going!"

Remember who God is, what He has said, and who He has made you to be—not a bad starting point for defining preaching! Unless they stand before good, Biblical preaching, the people of God will not stand at all. "With its preaching Christianity stands or falls," asserted P. T. Forsyth. And D. Martyn Lloyd-Jones declared, "When the church gives to prayer and preaching their true Biblical priority, she is able, under God, to meet the challenge of every generation."

Strategy #4: Prudence

To prayer, protection, and preaching, Nehemiah added a final, stabilizing leg to the believer's strategy of faith—prudence. Prudence describes a person wisely cautious in the practical affairs of life. Note the careful, prudent acts of faith that enabled Nehemiah and his contemporaries to forge ahead in the will of God despite the opposition of the world.

> From that day on, half of my men did the work, while the other half were equipped with spears, shields, bows and armor. The officers posted themselves behind all the people of Judah who were building the wall. Those who carried materials did their work with one hand and held a weapon in the other, and each of the builders wore his sword at his side as he worked. But the man who sounded the trumpet stayed with me.
>
> Then I said to the nobles, the officials and the rest of the people, "The work is extensive and spread out, and we are widely separated from each other along the wall. Wherever you hear the sound of the trumpet, join us there. Our God will fight for us!"
>
> So we continued the work with half the men holding spears, from the first light of dawn till the stars came out. At that time I also said to the people, "Have every man and his helper stay inside Jerusalem at night, so they can serve us as guards by night and workmen by day." Neither I nor my brothers nor my men nor the guards with me took off our clothes; each had his weapon, even when he went for water. (vv. 16–23)

Nehemiah and the people were prudent about organization (v. 16), their methods (v. 17), their preparedness (v. 18), and their systems (vv. 19–20). They were prudently cautious about their every move, even in the most mundane details of life (vv. 22–23).

We can easily mistake any risk for the risk of faith-filled obedience. It *is* a sign of faith to take any risk required by *obedience*. To take a risk *not* required by obedience may be a sign of something entirely different. Nehemiah was not afraid to risk everything in obedience to God, but he was not quick to risk simply for the adrenaline rush risk brings.

The world has a strategy to discourage you from living in the fullness of Christ. You, as a believer, have been given a strategy for walking by faith.

It is not a question of whether you will encounter opposition as you pursue the will of God; it is what you will do when opposition comes. Will you cower and hide? Whine and complain to God? Or will you face it, praying your way through? Will you prudently guard your life and ministry, returning again and again to the basic questions of who God is, what He has said, who He has called you to be and what He has called you to do?

Choose this latter course and God will "keep you from falling"; He will make certain "to present you before his glorious presence without fault and with great joy" (Jude 24). Take up the strategies of faith He has given you and He will guarantee that you "stand firm in all the will of God, mature and fully assured" (Col. 4:12).

Reaching Toward Revival

1. Is anything of real significance ever accomplished without opposition? Why?

   _____

   _____

2. How have you faced ridicule or taunts for doing God's will? What effect did it have on you?

   _____

   _____

3. In what ways might intimidation, propaganda, paranoia or rumor show up as opposition for God's people today?

   _____

   _____

4. How do Nehemiah's prayers (vv. 4–5, 9) challenge our conception of prayer? How might his example transform our praying?

   _____

   _____

5. How should Nehemiah's model of practical protection (vv. 12–13) be applied in our circles today?

   _____

   _____

6. What part does strong, Biblical preaching play in overcoming opposition to God's work?

   _____

   _____

7. What does prudence look like when God is moving in revival? How might a failure in prudence affect the approaching revival?

   _____

   _____

7

Flawed Foundations

Much has been written about our transformation into a postmodern culture. Postmodern thought denies absolute truth, which leaves us with no fixed point of reference—no standard by which we can define good and evil. Life becomes incoherent, and ultimately meaningless. The postmodernist concludes that we each can do whatever we want, without recrimination, judgment or guilt. Guilt is considered to be nothing more than the preconceived notions of a morality left over from an earlier and uninformed age.

Ideas will ultimately demand expression, and so we find the aimlessness of postmodern thought expressing itself in popular music, in cutting-edge art, and even in progressive architecture. In fact, postmodern architects have done us a great favor, for their work may provide one of the easiest places to spot the inconsistencies of their worldview. Tour a postmodern structure and you will find a building without rhyme or reason. Staircases will lead to nowhere. Windows may look into walls, not the world outside. Doors might open into nothing.

Why? Because life doesn't make sense, and, "After all," they ask, "shouldn't reality be portrayed in the buildings in which we live?" Proponents of postmodernism become almost giddy over this triumphant expression of "reality." Perhaps we should ask, as Dr. Ravi Zacharias once inquired of a tour guide directing his group through a postmodern structure, "Did the designer do the same thing with the foundation?"[1]

A building can abide with quite a lot of nonsense on the top floor as long as the foundation is secure. But if the foundation is incoherent and flawed, everything above ground is worthless, no matter how well it's put together. Foundations, apparently, are not as meaningless as postmodern thought would have us believe.

Nehemiah knew that if the foundation is flawed, everything built upon it is pointless. In his day the flawed foundation was not under the wall he was called to rebuild around Jerusalem. It was the bedrock of the people's hearts toward God and one another that was unsound. He addresses this in chapter 5.

Nehemiah and his crew faced many obstacles in rebuilding the wall, not the least of which was the hostile opposition of their pagan neighbors. As we saw in chapter 4, death threats were issued; rumors were spread; paranoia had begun to settle in. It was no small task to remain focused and keep building.

But an even more dangerous problem confronted Nehemiah and the people. It came not from the outside pressure of an unbelieving community but from a previously undetected internal flaw in the foundation of their relationships. The character and conduct of these Jewish rebuilders was threatening to damage the ministry to which God had called them. It threatened not only to bring the whole project to a halt but to destroy what had already been accomplished.

The message of Nehemiah 5 is simply this: *No revival of God's people ever rises above the level of the integrity of their relationships.* Our relationships to God and one another are the bedrock upon which the superstructure of ministry is built. If there is a crack in the relational foundation, all else simply awaits its appointed collapse.

> *No revival of God's people ever rises above the level of the integrity of their relationships.*

The fatal flaw in the foundation of the builders' relationships was exposed by a threefold problem: unpredictable weather patterns created drought conditions and a devastating crop failure (v. 3); unparalleled taxation by the Persian king created an economic crisis (v. 4); and unprincipled interest rates buried people in insurmountable debt (vv. 3–5).

Under this outward pressure three groups of people began to cry for relief. Their complaints are marked out by the repeated phrase, "Some were saying" (v. 2), "Others were saying" (v. 3) and "Still others were saying" (v. 4).

The first group to lift their lament were the working poor (vv. 1–2) who didn't own a house or property. There was no family farm. They labored daily for someone else in order to get a bit of money, buy food, and feed their families. Like the others, they had heard Nehemiah's call to rebuild, responded in faith, and spent their days working on the wall. But because they had given up their day jobs, they weren't receiving an income and their families were going hungry.

The second group to complain were the land owners. "Others were saying, 'We are mortgaging our fields, our vineyards and our homes to get grain during the famine" (v. 3). Though they owned land, they too were so busy rebuilding the walls of Jerusalem that they were losing out on their regular income. Their crops weren't coming in, and they began to mortgage their homes just to buy food to put on the table.

A third group to protest were the farmers. Oppressed by the high taxes imposed by the Persian king, they were forced into debt. "Still others were saying, 'We have had to borrow money to pay the king's tax on our fields and vineyards. Although we are of the same flesh and blood as our countrymen and though our sons are as good as theirs, yet we have to subject our sons and daughters to slavery. Some of our daughters have already been enslaved, but we are powerless, because our fields and our vineyards belong to others.' " (vv. 4–5).

Persian kings were renowned for their generosity in religious liberties toward the captive people they ruled, but were harsh in matters of taxation. When Alexander the Great conquered the kingdom of Persia and took the capital city, Susa, he discovered a storage hold of 270 tons of gold, and 1,200 tons of silver, all apparently acquired through heavy taxation.

These ordinary folks said to Nehemiah, "We can't take it anymore! The drought is killing our crops. When tax time came, we were forced to mortgage everything to pay the king. We can't pay back what we owe and in lieu of payment the creditors are taking our children away!"

What a horrible plight! When God's people give themselves to God's work, they often suffer when hard economic times hit. Yet their problem was not simply economic—in fact, Nehemiah insisted, it was not even *primarily* economic. Something far more serious than drought, taxation, or high interest rates threatened them. Their primary obstacle was relational—how they were treating one another. If God's people stand together, they can withstand almost anything, but when they turn on one another, God no longer stands with them.

> *REVIVAL IS STALLED BY FRACTURED RELATIONSHIPS WITHIN, NOT FEROCIOUS ATTACKS FROM WITHOUT.*

Those who called themselves by God's name permitted a climactic, economic, and agricultural crisis to destroy their relationships. Who were they crying out against? Not the Persian king, but their Jewish brothers (v. 1)! Revival is stalled by fractured relationships within, not ferocious attacks from without. What was derailing the work of God was not an evil, pagan government that was demanding exorbitant taxes; it was the opportunistic brothers who used calamity to prey upon their own people.

Perhaps a bit of background will enable us to see even more clearly the real issue. Jewish law did not prohibit a Jew from loaning money to another Jew, but it *did* prohibit loaning the money *at interest*.

> If you lend money to one of my people among you who is needy, do not be like a moneylender; charge him no interest. . . . Do not charge your brother interest, whether on money or food or anything else that may earn interest. You may charge a foreigner interest, but not a brother Israelite, so that the LORD your God may bless you in everything you put your hand to in the land you are entering to possess. (Exod. 22:25; Deut. 23:19–20)

Notice that the Law did not prohibit a Jew from loaning money at interest to a *non*-Jew, but only to a fellow Jew. There was to be something different about the internal relationships of the people of God with one another. This is not an indictment against *taking* or *making* a loan, or even against making a loan *with interest*. It is an indictment upon the people of God for a breakdown in their special, peculiar relationship to one another. They were not behaving toward one another as the Scriptures demand of God's people.

Can you imagine? Certain Jews were actually taking the children of other brother Jews in payment for debts, and then treating them as slaves (v. 5)!

During captivity in Persia some of the Jewish people had become enslaved to the Gentiles because of economic hardship. Nehemiah and other Jewish people of means had begun to redeem these people from captivity out of their own funds (v. 8). But now some of the Jews were enslaving again their brothers just as the pagan people had.

Though the external pressures of life were great, these were not the greatest problems facing God's people. The fundamental trouble was that they allowed these external forces to lay bare the internal flaw that existed in their hearts. *The people of God were acting like pagans!*

God, through Nehemiah, was doing more than condemning bad economic practices. He was expressing His deep concern for how His people relate to one another. Even today, the unique relationship we share together as the people of God is under attack on many fronts. Unforgiveness, bitterness, sexual impurity, unresolved conflicts, gossip, the inability to distinguish between opinion and Biblical absolutes—the enemies of our unique calling are legion!

In this case it was financial. As much as any other area, finances can be a stumbling block to God's people. Then, as now, God called His people to a higher standard.

> If one of your countrymen becomes poor and is unable to support himself among you, help him as you would an alien or a temporary resident, so he can continue to live among you. Do not take interest of any kind from him, but fear your God, so that your countryman may continue to live among you. You must not lend him money at interest or sell him food at a profit. I am the LORD your God, who brought you out of Egypt to give you the land of Canaan and to be your God.
>
> If one of your countrymen becomes poor among you and sells himself to you, do not make him work as a slave. He is to be treated as a hired worker or a temporary resident among you; he is to work for you until the Year of Jubilee. (Lev. 25:35–40)

In the face of such relational breakdown, Nehemiah said, "When I heard their outcry and these charges, I was very angry" (v. 6). Notice that he was not angry at the Persian king for the high taxation rates. High taxes were a fact of life for them—it is what you would expect of a government that has no claim on God. Nor was Nehemiah angry with God over the drought that allowed the famine to take place.

But Nehemiah was incensed! He was livid because the people of God were living like ordinary people and not according to their high calling. The arena in which their failure was on display was within the circle of their relationships.

They were behaving no better than the money-grubbing opportunists who jack up prices on bottled water during a natural disaster or sell generators and chain saws for five times their regular price after a hurricane or tornado tears through town.

Don't fool yourself into thinking that the plea "It's just business" will pacify God. God has a claim upon your business life as much as your devotional life. We are not to behave like everyone else, for we are not like everyone else. We have been bought at a price and we are not our own.

Paul and Peter both demanded that our relationships under the new covenant must bear the mark of Christ's presence.

> As a prisoner for the Lord, then, I urge you to live a life worthy of the calling you have received. Be completely humble and gentle; be patient, bearing with one another in love. Make every effort to keep the unity of the Spirit through the bond of peace. (Eph. 4:1–3)

> You are a chosen people, a royal priesthood, a holy nation, a people belonging to God, that you may declare the praises of him who called you out of darkness into his wonderful light. . . . Dear friends, I urge you, as aliens and strangers in the world, to abstain from sinful desires, which war against your soul. Live such good lives among the pagans that, though they accuse you of doing wrong, they may see your good deeds and glorify God on the day he visits us. (1 Pet. 2:9, 11–12)

The flaw in the foundation of God's work was relational (vv. 1–6), and God used Nehemiah to fix it (vv. 7–13). What are we to do when we discover a fundamental flaw in the foundation of our relationships as God's people? Nehemiah illustrates a godly approach to righting wrong relationships.

1. Control Your Temper

First, you are wise to collect yourself. Nehemiah was furious (v. 6), and yet what was the first thing he did? The NIV says simply, "I pondered them [the charges of vv. 1–5] in my mind" (v. 7). That seems to weaken the power of the Hebrew text, which literally reads, "My heart took counsel upon me."[2] Perhaps the translation "I consulted with myself" (NASB) is as close as any here.

Picture it in a modern setting: Nehemiah is sitting in his of-

fice surrounded by co-workers when the memo arrives, informing him of the people's actions. The roar, "They did *what!?!*"
can be heard through the walls of his office. The Venetian blinds
over the glass flutter from the force of the words. The windows
rattle in their frames. Every head in every cubicle snaps upward,
eyebrows raised in surprised wonder. And just as quickly, all
heads shoot downward as the employees bury themselves in
their work, to avoid eye contact when the boss bursts through
the door.

Nehemiah was indignant. But before he lost his temper he
took a deep breath, counseled with himself, and carefully considered the most prudent course of action. Nehemiah knew he
had to deal with the problem, but he was wise enough to know
that he'd achieve nothing for the glory of God in his anger.
"Man's anger does not bring about the righteous life that God
desires" (James 1:20).

> *CONFRONTING THE RELATIONAL FLAWS THAT HINDER REVIVAL REQUIRES A GODLY APPROACH — AND THAT BEGINS WITH A CONTROLLED TEMPER.*

If you can't go forward in control, wait until you can. It may not
mean your pulse will have completely returned to normal, but you
will be controlling your anger
rather than it controlling you.
"Brothers, if someone is caught in
a sin, you who are spiritual should
restore him gently. But *watch
yourself*, or you also may be
tempted" (Gal. 6:1).

2. Confront Privately

After you have collected yourself, you should confront the
problem privately. "I pondered them in my mind and then accused the nobles and officials. I told them, 'You are exacting
usury from your own countrymen!' " (v. 7).

Apparently Nehemiah went to the offending parties personally,
or dealt with them privately as a group, regarding their guilt. It is
no small detail that Nehemiah dared confront the problem at all.

There was a great deal at stake. They were in the midst of an over-whelming building project. They had received death threats from their enemies, who were marshaling Gentile armies around the city. They had people standing watch day and night to protect the workers from being overrun. In the midst of all these pressures, dis-unity began to show itself.

During his self-consultation Nehemiah could easily have reasoned, "Maybe we ought to deal with this later. Maybe it's not really that big a deal. Maybe it will all go away when we're done with this building project." Nehemiah didn't think that way because he knew that the ministry of God's people never rises above the level of the integrity in their relationships with one an-other. This wasn't just about rebuilding a wall; it was about re-storing God's people. A nice fence would never make them the people God wanted them to be. No, this was sin and it had to be dealt with! So Nehemiah confronted those responsible.

These were not easy folks to approach; they were power peo-ple—"the nobles and officials." They were community leaders who bore the respect of the populace, and were not used to having other people in their face. They had also been around Jerusalem a lot longer than Nehemiah had, and this problem had started long before he came on the scene. It was Nehemiah's visionary leader-ship and challenge to the people that laid bare what these other leaders had permitted and perhaps even participated in.

Long before Jesus walked the earth, Nehemiah anticipated the Lord's advice for resolving conflict: "If your brother sins against you, go and show him his fault, *just between the two of you*. If he listens to you, you have won your brother over" (Matt. 18:15).

3. Confront Publicly

What if those confronted do not repent? Jesus prescribed an-other step to be taken—confront the problem publicly (Matt. 18:17). That was just what Nehemiah did. "So I called together a large meeting to deal with them" (v. 7). Apparently the guilty parties had been unwilling to listen to Nehemiah or they determined that the sin was of such a public nature that there was nothing else to do but deal with it publicly.

Perhaps Nehemiah signaled "the man who sounded the trumpet" (4:18) to issue a blast on the shofar. Did all the workers abandon their work on the wall and rally to the site of the sound with swords drawn, ready to engage the enemy? If so, when they arrived they found themselves confronted by a more dangerous enemy—an internal one.

Nehemiah told those gathered, "As far as possible, we have bought back our Jewish brothers who were sold to the Gentiles. Now you are selling your brothers, only for them to be sold back to us!" (v. 8). The dumbfounded citizens-turned-construction workers "kept quiet, because they could find nothing to say" (v. 8b). Nehemiah continued,

> What you are doing is not right. Shouldn't you walk in the fear of our God to avoid the reproach of our Gentile enemies? I and my brothers and my men are also lending the people money and grain. But let the exacting of usury stop! Give back to them immediately their fields, vineyards, olive groves and houses, and also the usury you are charging them—the hundredth part of the money, grain, new wine and oil. (Neh. 5:9–11)

Forced by unrepentant sinners and rampant sin, Nehemiah made the charges public, outlining three areas of their failure.

The first and most fundamental problem Nehemiah identified was their *lackadaisical attitude toward God*. He asked the people, "Shouldn't you walk in the fear of our God?" (v. 9). The question was rhetorical because all God's people should know that all we are and do—everything about everything in our lives—is determined by what we think of God. Their relational failures were a sign of an even more fundamental failure in their individual relationship with God.

The second charge against them was an *uncaring attitude toward their mission*. Nehemiah warned them that their failure was bringing the "reproach of our Gentile enemies" (v. 9).

Remember, their mission was not primarily to rebuild the wall. That was only a means to fulfilling their mission. The call of Israel, like that of the Church today, was to glorify God in the midst of a world that does not recognize or honor Him. Whatever the assignment, the glory of God is always the ultimate mission. Instead of living together in such a way that the nations would give glory to God, they had by their conduct brought the reproach of the nations upon themselves.

The third accusation Nehemiah made against them was their *callous attitude toward their brothers*. Instead of serving their fellow believers, they enslaved them (v. 8). We are called, even in this age of grace, to glorify God by living with one another in such a distinctively different way that people say, "God is among them." Jesus said, "By this all men will know that you are my disciples, if you love one another" (John 13:35).

4. Provide a Process for Restoration

Nehemiah collected himself. He then confronted the problem—first privately, and then publicly. Nehemiah then illustrated the fourth step of fixing flawed relationships: creating a specific process for restoration of the repentant. He gave the offenders four specific things to do.

First, make up your mind to stop. Nehemiah stressed the simplicity of the fix: "Let the exacting of usury stop!" (v. 10). Whatever sin you are struggling with, make up your mind to stop it.

"It's not that easy!" you object.

God, by authoring Nehemiah's words, dared to disagree. God views us as fully able, by His grace, to make up our minds to discontinue whatever it is we have been doing. We are not weak victims, helplessly paralyzed by another's wrongdoing.

Second, make all restitution necessary. Nehemiah ordered the offenders, "Give back to them immediately their fields, vineyards, olive groves and houses, and also the usury you are charging them—the hundredth part of the money, grain, new wine and oil" (v. 11).

Nehemiah demanded they return all properties they had seized (v. 11a) along with all the interest they'd collected on the loans they'd issued (v. 11b). The "hundredth part" apparently means that they were charging one percent interest per month, which totaled twelve percent annually. Actually, compared to the interest rates the Persian loan brokers were offering, this was not exorbitant, but nevertheless it was burying the people of God in debt. God saw His own people using calamity to pillage their own and He called them to repentance and restitution.

Nehemiah didn't offer the loan sharks the option of simply forgiving future interest payments, or tell them to work out an easier repayment schedule. He demanded that they make restitution and that they do so immediately.

Simply doing things differently from this point on is not sufficient. To the degree that you are able to go back and make the past right, do it—*now*. Obviously, there are some sins one cannot make restitution for, which makes them all the more grievous.

If you begin a rumor about someone, you can never gather up the thousand repercussions of that act. You should try. You must go to every person you know and make it right. Yet you could spend the rest of your life tracking down all those infected by your gossip and still not be able to retrieve it fully. If you have violated the vows of your marriage, you have trampled something sacred that can never be returned. You can be forgiven, but you cannot make full restitution.

Yet as far as you are able you must make restitution to those wronged. Nehemiah knew that the things taken were physical and monetary. These were returnable. He demanded such returns be made, immediately.

We don't hear much about restitution these days, yet there are few things that evidence the reality of repentance and the approach of revival more than making restitution.

As a demonstration of the reality of their contrition, the offenders said, "We will give it back. . . . And we will not demand anything more from them. We will do as you say" (v. 12a).

When people own up to their sins through repentance *and* restitution it is a sign revival is on the way. But it does not necessarily mean it has fully arrived.

Nehemiah wasn't buying it yet. "Then I summoned the priests and made the nobles and officials take an oath to do what they had promised" (v. 12b). By doing this, Nehemiah was making the offenders take the third step in the path of restoration: *Make a promise to God and others.*

Nehemiah heard their promises, now he wanted them to sign on the dotted line. He knew how easy it is to say to God, "I'll never do it again!" He was cognizant of how simple it is to promise others, "I'll change!" He was also aware that it is sometimes of tremendous help to tell not only God, but a trusted friend in Christ as well.

The final step of restoration is to *meditate on the consequences of disobedience.* "I also shook out the folds of my robe and said, 'In this way may God shake out of his house and possessions every man who does not keep this promise. So may such a man be shaken out and emptied!'" (v. 13a).

> *T*HE PATH TO TRUE RESTORATION: MAKE UP YOUR MIND TO STOP SINNING; MAKE ALL RESTITUTION NECESSARY; MAKE A PROMISE TO GOD AND OTHERS; MEDITATE ON THE CONSEQUENCES.

This was a prophecy acted out in dramatic form, designed to say, "This is what God will do to you if you betray Him and these people again." It was a warning—vivid, picturesque, and graphic—of God's discipline for repeated sin. It forced them to face the consequences of failure.

The result of these steps of restoration? The people added a hearty "Amen! . . . And the people did as they had promised" (v. 13b). That is restoration. Their relationships started to become what they were designed to be.

The Remedy: Being an Example

The best remedy for failed relationships is a living example of the right way to do it. A prescription is wonderful, but a three-dimensional testimony in walking, breathing form is even better. Books are a help, but a brother who is a "living letter" is better when it comes to teaching us how to live in relationship with others.

It is just such an example that Nehemiah gives us next. He holds up the form of his relationships throughout his ministry in Jerusalem. What follows (vv. 14–19) was written in retrospect, looking back over his twelve years as governor of Jerusalem. He cleared his voice and declared, "Here is how I lived among my fellow believers."

1. Give Up Your Rights

Nehemiah glorified God in his relationships by following four principles. The first is this: *Give up your rights, don't demand them.* "Moreover, from the twentieth year of King Artaxerxes, when I was appointed to be their governor in the land of Judah, until his thirty-second year—twelve years—neither I nor my brothers ate the food allotted to the governor. But the earlier governors—those preceding me—placed a heavy burden on the people and took forty shekels of silver from them in addition to food and wine. Their assistants also lorded it over the people. But out of reverence for God I did not act like that" (vv. 14–15).

Persian governors were allowed to tax the people, not merely to benefit the Persian king but also for their official budget. Through such taxation a Persian governor provided for the material needs of his household and funded the entertainment of the many dignitaries he was expected to host.

Nehemiah had the right to do that, but he chose not to "out of reverence for God." Nehemiah governed his relationships not by what he could legally do but by what he should morally do before God.

Apparently Paul had studied Nehemiah carefully, for in First

Corinthians 9 he describes in detail his commitment to this same principle in his ministry as an apostle for Christ. Paul and Nehemiah did not see others as things to be used, but as people to be served. The "fear of God" (Neh. 5:15, NASB) is what leads a person to live like this.

2. Work Alongside, Not Over

Nehemiah's second guiding principle for relationships is: *Work alongside people, don't stand over them.* After over a decade of leadership, Nehemiah could honestly say, "I devoted myself to the work on this wall. All my men were assembled there for the work; we did not acquire any land" (v. 16).

Nehemiah got down in the trenches next to the people working on the wall. He helped clear away the rubble and stone of the broken wall. He got dirty moving rocks and debris. He mixed mortar. He carried stones. He helped them in the physical labor of rebuilding. Nehemiah didn't consider himself above the people, but one of them. He didn't gobble up land from disadvantaged people who would have sold it to him for a song. He and his servants were not expending their energies on that which would render them profit, but on that which would benefit all of God's people.

3. Serve People, Don't Use Them

His third principle comes, then, as no surprise: *Serve people, don't use them.* Isn't that what it means when we read, "Furthermore, a hundred and fifty Jews and officials ate at my table, as well as those who came to us from the surrounding nations" (v. 17)? Nehemiah took in needy people and fed them—not just Jews, but Gentiles also. These were individuals from the very groups plotting to overthrow and murder them, yet he fed them when they were hungry.

Nehemiah's commitment to service was costly. "Each day one ox, six choice sheep and some poultry were prepared for me, and every ten days an abundant supply of wine of all kinds" (v. 18a). It is estimated that this would have provided food for

600–800 people a day—all at his personal expense![3] "In spite of all this, I never demanded the food allotted to the governor, because the demands were heavy on these people" (v. 18b).

Nehemiah served people. It cost him to live such a principled life. He didn't have to conduct himself like this. But with the debt and economic pressures upon his people, he couldn't live with himself unless he lived with them from a position of servanthood. In doing so, did he not anticipate the heart of his Savior? "For who is greater, the one who is at the table or the one who serves? Is it not the one who is at the table? But I am among you as one who serves" (Luke 22:27).

Nehemiah knew that when you bend in service you wield more authority than when you rise to dominate. Jesus crystalized this truth in these words:

> You know that the rulers of the Gentiles lord it over them, and their high officials exercise authority over them. Not so with you. Instead, whoever wants to become great among you must be your servant, and whoever wants to be first must be your slave—just as the Son of Man did not come to be served, but to serve, and to give his life as a ransom for many. (Matt. 20:25–28)

4. Look to God, Not Others

Nehemiah's fourth principle of relationships was this: *Look to God for your reward, and not to others.* In the end he prayed, "Remember me with favor, O my God, for all I have done for these people" (v. 19).

Nehemiah knew that to conduct himself like this had been a sacrifice. He fully expected to be repaid, not by the people, but by God. Such living requires a commitment to measure life on an eternal continuum. Measuring life on a temporal continuum makes you vulnerable to anger, resentment, bitterness, and self-pity. But when you measure life on an eternal continuum, you're free from demanding that people repay you and you're at liberty to look to God for your reward.

Erwin Lutzer recounts a legend from the land of India that underscores this principle. One day a beggar caught sight of a wealthy rajah approaching him in a glorious chariot. Seizing his opportunity, the beggar took up his position at the side of the road with his bowl of rice extended. He was astonished, however, when the rajah stopped and, instead of making a contribution, demanded some of his rice!

Anger welled up within the beggar. Begrudgingly he placed one grain of rice in the rajah's hand.

"More!" was the demand from the rajah. An additional grain was placed in the wealthy man's hand.

"More please!" was the repeated request. Vexed beyond words, the beggar placed one additional grain in the man's hand and stormed away.

As the chariot rattled down the road, the beggar looked down into his rice bowl and saw something glimmering in the sun. It was a grain of gold! As he searched his bowl, he found two more just like it.

The lesson, says Lutzer, is simple: "For every grain of rice, a grain of gold." And he adds, "If we clutch our bowl of rice, we shall lose our reward. If we are faithful and give God each grain, He gives us gold in return."[4]

We do well to look to God for our reward. It begins to transform our perspective on life and the people we travel with through it.

The point of this chapter in the book of Nehemiah is this: *No revival of God's people ever rises above the level of the integrity of its relationships*. If the foundation is flawed here, it matters little how well constructed the top floor is.

Is the revival you long for held at bay by the way you relate to others? What next steps must you make toward others before you can make a move toward God?

Reaching Toward Revival

1. Why is revival so closely tied to the integrity of our relationships?

   _____

   _____

2. How do internal, relational problems present a greater challenge to revival than external problems?

   _____

   _____

3. What price do God's people pay when they (or their leaders) fail to confront sin?

   _____

   _____

4. Why should we confront privately before publicly exposing sin?

   _____

   _____

5. What needs to be confronted publicly? What is to be gained that can't be achieved through private confrontation?

   _____

   _____

6. What is the relationship between repentance, restitution and revival?

   _____

   _____

7. Who is there in your life that provides a model of relational integrity?

   _____

   _____

8

A Bull's-Eye on Your Back

*I*t has been said that if you want to lead the orchestra you have to turn your back on the crowd. How true. It also means that by the time you reach the podium and take up the baton, someone will have painted a bull's-eye on your back. If they don't like the music, they'll likely take aim at the guy flapping his arms.

Leadership draws opposition. To accept leadership is to invite antagonism, criticism, and complaints. It's always been true. When people didn't like the civil rights movement, who was shot? Martin Luther King, Jr. When people didn't like the outcome of the war between the states, who was shot? Abraham Lincoln. If people don't like the way the football team is playing, guess who gets fired? The head coach. When the economy slides, who is blamed? The President.

Nehemiah knew that leadership assures opposition. We too can mark it down as a maxim of life: if you lead, you'll be criticized.

Nehemiah had been divinely called to lead the way in revival. He accepted the assignment. He knew, therefore, he was also called to face contention. He had been called by God to return to the land of Judah and the city of Jerusalem, and to lead the people in restoring the city's walls. The temple had previously been restored under Zerubbabel (Ezra 1–6). Now Nehemiah was to restore the people and glory of that city. He was to make it a place where God would dwell with His people and from which they could be a light to the nations.

Nehemiah rallied his people and began the work. Their neighbors didn't appreciate it, and launched a broad, frontal attack upon the work and workmen generally (Neh. 4). But then the strategy changed. They concluded that if you can't stop the work, it may be best to shoot the leader! The cross hairs were focused on the bull's-eye on Nehemiah's back.

In one way or another, most of us have been placed by God in some position of leadership, whether in our homes, communities, schools, workplaces or churches. God has sovereignly positioned you and given you a measure of influence in others' lives. When you understand your call and seek to fulfill it to the glory of God, there will be opposition. Though the circumstances and methods of opposition may vary, they often fall into one of four categories. Nehemiah faced them all.

> *WARNING TO ALL LEADERS: WHEN YOU UNDERSTAND YOUR CALL AND SEEK TO FULFILL IT TO THE GLORY OF GOD, THERE WILL BE OPPOSITION.*

One form of attack is *diplomatic ambush*. Nehemiah's old enemies had joined forces once again in a final attempt to destroy him and the work he sought to accomplish (6:1). This was a last-ditch effort, because they saw that Nehemiah "had rebuilt the wall and not a gap was left in it," though he "had not set the doors in the gates." Realizing the time was short, they sent a message to Nehemiah saying, "Come, let us meet together in one of the villages on the plain of Ono" (v. 2a).

The "plain of Ono" was about twenty-five miles northwest of Jerusalem, on the border between Judah (Nehemiah's jurisdiction) and Samaria (Sanballat's jurisdiction). Their message went something like this: "Listen, we've been bickering back and forth a lot. Why don't we meet on neutral ground for a peace accord?" Though the approach was conciliatory, the intent was caustic.

Nehemiah saw through their ruse. "But they were scheming to harm me" (v. 2b). He realized this was a diplomatic ambush. Under the hypocritical guise of diplomacy, their goal was to get rid of Nehemiah; they probably planned to murder him. For to-day's leader, however, the danger is less likely to be physical. The goal is usually to discredit, disqualify or otherwise destroy the leader in the eyes of those he leads.

If it fails the first time, a diplomatic ambush may be reused repeatedly. Nehemiah didn't snap at their lure, so Sanballat and Geshem cast it his way three more times (v. 4).

A leader may also be attacked via *political blackmail*. A fifth attempt at wooing Nehemiah into a peace accord was is-sued, but this time the messenger also carried something else —"in his hand was an unsealed letter" (v. 5). It read:

> "It is reported among the nations—and Geshem says it is true—that you and the Jews are plotting to revolt, and there-fore you are building the wall. Moreover, according to these reports you are about to become their king and have even ap-pointed prophets to make this proclamation about you in Jeru-salem: 'There is a king in Judah!' Now this report will get back to the king; so come, let us confer together." (vv. 6–7)

Several cues tip us off that this was not born of sincere con-cern but was a politically motivated strategy. First of all, the let-ter was unsealed. In that day, a letter was normally composed on a scroll and sealed with a spot of wax or soft clay. The sender then impressed his insignia in the wax or clay before it hard-ened. This showed that the letter was for the eyes of only two people—the sender and the recipient. The unbroken seal was proof that no one else had read it.

But this letter was unsealed—purposely left open so the messenger would read it and blab it to everyone he met. This unsealed letter was addressed to Nehemiah, but the contents were for public consumption.

You think God's people are above such tactics? Don't you believe it! Consider the experience of Pastor Brian Wells. As he left the sanctuary after the morning service, he bent down to pick up a piece of paper lying on the floor. When he glanced at it, he groaned. This is what it said:

RESTORE COMMUNITY CHURCH TO ITS HISTORY OF BIBLICAL INTEGRITY! REMOVE PASTOR WELLS!

The flyer went on to say, "Brian Wells is bent on imposing his liberal views on our church. His utter disregard for the inspiration of Scripture will tear Community Church from its cherished Biblical moorings—unless we act now. . . ." The bottom of the page contained the urgent, final imperative: "ACT NOW!"[1]

Note also that the open letter to Nehemiah exaggerated the facts—"you and the Jews are planning to revolt . . . you are about to become their king" (v. 6).

"Everyone is saying . . ." "I've had a lot of people come to me . . ." "The whole church is worried about . . ." These are the stock phrases of political blackmail in the church.

A pastor recently told me of his early weeks as an associate pastor at his first church. New to the ministry, he was shocked when a church leader said during a board meeting, "Lots of folks are complaining about . . ." He was even more surprised when the senior pastor responded, "'Lots of folks'? Come on, it's you and your wife! That's all it is. You've always been upset about it and everyone knows it. Don't tell me it's 'lots of folks' when we all know it's just you two!" The pastor saw through the exaggerated facts and exposed them to the light of truth.

Political blackmail not only exaggerates the facts, it fabricates lies—"you are about to become their king and have even appointed prophets to make this proclamation about you in Jerusalem: 'There is a king in Judah!'" (v. 6–7a). The accusation was absurd, of course; Nehemiah had no aspirations for the throne, and no plans for a revolt against Persia. But someone not living in Jerusalem might believe the lie.

And that is one of the signs of political blackmail: its lies are accompanied by a threat. The open letter closed by saying, "Now this report will get back to the king; so come, let us confer together" (v. 7b). They were basically saying, "You know, if we are to be good subjects to the king, we must report this!" Can you hear the insincerity dripping from their words?

Don't let the word "political" throw you. You don't have to be a politician to be the target of political blackmail. Anywhere leadership is required, matters degenerate to the political level eventually. And those who do not like the direction the leadership is headed are often not above political blackmail.

A leader may also face attack through *religious manipulation*. Nehemiah reports,

> One day I went to the house of Shemaiah son of Delaiah, the son of Mehetabel, who was shut in at his home. He said, "Let us meet in the house of God, inside the temple, and let us close the temple doors, because men are coming to kill you— by night they are coming to kill you." (v. 10)

Who is Shemaiah? And what is he up to?

Why was he confined to his home? Some suggest that he was ritually unclean and was obediently waiting out his time of impurity at home. Others speculate that he was physically unable to leave his home for some reason. Yet neither of these seems to fit the facts. If either was the case, why then did he invite Nehemiah to go with him to the temple? If Shemaiah was ritually unclean, he wouldn't be allowed in the temple. And if he was physically unable to leave his home, how was he planning on getting to the temple?

I believe a better explanation is that the confinement was self-imposed, to symbolize danger. Shemaiah was pleading in tones of contrived fear: "Listen, Nehemiah, these people are trying to kill you. Now they are trying to kill me because I've been associated with you. We've got to stick together. Let's flee to the temple and find refuge together there!"

Nehemiah had heard that Shemaiah had barricaded himself within his home. This man was likely a priest (cf. Ezra 2:60; 1 Chron. 24:18) and thus may have been a person Nehemiah had come to trust. So this confidant, with panic in his voice, cried, "I need to see you!" Nehemiah went to his aid. When he arrived, Shemaiah delivered a "prophecy" (v. 12) that supposedly divulged divine direction for their plight. But the message wasn't from God.

DON'T BE TAKEN IN BY EVERYONE WHO SAYS, "GOD TOLD ME . . ." OR "GOD SENT ME TO TELL YOU . . ." NOT ALL WHO USE HIS NAME REPRESENT HIS INTERESTS.

This was an effort of the enemy to manipulate Nehemiah's religious commitments in order to get him to fall. Of all the strategies to bring down a leader, the manipulation of his love for spiritual things is perhaps the most vile.

Don't be taken in by everyone who says, "God told me . . ." or "God sent me to tell you . . ." How can you argue with God? You can't, but not all who use His name represent His interests.

A fourth attack upon leaders is *relational leverage*:

> Also, in those days the nobles of Judah were sending many letters to Tobiah, and replies from Tobiah kept coming to them. For many in Judah were under oath to him, since he was son-in-law to Shecaniah son of Arah, and his son Jehohanan had married the daughter of Meshullam son of Berekiah. Moreover, they kept reporting to me his good deeds and then telling him what I said. And Tobiah sent letters to intimidate me. (vv. 17–19)

Tobiah was using relationships to gain a foothold among the people that Nehemiah was called by God to lead. His father-in-law was Shecaniah, probably to be identified as one of the Jewish returnees under Ezra (Ezra 2:5). His son married the daughter of Meshullam, an unknown but influential person in Jerusalem. We will discover that Tobiah had so infiltrated the high priestly families that he acquired personal living quarters within the temple (Neh. 13:4, 7).

It is a painful day when you discover that those you trust are being lobbied by those who want to get rid of you. But it's infinitely more painful when you find out that it's your own kin that have been targeted for relational leverage.

It all hurts. Whether it be diplomatic ambush, political blackmail, religious manipulation or relational leverage, it hurts. One pastor honestly confessed,

I just feel angry sometimes. Angry at that individual, angry at the congregation and the leaders for seemingly deserting me, angry at myself, and sometimes livid with God for allowing this to happen.

Mostly though, I feel afraid. Very much afraid. I'm afraid of being unable to cope. Afraid of what people will say. Afraid I'll loose my job—and yet sometimes I feel like quitting, just throwing in the towel and saying, "There, God. If you won't take care of me, then forget about me taking care of them."

And I feel sorry for myself, then ashamed when I realize I'm dreaming about revenge. That's not me. But it *is* me. The whole thing upsets me so much that I'm obsessed with it. I get so I can't sleep at night. The longer it has worn on, the more tense I have grown. Sometimes I feel like I'm going to explode. It has spread slowly, like poison, to contaminate every part of my life. I'm irritable at home and church, suspicious of almost everyone. It seems as if I'm turning into the kind of person the antagonist says I am.

And then the awful doubts come. Maybe the antagonist is right. Maybe I should leave and let someone else take over. So I slip into depression until I get so angry that I fight my way out of it. And the process repeats itself like a hideous roller coaster ride that never ends.

I don't know what to do.[2]

Amy Carmichael penned words every would-be leader should hear:

Hast thou no scar?
No hidden scar on foot, or side, or hand?
I hear thee sung as mighty in the land;
I hear them hail thy bright, ascendant star.
Hast thou no scar?

Hast thou no wound?
Yet I was wounded by the archers; spent,
Leaned Me against the tree to die; and rent
By ravening beasts that compassed Me, I swooned.
Hast *thou* no wound?

No wound? No scar?
Yet, as the Master shall the servant be,
And piercèd are the feet that follow Me.
But thine are whole; can he have followed far
Who has nor wound nor scar?[3]

Lead and you will be attacked. But how can I do more than just react emotionally to such attacks? How can I respond in the wisdom of the Spirit? Nehemiah models the wisdom we need.

One response must be *determination*. When faced with a diplomatic ambush designed to divert him away from his God-given work, Nehemiah retorted, "I am carrying on a great project and cannot go down. Why should the work stop while I leave it and go down to you?" (v. 3). That did not, however, end the matter. "Four times they sent me the same message" (v. 4a). Yet Nehemiah's resolve was unwavering: "Each time I gave them the same answer" (v. 4b).

Nehemiah had been invited to the supposed peace summit in a village on the plain of Ono. And his response was, "Oh, no! I've got work to do. I'm not coming!" He had been given a task by God and he would not be turned away from it. That is determination. Sometimes the secret to success is as simple as refusing to give up. Victory often comes by simply refusing to be distracted, dissuaded or turned away from the thing God has called you to do.

When I think of determination, a friend named John comes to mind. He grew up in West Africa and has now spent nearly his entire adult life there as a missionary. As they prepared to leave Africa to return to the United States, John and his wife Betty were visited by a delegation from the Dafing-Marka tribe. God had powerfully used John and his wife to plant numerous churches among this people, and the delegation was sent to officially bid them farewell and present them with a gift. The Dafing-Marka are known for a particular fabric that they weave, and the gift prepared for John and Betty at their departure was made from this material.

Another thing that this tribe is known for is the special names that the people give to each missionary. The missionaries seldom know what those names are or what they mean, for the people use them only when the missionaries are absent.

John and Betty's special gifts had been woven in such a way as to reveal the names they had been given by the people. Betty later reported, "John's pattern means 'the man who says nothing.'" Then she explained, "They said that this means he is a man who works on, no matter what is happening around him. If he is criticized, encounters problems or difficulties, is persecuted, or even ill, he says nothing, but continues to work, no matter what."

A man with determination saw a people largely unreached with the gospel. A largely unreached people saw a man with a God-given determination. The result was people won to faith, churches built, and light coming in a dark place. The road was not easy, but God's will was done. Many more people will inhabit eternity because a couple refused to be turned back from doing God's will.

A second necessary response to attack is *discernment*. Nehemiah possessed and exercised it. In the face of his enemy's ruse, he concluded, "they were scheming to harm me" (v. 2b). How did he know? And when a supposed ally tried to lure him into the temple under the banner of friendship and spirituality, Nehemiah saw right through it.

> But I said, "Should a man like me run away? Or should one like me go into the temple to save his life? I will not go!" I realized that God had not sent him, but that he had prophesied against me because Tobiah and Sanballat had hired him. He had been hired to intimidate me so that I would commit a sin by doing this, and then they would give me a bad name to discredit me.
>
> Remember Tobiah and Sanballat, O my God, because of what they have done; remember also the prophetess Noadiah and the rest of the prophets who have been trying to intimidate me. (vv. 11–14)

He discerned that the message, though cloaked in religious terms, was not of God. How did he know that?

It wasn't all mysticism. Two things help us see how he knew Shemaiah's invitation was not of God. For one thing, it was contrary to the Word of God. We could easily mistake Nehemiah's reply, "Should a man like me run away?" (v. 11), as arrogance. But that would miss his intention. He was saying, "I'm a layman, and only priests are allowed to go into the inner chambers of the temple. You're a priest, a student of the Bible. You know your plan is contrary to the Word of God. I won't go!"

Nehemiah's words, rather than a flash of arrogance, were a confession of humble discernment, as well as a recognition that Shemaiah's plan was inconsistent with God's call on his life. He was saying, "God called me to rebuild this wall. He's enabled me to rally the people to build it with me. You are suggesting that a man with such a call on his life should run away. That would dishonor God!"

> *A* DISCERNING AND DETERMINED MAN OF GOD IS NOT DISTRACTED BY PROPOSALS THAT ARE CONTRARY TO GOD'S WORD AND INCONSISTENT WITH THE CALL OF GOD ON HIS LIFE.

Nehemiah was able to discern the truth about the invitation because it was contrary to God's Word and inconsistent with God's call on his life.

A wise mentor once told me, "You have to make up your mind who you're going to listen to." His point was that leaders never lack for people with "a word from God" for them. There are always those who are sure they know God's mind and are dying to let you in on the secret. But not everyone who says, "Thus saith the Lord" has truly heard from God.

We need discernment. To consistently find it may be a leader's greatest accomplishment. "But solid food is for the mature, who by constant use have trained themselves to distinguish good from evil" (Heb. 5:14). J. Oswald Sanders underscored the challenge of living such a perceptive life:

> It might be thought by those who have not found themselves in a position of leadership that greater experience and a longer walk with God would result in much greater ease in

discerning the will of God in perplexing situations. But the reverse is often the case. God treats the leader as a mature adult, leaving more and more to his spiritual discernment, and giving fewer sensible and tangible evidences of His guidance than in earlier years. This perplexity adds to the inevitable pressures incidental to any responsible office.[4]

Nehemiah also shows us that a plain, pointed *denial* can at times be a leader's best response to unjust attack. In the face of political blackmail, false accusations and outlandish rumors, he simply replied, "Nothing like what you are saying is happening; you are just making it up out of your head" (v. 8).

The letter of response said simply, "Not true. You're making it up." Period. End of story. Sanballat got an *A+* for creativity, but an *F* for his research.

Nehemiah didn't dignify the accusation with more discussion. He gave a limited, measured denial of all charges.

"It's not true. Don't bother writing back."

He held no press conference. He didn't frantically try to find every person who might have heard the rumor and clarify the issue. Nehemiah didn't descend into self-defense. He didn't engage in arguments. He simply denied the charges and got back to work.

C. H. Spurgeon, the renowned English preacher, came to a disagreement with the equally well-known Joseph Parker. It was largely a private matter, but Parker made it public by publishing an open letter to his colleague in the newspaper. The press had a heyday with the public charges leveled by one pastor against another. Spurgeon's response? Silence. He never made mention of the matter in public. He just let it go and got on with his work.[5]

When unjustly attacked, a leader's response must also be one of renewed dependence on God. Through it all Nehemiah knew his one unfailing Source of strength. Repeatedly he turned to that one Source through prayer.

> They were all trying to frighten us, thinking, "Their hands will get too weak for the work, and it will not be completed." But I prayed, "Now strengthen my hands." . . .

Remember Tobiah and Sanballat, O my God, because of what they have done; remember also the prophetess Noadiah and the rest of the prophets who have been trying to intimidate me. (6:9, 14)

Whether in leadership or under it, you and I will both be burned by people. You're going to get used; I'm going to be disappointed. We should not be surprised. But instead of backing away from people, we need to draw near to God.

G. Campbell Morgan said, "What we do in the crisis always depends upon whether we see the difficulties in the light of God, or God in the shadow of the difficulties." The ability to consistently view life in light rather than shadow is largely a matter of remembering and consistently reasserting our dependence upon God.

What results when leaders continue to lead in the face of resistance? For one thing, they get the job done.

Obvious, right?

Don't let the plainness of the observation obscure its profundity. The greatest single thing a leader can do to stop his enemies is to finish the job he's been given to do.

Nehemiah matter-of-factly reports with an unimaginative, utilitarian use of words, "So the wall was completed on the twenty-fifth of Elul, in fifty-two days" (v. 15). Kidner aptly says, "After the high emotions on both sides, there is a pleasing dryness about the words."[6] The biggest news about Nehemiah's leadership is reported on the back page with an unobtrusive byline!

But that's just like a leader. They get the job done. That's their biggest credit. They finish what they're called to do.

Churchill, in his first speech as Prime Minister, established the only acceptable measurement of his leadership—victory!

We have before us an ordeal of the most grievous kind. We have before us many, many long months of struggle and suffering. You ask what is our policy? I will say: It is to wage war, by sea, land and air, with all our might and with all the strength that God can give us; to wage war against a monstrous tyranny, never surpassed in the dark, lamentable catalogue of human crime. That is our policy. You ask, What is our aim? I answer in one word: Victory—victory at all costs, victory in spite of all terror, victory, however long and hard the road may be; for without victory, there is no survival.[7]

I think Nehemiah would have liked Churchill. But Nehemiah would add another indispensable result of a leader's work: giving glory to God. When you've fulfilled your calling and finished your assignment, give God the glory that is due His name.

> *GREAT LEADERS FULFILL THEIR CALLING, FINISH THEIR ASSIGNMENT, AND THEN GIVE GOD THE GLORY DUE HIS NAME.*

Think of it: only fifty-two days to completely rebuild the wall of Jerusalem. Amazing! And Nehemiah reports, "When all our enemies heard about this, all the surrounding nations were afraid and lost their self-confidence, because *they realized that this work had been done with the help of our God*" (v. 16).

We all have our dreams, aspirations and ambitions. But has it ever struck you that the only glory you can ever bring to God is to do His will, in His way, in His time, by His strength? I can't give God glory by doing *your* job. You can't give Him glory by finishing *my* assignment. Neither one of us can glorify God by doing someone else's duty.

There is no greater glory you can bring to God than by finishing the work He has called *you* to. I can only glorify God by knowing and completing His individual will for my life. Along that path we each will face resistance and suffer attack. If you are contemplating backing off, giving in or jumping ship, consider this—it's not just self-protection you are considering, you are attempting to rob God of the glory due His name.

Leadership draws opposition. To accept leadership is to invite antagonism, criticism, and complaints. It's as true for you and me as it was for Nehemiah. The only question that remains is, how well will we wear the bull's-eye on our backs?

1. Why does being in leadership assure opposition?

   _____

   _____

2. What should a leader's response be when falsely accused?

   _____

   _____

3. How can you identify religious manipulation? How can you tell it is insincere and hypocritical?

   _____

   _____

4. How have you been the victim of relational leverage by those who oppose God's work through you?

   _____

   _____

5. How does a leader know when to ignore opposition and move ahead and when to stop and deal with it?

   _____

   _____

6. What are the effects of long-term opposition upon a leader and his people?

   _____

   _____

7. How do you know whether you are being determined or stubborn?

   _____

   _____

9

We've Got It All—

But Something's Missing

*O*ccasionally I'll be driving with my family, spot a building along the road and ask, "Anybody know what that place used to be?" Invariably someone will shout, "Pizza Hut!" or "Dairy Queen!" or another restaurant chain that has a distinctive building design.

A building like that always seems a bit out of place because it continues to display a subtle hint of its former life. It may have been remodeled and have a fresh coat of paint; a new sign is hanging out front; a new product is for sale under that familiar roof. But something is missing. Something is just not right.

Saddest of all is a former church building. Though abandoned for its original purpose, it is not unused. It may have a new roof; some windows may have been replaced; it may have a new coat of paint. But instead of serving as a house of worship, it is an office building, a karate studio or a local museum. The lawn may be mowed, the shrubs trimmed and the flowerbeds manicured, but something is missing. Something is just not right.

As Nehemiah 7 opens, we find that the city of Jerusalem has been restored. A new wall is around its perimeter. New doors hang at its gates. A relatively new temple is housed within those walls.

145

Thousands of Jewish people are now repopulating the city, having come back from exile. It's an exciting time to be in Jerusalem, but something's missing. Something's not quite right about it all.

The building project is over. The wall is rebuilt, the temple is up, the people are returning. Why isn't that enough? What's missing?

The trouble was, they had a great physical structure but they were not fulfilling God's purpose for their lives. They had rebuilt the city of God, but they did not yet have the promised revival of the Spirit of God. They had a nice new wall, shiny new gates, a beautiful temple, people who were excited, sacrificial, motivated. All the externals were right, but something internal was missing.

PHYSICAL STRUCTURE IS NO PROOF OF REVIVAL. GREAT FACILITIES, EFFICIENT ORGANIZATION, STELLAR STAFFING AND A CAREFULLY MARKETED MINISTRY DON'T EQUAL A MOVING OF GOD'S SPIRIT.

It helps to see this seventh chapter in context. The first six chapters of Nehemiah describe the excitement and sacrifice of rebuilding the walls of Jerusalem. Later chapters describe the revival of God's Spirit in the people of Jerusalem. Sandwiched between an exciting, and now completed, building project (chapters 1–6) and a life-changing move of God's Spirit (chapters 8–10) is chapter seven. This chapter reminds us that *just because the physical structure is completed doesn't mean the revival has started*. To put it in our context: Programs don't equal life. Great facilities, efficient organization, stellar staffing and a carefully marketed ministry don't equal a moving of God's Spirit.

The excitement of a building project is not necessarily the same thing as a move of God's Spirit in revival. You know unbelieving people who have built homes and become very excited in the process. A natural, man-made excitement is generated over new things. A human hype rises up when we join hands and accomplish a project together. It's a great thing to be drawn together as a church family in a building project. Yet we cannot mistake the natural excitement of doing God's will in building a physical structure with the enduring work of His Spirit that comes through revival. He may sovereignly choose to wed a building project and a revival into one time period, or one may precede the other.

How do we begin to see God's spiritual purpose fulfilled in our new physical plant? Just because we have a nice location, lovely property, ease of access, plenty of parking, a functional and beautiful building, a sign out front, an ad in the Yellow Pages and a listing with the chamber of commerce doesn't mean that God's purpose is being fulfilled among us.

The goal in Nehemiah's day was the restoration of Israel to God's high purpose for them. They were to be a light to the nations. They would be the channel through which the Savior of the world would come. Fulfilling such a high calling required a repopulated nation. Many had come out of exile and returned to Judah and Jerusalem. It required a rebuilt temple. Zerubbabel and Ezra had made sure it was finished. God's high purpose required a restored capital city. That had been Nehemiah's first assignment. But a repopulated nation, a rebuilt temple, and a restored capital did not necessarily mean God's purposes were being fulfilled through them.

What was missing? Revival. God's Spirit. God's reign in the lives of His people. God's presence in the midst of His regathered people.

How do we get from chapter six to chapter eight? That is to say, how do we get from fine facilities to a spiritual revival? How do we put ourselves in a position to receive the revival God desires to send?

Nehemiah seven gives a partial answer to that. It doesn't delineate everything that could be said in that regard. Yet it does outline how to begin to move from the excitement of constructing a wonderful building to seeing God's spiritual purpose fulfilled.

One thing required will be the raising up of godly leaders. It often takes a singular, dynamic leader to spearhead a large building project. He can't do it alone, for sure, but he becomes the point man, the one to cast vision, motivate people, challenge them to sacrifice, inspire commitment, and to encourage the weary. If a building project is to rise from the soil of one's property, it requires a strong leader.

Such leadership is vital in the limited span of a building project, but it is often short-lived. Statistics reveal that most pastors who lead their churches through major building programs leave within a year or two of the building's completion. The sacrifices necessary are costly to a leader. Emotional, physical, and mental reserves are spent. It is, for this reason, critical to the long-term fulfillment of God's purposes to build a plurality of leaders around the key leader.

Nehemiah seems to have understood the critical need for shared leadership, for he writes that

> After the wall had been rebuilt and I had set the doors in place, the gatekeepers and the singers and the Levites were appointed. I put in charge of Jerusalem my brother Hanani, along with Hananiah the commander of the citadel, because he was a man of integrity and feared God more than most men do. (vv. 1–2)

The last stone was barely cemented into place and the last gate door barely hung before Nehemiah busied himself with raising up godly leaders to help him lead God's people. From the initial success of a remarkable building project they were to move on to the fulfillment of God's purpose through them.

Nehemiah was still the governor of Judah, but he knew that he must share the leadership load if the work was to be all God wanted it to be—and if he was going to personally survive. Notice how he went about raising up these fellow leaders.

Appointed by Calling

They were *appointed by calling*. He looked for those who were already known as gatekeepers, singers and Levites (v. 1). Nehemiah couldn't work all day and stay awake all night guarding the city gates. He could attend worship services, but he couldn't lead in the singing too. If the priests were to perform their functions they needed the support ministries of the Levites. Leaders need to be called and have that call recognized by others, who then affirm that calling and release them to ministry.

Notice that these leaders were called, but also flexible. It appears that "the gatekeepers and the singers and the Levites" were appointed not only to the work they were trained for, but also to guard the city (v. 3). The gatekeepers were normally to be positioned at the gates of the temple, but here they were redeployed to the gates of the city. The singers could easily have argued, "I can handle the harp, but forget the sword!" The Levites were laborers in the daily affairs of the temple, but here they were armed and given night watchman duty. They were called, but flexible.

Nehemiah didn't just share the areas of ministry for which he had little competence or calling, but he also distributed his administration of the city of Jerusalem itself. He appointed two V.P.'s to oversee Jerusalem's day-to-day functions.

Nehemiah knew that shared leadership was essential to seeing growth in the ministry God had entrusted to them. One man has only so many hours and so much heart. If everything has to funnel through a single leader (or even a single group of leaders), we predetermine the maximum extent of God's work through us. Nehemiah didn't want to limit God, so he started sharing the load as soon as it was feasible to do so.

> *SHARED LEADERSHIP IS ESSENTIAL TO SEEING GROWTH IN THE MINISTRY GOD HAS ENTRUSTED TO YOU. IF YOU DON'T WANT TO LIMIT GOD, SHARE THE LOAD.*

Assessed by Their Character

These leaders were also *assessed by their character*. Nehemiah says of Hananiah "he was a man of integrity and feared God more than most men do" (v. 2b). He looked for "a man of truth" (a literal translation) who could be trusted. Nehemiah was surrounded by certified enemies and mask-wearing "friends" who conspired with them. Then and now our calling is to find "reliable men" (2 Tim. 2:2) who can be entrusted with important responsibilities in God's work. Such men must not only be trustworthy on the horizontal plane, but connected on the vertical as well. Nehemiah knew that "the fear of the LORD is the beginning of wisdom, and knowledge of the Holy One is understanding" (Prov. 9:10) so he looked for such a man to share the load of leadership.

Nehemiah had been the cupbearer to the king (1:11). The cupbearer protected the man in charge. By sipping his drinks and tasting his dinners, Nehemiah had preserved the top man. He had known what it was to serve in a support role and now he knew what to look for in such support staff. As governor of Judah he knew there were people out there that wanted to kill him, so he looked for somebody to fill the position that he once filled for the king. He was looking for men who were as faithful as he had been.

One of those he chose was Hanani, his brother. He's the one who traveled all the way from Jerusalem back to Persia and reported to Nehemiah about the desolation of the city (1:2). Hanani had been burdened for Jerusalem before Nehemiah was! And he cared just as much about God's work there.

The other appointee was Hananiah, "the commander of the citadel"—already a proven leader. "He was a man of integrity and feared God more than most men do." Not a bad summation of one's life! He was not only tested but also true. A man could do worse for an epitaph.

In any ministry the purposes of God rise and fall with the integrity of the leaders. Faithful leaders, over time, lift a not-so-faithful people to a higher plane. But a faithful people often give way before less-than-faithful leaders. It takes more than faithful, godly leaders to see the will of God done, but you'll never see it achieved without them.

Alert to Conflict

These leaders were also *alert to conflict*. "I said to them, 'The gates of Jerusalem are not to be opened until the sun is hot" (v. 3a). In the ancient world a city's gates were normally opened early in the day. As the sun rose people began to come and go, passing in and out of the city. Nehemiah charged the sentries with changing that convention. Why? Because some would be just getting out of bed and in no position to fend off an attack from their enemies. The strategic time for attack might come as the citizens wiped sleep from their eyes and poured their first cup of coffee. He wanted leaders who knew the times and were alert to danger.

Furthermore Nehemiah commanded that "While the gate-keepers are still on duty, have them shut the doors and bar them" (v. 3b). He wanted the doors closed while there were still guards on duty so that they could make certain that from the moment the doors were open to the moment they were shut someone was on guard.

Additionally he commanded, "Also appoint residents of Jerusalem as guards, some at their posts and some near their own houses" (v. 3c). Why "near their own houses"? It was the same principle as having people build in front of their homes (3:23–24, 28–30)—they would own the cause more if they had something personally at stake in it.

Of all the things that the Spirit of God could have moved Nehemiah to write, why focus on these administrative details? They are included to show us that we need leaders who are not only appointed by calling and assessed by character, but also alert to conflict. They needed to be watchful in order to preserve the gains that had already been made in their rebuilding project.

Jerusalem had a marvelous new wall around it. New doors hung in its gates. A rebuilt temple resided within its boundaries. They may not have yet tasted of true revival, but they had come so far! And they wanted to preserve the gains God had given them to that point.

Have you ever tried to tie a string around a package by yourself? You pull the string tight and then glance around for someone to place his or her finger on it so you can finish the knot. But no one is in sight. No one responds to your cries. The string is tight, but when you try to finish the knot on your own, it begins to loosen. Again and again you try, but on your own you are never able to preserve the tension on the string.

Nehemiah knew that God had more He wanted to do in and through the people. He also knew that they were a great deal farther along than they had been in many centuries. In order to embrace all that God had yet to give and not lose anything He had already granted, Nehemiah began raising up godly leaders around himself.

Such organizational refinements are not revival. They are not unspiritual, but they simply cannot produce that which is spiritual. Organization is good, but it should never be equated with a release of God's Spirit. It can help prepare for the outpouring of God's Spirit; it can also help preserve the gains of such a heaven-sent move of God. But in the end something more than refined organization is needed. For this reason Nehemiah also began refining the membership of God's people.

> *ORGANIZATION CAN HELP PREPARE US FOR THE MOVE OF GOD'S SPIRIT AND PRESERVE THE GAINS MADE. BUT IT IS NOT THE SAME AS REVIVAL. IN THE END SOMETHING MORE IS NEEDED.*

A brief glance at Nehemiah 7 reveals a long list of difficult-to-pronounce names in the greater portion of the chapter. It is one of those sections of Scripture that we may yawn over and flip through so we can get on to something more interesting and seemingly relevant.

Why are all these names here? One reason is because *God's work is always about people.* Organization is necessary. God commands it. But ultimately God's work is not found in well-oiled organizational machinery, but in the lives of real people. Every one of them has a name. Eternal souls that are precious to God are listed here.

Nehemiah 7 is a repeat of the list of returnees under Zerubbabel found in Ezra 2. Why suddenly introduce a group of names that is almost a century old? The list is given here to establish heritage, to identify the rightful heirs of the city.

Jerusalem was filled with people who claimed to worship

the one true God, but not all were genuine believers. Commitment to Yahweh was for many a cultural, comfortable convenience. It enabled them to get along, to do business, to thrive in the melting pot of faiths that had become the land of Judah. Even Tobiah, who plotted Nehemiah's murder, laid claim to faith in the God of the Jews. He was "closely associated" with one of the priests, and even manipulated the religious system to acquire living quarters in the temple (Neh. 13:4–5)!

Nehemiah, however, knew that living in Jerusalem didn't make you a true Jew any more than working at a bagel shop makes you a bagel. If God was to move among His people, it had to be established just who His people actually were. Nehemiah needed to know who claimed God's name out of deep, personal conviction and who did so merely out of convenience. To accomplish this Nehemiah called for the official list of verifiable Jewish people and began asking, "Is your name on the list?"

To make accurate application we must remember that Nehemiah was checking for true citizenship to a physical nation. We live on the other side of the cross and under a different covenant. God calls us to clarify who is a part of His *spiritual* nation. Peter said we "are a chosen people, a royal priesthood, a holy nation, a people belonging to God" (1 Pet. 2:9). As such we must live up to God's choice of us. We must live in light of our high calling. We must walk holy, as God is holy. We must behave as those who belong to the Lord. In revival God's people begin to own up to their high calling.

When a genuine revival arrives, when the Spirit of God moves in a fresh way to achieve His purposes through a gathered local body of believers, it will always be accompanied by a movement in which God purifies His people. When revival comes there will come with it a powerful clarification of just what it means to belong to Jesus Christ. There will be a renewed urgency pressed upon every heart to answer the question: Are you in or are you out? Revival always brings its subjects to an hour of decision.

Let's make it simple: God desires our purity.

To such simple truth, some object. "How can He? How dare

He? Doesn't He know how intolerant, narrow-minded, judgmental, and bigoted the word 'purity' sounds?"

Those immersed in contemporary thought revolt against even God's right to place before them a moral standard of measure. How violent, then, is the reaction when a mere human dares announce and enforce that divine concern? But Nehemiah makes clear that this refining of Israel's membership was God's idea, not his own. "So *my God put it into my heart* to assemble the nobles, the officials and the common people for registration by families. I found the genealogical record of those who had been the first to return. This is what I found written there" (v. 5).

We must realize that the God of the Scriptures is not one option among many. He is not a mere selection on the spiritual smorgasbord of life. This world arose out of God's heart and at His command. His nature, character and Person are the objective standard by which this world is and will be judged. There is but "one God" (1 Tim. 2:5). He is "the only Ruler, the King of kings and Lord of lords" (1 Tim. 6:15). He is "our only Sovereign and Lord" (Jude 4). He is "the eternal God" (Rom. 16:26). "Salvation is found in no one else" and there is "no other name under heaven given to men by which we must be saved" (Acts 4:12).

These are God's words, not mine. You may want to debate the truthfulness of His words, but you do not have the liberty to craft a god of your own making and then designate him the God of the Bible. God has spoken; we must meet Him on His terms and employ His revelations, declarations, and definitions. According to His words He desires our conformity to His character.

Thus we must realize that not only does God desire purity, but He defines what purity means.

Allow me to thrust us into the midst of this long list of names. "And from among the priests: the descendants of Hobaiah, Hakkoz and Barzillai (a man who had married a daughter of Barzillai the Gileadite and was called by that name)" (v. 63). Nehemiah is simply listing those who came and said, "We are among God's people!" Then he says, "These searched for their family records" (v. 64a). They were asserting that they wanted to be counted among God's people. But "they could not find them and *so were excluded* from the priesthood as unclean" (v. 64b).

Some bleeding-heart cries, "What do you mean they 'were excluded'!? That is not fair! Just because they couldn't find their name on the list they couldn't be priests? Who made up that rule?"

God did. This wasn't Nehemiah's idea. Nor was this Nehemiah's standard. God defines what it means to be a purified people.

Priests came from the family of Aaron (Exod. 28:1, 4, 41; 29:9). It was God who drew these lines. These folk could not verify their descent from Aaron, so they were not allowed to be among the priesthood.

Remember, they were dealing with a priesthood determined by physical descent. We are called according to a spiritual lineage, for a spiritual priesthood. We do not have an ancestral registration in which to check for our name. Under the New Covenant all God's children serve in the priesthood of all believers (1 Pet. 2:5). It is rightly called the priesthood of *all* believers. But realize, it is the priesthood of all *believers*.

God not only *desires* and *defines* a purified people, He alone *discerns* that purity in people. In other words, ultimately only God knows who truly believes and therefore belongs. That is precisely what Nehemiah means when he wrote, "The governor, therefore, ordered them not to eat any of the most sacred food until there should be a priest ministering with the Urim and Thummim" (v. 65).

> *TRUE REVIVAL ALWAYS CALLS US TO PURITY, TO MAKE A CHOICE: ARE WE IN OR OUT? BUT WE MUST ALSO REALIZE THAT GOD DEFINES WHAT PURITY IS, AND ONLY GOD KNOWS THE HEART.*

The exact nature of the Urim and Thummim eludes us. We know that they were a component of the breastplate worn by the High Priest (Exod. 28:30). We know that it was used to discern God's will in unclear matters (Num. 27:21; 1 Sam. 28:6). We are not certain just exactly what form they took, nor how they were used. Some suggest that they were like dice and were rolled in an act of trust in God's providence. The outcome of the roll would determine God's mind in a given matter. Whatever the exact form, in a day and age before the gift of God's Spirit to all His people and a completed canon of Scripture, the Urim and Thummim functioned as a means to discovering God's will in disputed matters (cf. Acts 1:23–26).

When a dispute arose concerning who was truly among the servants of God, the leaders of Nehemiah's day said, "Let's have God decide." They didn't have the recognized and God-given means at their disposal, so they determined to wait until God's thoughts could be discovered.

They decided that purity was worth waiting for. They didn't say, "Until we can hear from God, why don't we just let everyone in!" In revival God makes clear to His people that only a purified people participate in His purposes.

They made no arbitrary decisions; they had no personal agendas or vendettas. All they wanted was to know God's will and to do it. They didn't need to worry about the marketability of the idea or the popularity of their decision. All they needed to know was what God said about purity and what that revealed about their lives. That's all we need to know today.

Again remember, they looked to a physical linage to determine a physical priesthood. We, however, look to a spiritual lineage as a determiner of a spiritual priesthood. Leaders are given to the Church and charged with making clear what the Scriptures declare about being a believer in Jesus Christ. No pastor, preacher or teacher has the right to inject personal opinion, judgment or feelings in this regard. All that matters is what God says it means to believe and obey Jesus Christ. Leaders hold forth God's standard. They do what they can to see that it is honored among the people. In the end, however, it is God who discerns true faith in a person's heart.

They left it to God, and so should we. I don't decide who goes to heaven and who doesn't. You don't determine who is fit to serve God. God decides. Only God knows the heart.

To move us beyond the jubilant celebration of a completed building project and into the fulfillment of His purposes, God begins raising up godly leaders and refining the membership of God's people. There is another accompanying sign of a coming revival— God releases a spirit of generosity in His people. Does that seem strange? Out of sync with the first two signs? Nehemiah wrote,

> Some of the heads of the families contributed to the work. The governor gave to the treasury 1,000 drachmas of gold, 50 bowls and 530 garments for priests. Some of the heads of the families gave to the treasury for the work 20,000 drachmas of gold and 2,200 minas of silver. The total given by the rest of the people was 20,000 drachmas of gold, 2,000 minas of silver and 67 garments for priests. (vv. 70–72)

Erwin Lutzer, pastor of Moody Church in Chicago and a careful student of revival, lists a spirit of generosity as one of the four sure signs of a true revival.[1] It ought not surprise us, then, to discover that God moved the leaders to a new level of generous giving to His work. The "heads of the families" and the "governor" (v. 70) all led the way in giving. They didn't do all the giving, but they showed the way. It was understood—if you were a leader, you gave. Anyone who is unwilling to make committed, regular, sacrificial giving a part of his ministry should not be in leadership.

Leaders led the way in giving. But notice the people also were committed to giving. Nehemiah then lists "the rest of the people" (v. 72) as following their leaders in giving.

Notice that this giving was "to the work" (v. 70) and "to the treasury for the work" (v. 71). What was "the work" to which they gave? Logic might lead us to conclude it was the building project, and it may have been. Certainly the walls would never have been built without sacrifice on everyone's part. This generosity, however, went well beyond the weeks of the building project and was sustained in ongoing, committed giving. We know this because the giving went at least in part to supply "garments for priests" (vv. 70, 72).

These weren't work clothes for construction, but the pre-scribed garments for leading worship in the temple (see Exod. 28). This movement of giving was not simply to a temporary building fund, but to a general fund which financed the ongoing ministry of God's people. The kind of giving true revival engenders is not simply an emotional response to a fleeting feeling of generosity but an enduring discipline.

It is relatively easy to give when caught up in the sweeping excitement of a building project. It is more difficult, but just as necessary, to continue to give for the daily, weekly, monthly and yearly flow of ministry. The trouble is we are often impulsive (immature) in our giving, rather than regular (mature). We ought to give as the Lord prompts us. We ought to so budget our re-sources that we are in a position to do so when a special need arises. But these free-will offerings ought to grow out of an es-tablished, regular pattern of giving to the ongoing needs of the ministry of which we are a part.

Note that revival giving is not only enduring but sacrificial. The governor gave 1,000 drachmas of gold (v. 70), or about nineteen pounds. At today's prices that means one man gave over $120,000! There would be very few for whom that would not be sacrificial.

The heads of families gave 20,000 drachmas of gold, or about 375 pounds. That would add up to $2.4 million in today's economy! They also gave 2,200 minas of silver, which, believe it or not, equals about 1.3 tons, valued today at over $230,000! The people followed their leaders and gave the same amount of gold, and almost as much silver (v. 72).

Calculate it any way you like, but the leaders and the people were all taken to sacrificial depths in their giving. Only revival can produce that. We wouldn't want it if it was brought about by any other means. When sustained, sacrificial giving comes it's a sure sign that God is releasing His Spirit in a fresh way through His people. People may give sacrificially out of mere excitement over something at the moment; such philanthropy is not the sole domain of people of faith. But giving that is sacrificial *and* sustained is a good indicator that a fresh wave of the Holy Spirit is breaking upon us.

Do you give? Regularly? Sacrificially? Not simply to the most recent, urgent and moving appeal that has come your way, but to the regular ministries that consistently feed your soul at a local level?

The people of Nehemiah's day had a repopulated country, a

> *THE LEADERS AND THE PEOPLE WERE TAKEN TO SACRIFICIAL DEPTHS IN THEIR GIVING. ONLY REVIVAL CAN PRODUCE THAT.*

rebuilt temple and a restored city, but they did not yet have the Holy Spirit moving in revival. If Nehemiah had ended his account here, we would be reading the average story of the average church in America. A nice property and a nice building, but not much else going on.

What story is your local church writing? What legacy will you all leave to the coming generations? Will the dust of the ages be wiped away to reveal a well-organized, efficiently run organization housed in a fine facility on a prime piece of land? Or will those yet to come find in you a legacy of Spirit-born revival? Will they find the remnants of a people who said to themselves, "We've got it all—building, property, pews, people—but something seems to be missing"? Or will they discover a heaven-sent intensity about the work of God's Spirit in and through you?

Reaching Toward Revival

1. What are some of the external trappings of "church" that we settle for instead of revival?

   _____

   _____

2. How does the size and strength of the leadership team affect the extent of a revival's impact?

   _____

   _____

3. How may leaders be alert to conflict without becoming controlling?

   _____

   _____

4. When God sends revival, how does He refine His people?

   _____

   _____

5. What appropriate steps can leadership take to refine the membership of a local church?

   _____

   _____

6. How is generosity tied to revival?

   _____

   _____

7. What does a person's giving signal about their readiness for revival?

   _____

   _____

Part III
The Profile of Revival

*Revival is the people of God living in the power
of an ungrieved, unquenched Spirit.*
—James A. Stewart

A revival means days of heaven on earth.
—D. Martyn Lloyd-Jones

What is true revival? Does all that claims the badge originate from heaven? How do we identify a genuine move of God?

Too often false fire is embraced as revival, and the Church gets burned. Satan is the master counterfeiter, and is saving his greatest deceptions for the end of time. We might anticipate, therefore, that the longer Jesus tarries the greater the discernment we will need. It is little wonder we need to think clearly about what marks a genuine revival of God.

10

The Power of God's Word

On an average weekend in America 55 million people attend worship services at a church. While there they listen to approximately one billion words spoken in what we call sermons.

Why?

Some might think the question irreverent, but the raw data demands we ask it. Why would so many people listen to so many words? Why would all those speaking spend countless hours to prepare those words?

It's more than sheer numbers that force the question. Despite the massive turnout, the leading complaint about church is that the sermons are boring and do not relate to life. So why bother?

I'll admit it up front: we preachers need help. After subtracting a few outstanding exceptions, we really are not all that good.

One of the first times I preached was in a tiny church not far from the college I was attending. My wife Julie and I were dating at the time, and she came along for moral support. As the service began, I glanced around at those who were about to hear the message I had labored over. I counted six—yes, six—including the pastor, his wife, their children, Julie, and me! No sooner had I taken my place and opened my Bible and my mouth, than the pastor promptly fell fast asleep in the front row. Bless his heart, he was trying to encourage me. He sat there with a silly grin on his face and kept trying to nod his head in agreement with my words, but he just kept drifting off into a better world.

There's no doubt about it, we preachers have a lot of room for improvement! Having admitted our weakness, just what kind of help is it we require? Do we need a new strategy for worship? A little marketing glitz? Would some vaudevillian theatrics make the time pass more quickly? Maybe some improved staging or a little choreography? Would any of those things radically change the effectiveness of our preaching? I don't think so.

> *EFFECTIVE PREACHING HAPPENS WHEN THE SPIRIT OF GOD TAKES THE WORD OF GOD AND TRANSFORMS US INTO THE PEOPLE OF GOD. IS THERE ANY BETTER DEFINITION OF REVIVAL?*

So what is the answer? What will it take to restore preaching? I believe Nehemiah 8 tells us, in one word: *revival*. Effective preaching happens when the Spirit of God takes the Word of God and transforms us into the people of God. Is there any better definition of revival?

Think of Nehemiah and those who served with him to rebuild the wall of Jerusalem. They had seen God's miraculous provision, worked under great opposition, faced death threats, starvation, drought, and internal strife. Yet somehow, in just fifty-two days, they were able to erect the wall and hang the gates. It was nothing short of miraculous. What drove their building project? One thing—the hope of revival.

How do we know this was the impetus behind their diligence? No sooner was the building project complete than the people made an amazing demand. The events of Nehemiah 8 began "on the first day of the seventh month" (v. 2). We are able to precisely date that event in history: it was October 8, 444 B.C. Do you remember when the walls were completed? On "the twenty-fifth of Elul" (Neh. 6:15). That too can be dated precisely—October 2, 444 B.C.

Do the math. Not even a full week passed after they completed the building project until "all the people assembled as one man" and began demanding that their leaders bring out the Bible and preach (8:1)! Ezra must have turned to his wife and said, "Pinch me!" The people were coming to the leaders and saying, "We want to hear what God says!"

Nothing had really changed in the preacher. By this time Ezra had been in Jerusalem for some fourteen years. Though we've heard nothing of him in Nehemiah's book, Ezra had been on the scene long before Nehemiah ever arrived in Jerusalem. "Ezra had devoted himself to the study and observance of the Law of the LORD, and to teaching its decrees and laws in Israel" (Ezra 7:10). Study, obey, teach—that was Ezra's whole life. Discover what God has said. Obey it personally. Pass it on to others. We have every reason to believe that Ezra had been doing that very thing for the past fourteen years among the very same people who were now coming to him and demanding that he take the Bible and preach to them.

Something changed on that first day of the seventh month in 444 B.C. What was it? Did Ezra finally deliver a decent sermon after fourteen years? Did something change in the preacher? No. Something changed in the people.

Scan the words of Nehemiah 8. Can you identify the main character(s)? Nehemiah is mentioned just in passing. Ezra is introduced, but he's certainly not the central figure. The main characters in this drama are the people! Fifteen times in this chapter "the people" are thrust before us (vv. 1, 3, 5–7, 9, 11–13, 16). Why? Because that's where the work of God was taking place. Something had changed in the people. It was God's Spirit moving afresh in them and it made them hungry for God's Word!

How does that happen? What is it like when it does come about?

When God's Word is proclaimed and heard through a fresh outpouring of God's Spirit, it is *clear*. This preaching was for "all who were able to understand" (v. 2). The Hebrew word translated "understand" means to make a distinction between two options. It has the notion of discernment in it. The goal was for people to hear the Word of God and be able to compare it with their current thinking and see the implications. "But solid food is for the mature, who by constant use have trained themselves to distinguish good from evil" (Heb. 5:14).

Clarity was the goal, and so Ezra set out to achieve it. He gathered around himself thirteen Levites and they too "instructed the people in the Law" (v. 7). Ezra read the Scriptures from the front. This went on for five to six hours (v. 3)! It is likely that he inserted breaks into the meeting and perhaps during those times these others would take turns translating or explaining for the assembly what had just been said. It is even possible that they moved around amid the people and gathered them into smaller discussion groups and helped answer their questions. "They read from the Book of the Law of God, making it clear and giving the meaning so that the people could understand what was being read" (v. 8).

The Old Testament is written almost entirely in Hebrew. But the people listening to the Scriptures had grown up in Babylon and Persia. It is possible they didn't speak Hebrew at all, or at least not as well as they would have liked. Not only did they struggle with the language, but they were more Babylonian and Persian in their thinking than they should have been. Many of them had intermarried with Gentiles (see Neh. 13). They were native Jews, but they were listening with foreign ears! They were Hebrews, but they thought in Gentile categories. It is likely that some stood there—just like many filling churches today—asking, "What does this book, written long ago in a language I don't understand and filled with customs and cultural ideas that are foreign to me, have to do with my life?"

Thus Ezra and his co-laborers were "making it clear" (v. 8). The Hebrew word literally means "to separate" or "to determine." It means, then, to make something clear by separating and clarifying its parts. It could be a reference to simply translating Hebrew into Aramaic ("translating to give the sense," NASB). It is more likely, however, that they were taking the Scripture that had been read and breaking it down into paragraphs, sentences and words, and then explaining to the people exactly what the text meant and how these things applied to their lives.

This is, in my estimation, the essence of expository preaching. The goal is to have the Holy Spirit use the text of the Scriptures He breathed out in order to shape and control the sermon. It is not stringing together thematic verses orphaned from their context; it is letting the Holy Spirit speak today as He spoke the words originally. He didn't breathe forth the Scriptures in a topical index but in running narratives, carefully reasoned epistles, and other literary forms that are given to us as whole documents, not fragments of thoughts.

When the Author of the Scriptures is released upon God's people He delights to make His words clear to them as He wrote them. Clarity should be the goal of every preacher and every sermon. Clarity is different from relevance. I don't aim to make the Bible relevant. It is already more relevant than I could ever make it. The Bible is the most relevant book in the world, because it has been written by the timeless, unchanging God. No teacher makes the Bible relevant. His highest aim is to clearly expose its relevance to those who are listening. That resulting clarity leads to changed lives. The people walked away from Ezra's preaching and lived differently "because they now understood the words that had been made known to them" (v. 12b).

When God's Word is proclaimed and heard through a fresh outpouring of God's Spirit it is also *compelling*. It is a powerful, gripping thing to sit under the Word of God as it comes clear to you with Spirit-fresh understanding. There's all the difference in the world in listening to a sermon and hearing from God! It's as distinct as eating pie is from consuming the plate it is served on. One taste and you are back for more!

Who started this preaching service? "*All the people* assembled as one man in the square before the Water Gate. *They told* Ezra the scribe to bring out the Book of the Law of Moses . . ." (v. 1). The people came to the preacher and said, "Teach us what God says!" When was the last time you told your pastor to preach longer? Do you take full advantage of the opportunities to take in God's Word at your church?

"Wait a minute!" you object. "They asked for a sermon *be-*

fore Ezra began preaching! How do we know they didn't change their tune once they got a taste of it?"

Remember, this was a change in the people, not in the preacher. Ezra was doing what he'd already been doing for fourteen years. Preaching is not compelling simply because of how the speaker presents the message but also because of how the people hear it. The tongue of the preacher and the ears of the people must be equally anointed by the Spirit. When both the man in the pulpit and the people in the pew have their hearts set afire, the preaching will be compelling.

> *I*N NEHEMIAH'S DAY, THE PEOPLE CAME EXPECTANTLY BEFORE GOD'S WORD AND ITS SPOKESMAN. THEY WANTED TO HEAR FROM GOD, AND EXPECTED IT TO CHANGE THEIR LIVES. *I* WONDER IF WE DO.

The people came expectantly before God's Word and its spokesman. They wanted to hear from God! They expected they *would* hear from God. They expected that it would change their lives. I wonder if we do.

"He read it aloud from daybreak till noon as he faced the square before the Water Gate in the presence of the men, women and others who could understand. And all the people listened attentively to the Book of the Law" (v. 3). The literal wording of the last line is "And the ears of all the people were to the Book of the Law." They hadn't come to hear what Ezra had to say. They didn't want his opinions. They didn't want a digest of that week's news, a social commentary or a political statement. They wanted to know what *God said*! And don't miss this—they knew they'd find it in His written Word!

When people come expectantly to encounter God in the preaching of His Scriptures you can bet the Spirit of God is in it. What, then, must it say about us when we fuss about a sermon running five minutes overtime? I have preached in Belarus, where every service has at least two or three preachers, each with a full message. I've proclaimed God's Word in South

America and in Africa where the services last for hours and the people feel cheated if the message isn't at least an hour long. We may be richer materially in America, but I have to wonder if we are not impoverished spiritually in comparison to what God is doing among His people in other lands.

Notice that the Scriptures were read and explained "from daybreak till noon" (v. 3; lit., "from the light until the middle of the day"). In an apparently spontaneous reaction to the sight of God's Word being unfurled before them, the people rose to their feet to listen (v. 5). For some five or six hours they *stood* and listened to the Word of God. It must have been compelling!

That does not mean we must stand every time the Bible is read; that can become as formal and empty as any ritual. It means that if our hearts do not come to attention whenever we hear God's Word, something is wrong. A cold chill has crept over our hearts and the Spirit has drawn back His hand.

So compelling was this proclamation of God's Word that the leaders of the people came separately and asked for further instruction (v. 13). As leaders they weren't arrogantly fixated on how much they already knew (1 Cor. 8:1); they were conscience-stricken over how much they did *not* know of God's Word. They came crying, "Teach us! Don't make us wait until tomorrow! Don't put us off until next week! Teach us what God says!"

The result was that Ezra held a Bible conference for a solid week. "Day after day, from the first day to the last, Ezra read from the Book of the Law of God. They celebrated the feast for seven days, and on the eighth day, in accordance with the regulation, there was an assembly" (v. 18). As they celebrated the Feast of Tabernacles, every day they set aside significant times for the exposition of God's Word.

When I think of people finding God's Word so compelling that they long to hear it taught in an understandable, life-changing way, I recall a night years ago when my wife and I were in Argentina. We were traveling about in ministry with a couple from Canada and a missionary, and had come that day to a community in the interior of the country. We'd been given the opportunity to minister in a church on that week night. We arrived early and were informed of our assignments. I was to preach, my wife was to sing, the other couple would share their testimonies. Curious people began to gather. When the service started the large sanctuary began to fill up. We sang for what seemed like hours, clapping till our hands felt raw. All the while as we were in the front pew we could hear more people arriving and finding places to be seated. As our friends gave their testimonies I realized the seats must be nearly filled, for the men began bringing in benches and placing them on the platform behind the pulpit. People were led in and filled the entire platform until the only room left was in a small circle around the pulpit. Julie shared in music. Then it was time for me to preach. I rose with the missionary who would translate, and as we made our way to the platform I resisted turning around to see how many had gathered. When I finally turned I saw every bench filled—South American style! There were more than twice the people on every bench than any American church could manage. The aisles were filled with a crush of people standing in every available space. I was encircled on every side by people who had gathered to hear God's Word. Then I saw the two windows in the back of the sanctuary. Where panes of glass should have been, there was instead a montage of faces pressing close to hear. As far as I could see into the street, people had gathered to try to catch the sound of God's Word being preached.

Honestly, I don't remember exactly what I preached that night. I do, however, recall the sight of so *many* people so *compelled* to hear what God says. And I remember the fear that I wouldn't be able to speak for weeping over the privilege of bringing God's Word to them.

When God's Word is proclaimed and heard through a fresh outpouring of God's Spirit it is clear and compelling. It is also *convicting*.

What happened when the people got what they wanted? When God's Word was proclaimed under the anointing of the Holy Spirit the people spontaneously came under conviction. "Then Nehemiah the governor, Ezra the priest and scribe, and the Levites who were instructing the people said to them all, 'This day is sacred to the LORD your God. Do not mourn or weep.' For all the people had been weeping as they listened to the words of the Law" (v. 9).

We are not told when the people began weeping; we are simply told that they were. At some point during the sermon they began to weep and could not control themselves. From time to time I'll have someone approach me and say, "I'm sorry about leaving the service. I just had to get up and go, otherwise I would have begun to cry." Occasionally I'll say something like, "You don't have to worry about crying during a service. That is permissible." Often the response is, "Oh, no! If I got started I might not have been able to control it!"

Maybe what we need is a few more tears. When was last time you wept over God's Word or in prayer before Him? Remember the shortest verse in the Bible? "Jesus wept" (John 11:35). What was He weeping over? The incongruity of what was before Him with what His Father desired. "During the days of Jesus' life on earth, he offered up prayers and petitions *with loud cries and tears . . .* " (Heb. 5:7a). If Jesus wept over how far things are from what God desires, don't you think we should too?

But we feel too self-conscious for such things. It's just not socially acceptable to cry at church. What will people think? They might conclude I don't have it all together!

We don't all respond in the same way emotionally, but perhaps God is giving you the ministry of tears. Remember, the revival that began in one heart full of tearful brokenness (Neh. 1:4) had now spread to the people for whom he wept. Maybe the brokenness in your heart is the precursor to the brokenness and blessing God longs to send to a wider circle of His people.

> *T*HE REVIVAL BEGAN IN *N*EHEMIAH'S TEARFUL, BROKEN HEART AND SPREAD TO THE PEOPLE FOR WHOM HE WEPT. *M*AYBE *G*OD LONGS TO USE YOUR TEARS TO SEND BROKENNESS AND BLESSING TO OTHERS.

The conviction was not manipulated. The Word was preached. The Spirit blessed the speaker and the hearers. In the midst of that encounter people came under the convicting work of the Holy Spirit. God was at work through His Word in the hearts of the people and they began to realize, "Our lives aren't right! If God said that, then my life has to change!"

Guess what triggered what arguably may be the greatest spiritual revival the English-speaking world has ever known? It happened when a stick-thin, austere pastor by the name of Jon went to his pulpit one Sunday. He'd gone into that pulpit many times over the eight years since he'd arrived at the church. Just like every other Sunday he stood in the pulpit, a sermon manuscript in one hand and a candle by which to see it in the other. He held the manuscript up close to his face because of his poor eyesight. His voice, as usual, was rather weak and seemed to drone on in the familiar monotone way he always did as he read word for word from his manuscripted message.[1] He was anything but animated, captivating and colorful. Yet through the series of messages he began that day, God did something in the hearts of the people listening to God's Word. Some began to weep over the distance between what God said and how they lived. As they came under conviction, God seemed to sweep through the congregation. The fire did not die down when the benediction was pronounced. Hardly! The blaze of conviction spread from that congregation and before long the embers of revival spread to surrounding churches as well.

As Pastor Jonathan Edwards began his message that day, few in his Northampton, Massachusetts, congregation could have anticipated that they were about to become the spark that would ignite the first Great Awakening. Little did they know that their response to the Spirit-anointed preaching of God's Word on that day would be the beginning of a movement that would see tens of thousands of people brought to faith in Jesus Christ, not only in America, but in England as well.

They likely didn't anticipate it. It wasn't hype. It wasn't coerced. *God* did it. On an otherwise ordinary Sunday morning that must have begun like so many other mornings had, God did it.

Will He do it again? If *He* isn't doing it, I don't want it. And if God's not doing it, we ought to weep and pray that He would.

When God's Word is proclaimed and heard through a fresh outpouring of God's Spirit, it is clear, compelling, and convicting. That is what the Spirit makes preaching to be, but what does He aim to accomplish through it? The revival of Nehemiah's day reveals that Spirit-anointed preaching informs the mind, moves the emotions, and activates the will.

When the Spirit ignites in the hearts of the people and preacher alike the Word He breathed out, He aims to *inform the mind*. Biblical preaching begins here. God wants to address the mind, the rational part of our being. Remember, the emphasis here is upon understanding (vv. 2, 3, 8, 12).

The ones who gathered for Ezra's preaching were those "who were able to understand" (v. 2), which was their goal. Ezra and his associates spoke from "the Book of the Law of God, making it clear and giving the meaning so that the people could understand what was being read" (v. 8). There was great joy over the preaching "because they now understood the words that had been made known to them" (v. 12). The mind had been addressed. The people learned something, gaining content they did not possess before the preaching.

Biblical preaching aims at *truth*. God is "the God of truth" (Ps. 31:5; Isa. 65:16) and when we take up the Bible we hold in our hands "the truth of God" (Rom. 1:25; 3:7; 15:8) in propositional statements. Jesus claimed to be the embodiment of and exclusive possessor of truth (John 14:6). He who breathed life into us physically (Acts 17:25) and spiritually (John 3:5–8) is the One who breathed out the Scriptures themselves (2 Tim. 3:16). He is "the Spirit of truth" (John 14:17; 15:26) and His great desire is to "guide [us] into all truth" (John 16:13). Causing us to know truth is the Holy Spirit's aim because He knows that only the truth can set us free (John 8:32).

The light of truth drives out the darkness of the lie. It dissolves the bonds of error, misperception, distortion, and deception. The fixed point of truth gives measure, perspective and proportion to reality. To depart from the rock of truth is to cut oneself adrift from reality and to sail into a self-defined dream world. Preaching aims to reveal the God of the universe who is the center and ground of all things. Its purpose is to impart to us what He declares is truth.

Truth is not an emotion ("It feels right!"). Truth is not a choice ("I choose to believe that . . ."). Truth is not an opinion ("It seems to me that . . ."). Truth is a Person. His name is Jesus. His character, Person, and attributes form the straightedge by which all things are measured. Proximity to Him distinguishes right from wrong, up from down, truth from error.

What if preaching aims at the *emotions* before thinking? There are those who attend worship services whose first and greatest desire is to escape the pain of their daily lives. They want to be moved emotionally to a different experience. Their desire is much like what Dobie Gray expressed in his rock-'n-roll hit from years ago: "Give me the beat boys and free my soul, I want to get lost in your rock-'n-roll and drift away." They want a moving experience. They are not searching for truth but an emotional fix.

What if preaching aims at the *will* before thinking? Unlike the escapist who cries, "Just take me away from all this!" this person demands, "Just tell me what to do!" Don't make me think. Don't make me grow. Don't make me reason through the issues. Just give me a checklist of what I should do.

I've had people come to me seeking counsel regarding God's will. In the course of the conversation I'll ask questions, probe motives, explore possibilities, check their thinking. We'll begin to examine what Scripture's statements have to say about their options. Suddenly they cut off the conversation and say, "No, no, no! Don't confuse me with all of that, just tell me what to do!"

What if, on the other hand, preaching aims first at informing the *mind*, without ignoring the emotions or will? The result is that truth structures have been built within our lives that can support the weight of free-swinging emotions. The strength of an informed mind, then, is capable of harnessing the stubbornness of the will.

We have two great resources available to us in ministry—the

Word of God and the Spirit of God. Dr. Stephen Olford put our options this way:

All Word and no Spirit—you dry up.
All Spirit and no Word—you blow up.
All Word and all Spirit—you grow up.

While we must understand the priority of informing the mind, Biblical preaching produces more than intellectual stimulation. Biblical preaching *moves the emotions*.

> Then Nehemiah the governor, Ezra the priest and scribe, and the Levites who were instructing the people said to them all, "This day is sacred to the LORD your God. Do not mourn or weep." For all the people had been weeping as they listened to the words of the Law.
>
> Nehemiah said, "Go and enjoy choice food and sweet drinks, and send some to those who have nothing prepared. This day is sacred to our Lord. Do not grieve, for the joy of the LORD is your strength." The Levites calmed all the people, saying, "Be still, for this is a sacred day. Do not grieve."
>
> Then all the people went away to eat and drink, to send portions of food and to celebrate with great joy, because they now understood the words that had been made known to them. (vv. 9–12)

When the Spirit of God anoints the servant of God to speak the Word of God, it has a powerful effect upon the listener's emotions. Such an encounter with the Spirit of truth may bring both deep sorrow (v. 9) and great joy (v. 12). Their sorrow arose because of exposure to the words of God's Law (v. 9). Exposure to God's truth exposed who they were in light of who God is—and tears and remorse were the result. Exposure to God's truth revealed who God is—and the result was great joy. When God's Word is proclaimed under the Spirit's influence it stirs one's affections.

I find great help from John Piper when he describes what worship is to be like. Apply what he says specifically to the proclamation and reception of God's Word:

The fuel of worship is the truth of God, the furnace of worship is the spirit of man, and the heat of worship is the vital affections of reverence, contrition, trust, gratitude and joy.

But there is something missing from this picture. There is furnace, fuel and heat, but no *fire*. The fuel of truth in the furnace of our spirit does not automatically produce the heat of worship. There must be ignition and fire. This is the Holy Spirit.

Now we can complete our picture. The fuel of worship is a true vision of the greatness of God; the fire that makes the fuel burn white-hot is the quickening of the Holy Spirit; the furnace made alive and warm by the flame of truth is our renewed spirit; and the resulting heat of our affections is powerful worship, pushing its way out in confessions, longings, acclamations, tears, songs, shouts, bowed heads, lifted hands and obedient lives.[2]

Biblical preaching aims *first* to inform the mind, but make no mistake, when God anoints the preacher to speak and the people to hear, the emotions will be stirred.

To counteract a chilling deadness to their worship, some churches have taken aim at stirring the emotions. Each congregation goes about it in its own way. Some use endlessly repeated choruses that drone on and on, working the worshipers up into a frothy frenzy of emotion. Others race back to the music many worshipers remember from a time gone by, in an attempt to dredge up nostalgic feelings of how things used to be "when God really moved." At every point along the spectrum of worship styles there can be found those who do what they do in an attempt to produce an emotionally pleasing experience. Whatever the style and whatever the emotion sought, the strategy is human, earthly, and carnal.

EVERY WORSHIP STYLE HAS THOSE WHO ATTEMPT TO PRODUCE AN EMOTIONALLY PLEASING EXPERIENCE. WHATEVER THE STYLE AND EMOTION SOUGHT, THE STRATEGY IS HUMAN, EARTHLY, AND CARNAL.

It is not that we do not want to experience emotion in worship. We do. But we desire the right kind of emotion, not that which is produced and manipulated. Authentic emotion in worship is the fruit that arises from an encounter with the truth. When heaven-sent truth embraces human hurt the result is often deeply emotional in nature. Jesus taught that "true worshipers will worship the Father in spirit and truth, for they are the kind of worshipers the Father seeks" (John 4:23). The worship our Father seeks involves the whole of our being—mind, emotions and will. But we must discern what makes for legitimate emotion in worship. Such a distinction is highly offensive to some, for to them emotion is something that happens automatically to them, something they cannot control. To them emotion is a wave you ride. You can no more choose your emotions than a swimmer adrift in the ocean can choose to bob up and down with the swelling surges of the surf.

That simply is not true. Legitimate emotion in worship springs from an encounter with the truth rather than being found in its absence.

When I am moved emotionally during worship, I often ask myself a simple question: "What truth have I just encountered that moves me so deeply?" I search my heart to see if there may be something other than truth that is pushing these feelings to the surface. I ask myself this because I know that emotion can be stirred by a variety of things. Emotions are a fact, but it does not mean they are all created equal.

There have been times during worship when I have been overwhelmed by deep emotions and as I examined my heart I knew it was because God had just opened my heart to fresh views of His truth and how it applies to my life. There have been other times that I have felt nearly identical emotions and discovered that they arose not from a fresh Spirit-given encounter with the truth of God but because I've been pushing too hard, not keeping an appropriate schedule, been under a lot of stress, been attacked by people or some other combination of events. Those events had combined to reduce my emotional reserves, and the feelings that broke to the surface could just as easily have been stirred by the sounds of "White Christmas" as by "O Come, All Ye Faithful." The emotions were stirred more by the melody line than by the truth content.

Any study of the history of revival reveals that true revival nearly always involves some intense emotions. Even the most staid and austere folk have found themselves strangely moved when God's Spirit is unleashed in a fresh way upon them. But such emotions spring *from* and are governed and perpetuated *by* the proclamation of the truth of God's Word.

In addition to informing the mind and moving the emotions, Spirit-anointed preaching *activates the will*. When the mind is opened by God's Spirit to understand His truth and when the emotions are stirred by a fresh understanding of the relationship of that truth to our lives, the will leaps to obey what God says. When God's Word is rightly preached and heard, people begin making wise, Biblical choices.

Preaching moves us to respond to the truth. "Ezra praised the LORD, the great God; and all the people lifted their hands and responded, 'Amen! Amen!' Then they bowed down and worshiped the LORD with their faces to the ground" (v. 6). The people verbally affirmed and assented to the truth proclaimed ("Amen! Amen!"). They were moved to bodily express their response ("all the people lifted their hands"). There was both an audible and physical response to the truth as God applied it to their needs.

Of course this is not to institute the saying of "Amen!" or the lifting of hands as the measure of response to God's Word or the indisputable sign of revival. Such outward tokens are too easy to fake. The unspiritual can employ them as easily as any other religious activity. On the other hand, we might want to ask ourselves when was the last time we ventured an "Amen!" to a truth proclaimed from the pulpit or when we last raised our hands to God in yearning prayer.

One way preaching moves us to respond is in *worship*. When the people heard the words of God, "they bowed down and worshiped the Lord" (v. 6). The Hebrew word translated "bowed down" is found fifteen times in the Old Testament, and always in connection with the word for worship. The proclamation of God's truth elicited a united response from the people toward God. They were not drawn to the preacher but to the God in whose name he spoke.

There was no "preacher cult" here. Ezra was simply a vessel. He hadn't changed his methods; for the past fourteen years, he'd been preaching God's Word to them in virtual obscurity. When God's Spirit moves upon His people, they have a powerful compulsion for God in worship, not for the preacher in adulation.

Preaching also moves us to respond in *humility*. The people bowed down before the Lord "with their faces to the ground" (v. 6). Who gets exalted when God's Word is proclaimed and heard under the anointing of the Spirit? God. Who gets humbled? Us! If the goal is to hold forth the Person of God in His glory, there can be no other outcome.

Preaching moves us to respond in *obedience*, as well. As Ezra led them in the study of God's Word they learned that on that day they were to be keeping a festival called the Feast of Trumpets (compare "first day of the seventh month," Neh. 8:2, with Lev. 23:23 and Num. 29:1–6). The trouble was that the Scriptures commanded this to be a day of celebration, not weeping. The Day of Atonement, on the tenth of the month (Lev. 23:27; 25:9), was the appropriate time for weeping, remorse and repentance. But this day was to be one of celebration, so the preachers commanded the people to rejoice!

How did the people respond? They did exactly the opposite of what they felt like doing.

> The Levites calmed all the people, saying, "Be still, for this is a sacred day. Do not grieve."
> Then all the people went away to eat and drink, to send portions of food and to celebrate with great joy, because they now understood the words that had been made known to them. (vv. 11–12)

When confronted with a command of God's Word that contradicted their emotions, they bent their wills to what God said rather than what they felt like doing. Don't miss the significance of this. How different the response might be in our day! Someone would object, "But I just don't feel like doing that! To rejoice would be emotionally dishonest. I would be a phony. To rejoice would be hypocritical. I just can't do what God asks of me because I don't *feel* that way." Too often when the word of the living God clashes with the emotions of a languishing believer, feelings win out. We have believed the lie that the will must answer to the emotions.

How different it was in Ezra's day, when the Spirit moved upon the people in fresh power! Ezra and the Levites assisting him told the people, "We understand how you feel. But we must remind you that God says rejoicing is our next step of obedience." And the people responded, "Okay. Let's rejoice!"

Preaching also moves us to respond in *ministry*. Fathers and family leaders came to Ezra and said, "Teach us! We've not been leading our families as we should. Show us what God says. Train us to lead our families!" (v. 13). Perhaps the Scripture reading included Deuteronomy 6:6–7: "These commandments that I give you today are to be upon your hearts. Impress them on your children. Talk about them when you sit at home and when you walk along the road, when you lie down and when you get up." Maybe God began awakening fathers in the crowd to realize they were responsible for the spiritual welfare of their wives and children. It wasn't the responsibility of "the guy on the platform" to reach their children. It was their God-given responsibility! These fathers and leaders were moved to respond in ministry, and not just sit back and take in the truth of God.

Preaching also moves us to respond in *unity*. Watch for the key phrases that signal a new unity in their midst:

> They found written in the Law, which the LORD had commanded through Moses, that the Israelites were to live in booths during the feast of the seventh month and that they should pro-

claim this word and spread it *throughout their towns and in Jerusalem*: "Go out into the hill country and bring back branches from olive and wild olive trees, and from myrtles, palms and shade trees, to make booths"—as it is written.

So *the people went out* and brought back branches and built themselves booths on their own roofs, in their courtyards, in the courts of the house of God and in the square by the Water Gate and the one by the Gate of Ephraim. The *whole company* that had returned from exile built booths and lived in them. From the days of Joshua son of Nun until that day, the Israelites had not celebrated it like this. And their joy was very great.

Day after day, from the first day to the last, Ezra read from the Book of the Law of God. *They celebrated* the feast for seven days, and on the eighth day, in accordance with the regulation, *there was an assembly*. (vv. 14–18)

The response the Spirit elicited from God's people was singular. It had not been humanly orchestrated. It didn't happen because of someone's administrative expertise. This was a God-ordained movement—and when He communicated new life to each heart, the people moved as one.

When God revives both the preacher and hearers of His Word, minds are informed, emotions stirred, and wills activated—and everything changes. The service times may be the same; the sign out front may not have been upgraded; nothing may have changed—and yet, everything is different!

Remember, the primary change that ushered in the revival of Nehemiah's day did not occur in the preacher but in the people. That change took place when they came together and expected God to do something when His Word was proclaimed (v. 1).

What would happen in our day if all the people worked at preparing their hearts to receive God's Word, just as they expect the one man to prepare a message from God's Word?

Who knows . . . the result might be revival.

1. What place does preaching hold in true revival?

    _____

    _____

2. What would be the result if God's people came to your church this weekend with prepared, expectant, Spirit-filled hearts?

    _____

    _____

3. What makes for compelling preaching?

    _____

    _____

4. What is the difference between Spirit-produced conviction and humanly-produced guilt?

    _____

    _____

5. What must God do in the hearts of the people and the preacher if His purposes for preaching are to be fulfilled? What happens when one or the other does not cooperate?

    _____

    _____

6. What is the relationship between preaching and worship?

    _____

    _____

7. How do you know when you've encountered God in the preaching of His Word?

    _____

    _____

11

It's My Fault!

As the Kansas State Senate convened for a new session of business on January 23, 1996, most of the Senators had their minds on the matters most important to them. No one expected much as the guest pastor approached the microphone to offer the opening prayer, as had been done for years on end. Such prayers were routinely generic and perfunctory. But when Pastor Joe Wright of Central Christian Church bowed his head, it raised a few eyebrows.

Heavenly Father, we come before You today to ask Your forgiveness and seek Your direction and guidance. We know Your Word says, "Woe on those who call evil good," but that's exactly what we have done. We have lost our spiritual equilibrium and inverted our values. We confess that we ridiculed the absolute truth of Your Word and called it pluralism; we have worshiped other gods and called it multiculturalism; we have endorsed perversion and called it an alternative lifestyle; we have exploited the poor and called it the lottery; we have neglected the needy and called it self-preservation; we have rewarded laziness and called it welfare; we have killed our unborn and called it choice; we have shot abortionists and called it justifiable; we have neglected to discipline our children and called it building self-esteem; we have abused power and called it political savvy; we have coveted our neighbor's possessions and called it ambition; we have polluted the air with profanity and pornography

183

and called it freedom of expression; we have ridiculed the time-honored values of our forefathers and called it enlightenment.

Search us, O God, and know our hearts today; try us and see if there be some wicked way in us; cleanse us from every sin and set us free. Guide and bless these men and women who have been sent here by the people of Kansas, and who have been ordained by You, to govern this great state. Grant them Your wisdom to rule and may their decisions direct us to the center of Your will. I ask it in the name of Your Son, the Living Savior, Jesus Christ. Amen.

Pastor Wright's prayer was met with something less than enthusiasm by most of the legislators. Some attempted to drop the requirement of prayer before their sessions. Some denounced it publicly. Others walked out before it was done.

Prayers of confession are not comfortable. Nehemiah 9 is one of those uncomfortable prayers of confession. It is the longest recorded prayer in the Bible—1,258 words.[1] But only once in over 1,200 words did they dare ask for anything. Eleven words were employed to make a request; 1,247 words were used to exalt God and make confession of their sins.

TRUE CONFESSION OF SIN IS THE PATH TO A FRESH WORK OF GOD. IT WON'T HAPPEN ANY OTHER WAY.

The physical security of the city through a rebuilt wall (Neh. 1–7) had been a concern, but it was secondary to their desire for a fresh outpouring of God's Spirit in revival (Neh. 8–13). As we saw in the last chapter, the wall was barely completed when the people demanded of their leaders, "Let's get to the matter of revival. Get that Bible and teach us!" When God brings revival He begins by calling His people back to His Word.

In Nehemiah 9 we encounter the second step of revival: admission of what the light of God's Word has uncovered. True confession is the pathway to a fresh work of God. It won't happen any other way.

Why is that so? Simply because *sin is worse than we think*.

It's My Fault!

Sin is not a popular subject. Never has been. We avoid it at all costs. We'll admit to a great deal, but seldom does it go so far as admitting sin. We make mistakes, but seldom commit sins. We make errors, but rarely rebel against God. We admit to lapses in judgment, but never to defiant arrogance. We make boo-boos, but we do not commit transgressions. We have made poor choices, but not iniquities. We will, if it is otherwise unavoidable, say we are sorry, but we avoid at all costs having to make the request, "Will you forgive me?"

We redefine our actions, thoughts, words, attitudes and motives. We spin. We massage. We recast the image of our sins. But the fact remains: sin is worse than we think.

There is much to be said about how horrific sin is, but this prayer highlights two great reasons that sin is worse than we think. One reason is that *we live with the consequences of the sins of others*.

It's a hard fact of life, but you know it's true. Right now you are experiencing some consequences that come to you not because you did something sinful but because someone else did. Someone made a choice that has affected your life negatively. You shout, "That's not fair!" Guess what? You're right. It's not fair. Ask anyone who has lost a child to a drunk driver, or suffered from child abuse. Ask the person dealing with a spouse's uncontrolled anger. Ask any parent of a rebellious child. Ask a Christian in the Sudan.

Is it fair? No, but it is a fact. It's a fact in a fallen world. Mark it down. Count on it. It's a maxim of life in a sin-laden world. We live with the consequences of others' sin.

"Why doesn't God just . . . ?"

It's not about God's refusal, but about our choice as a race to live separate from God.

This prayer was offered up to God around 444 B.C. It recounts Israel's history over the previous 1,500 years. Chew on that for a moment. All those events over fifteen centuries were shaping the way their lives were unfolding on that day, in that hour, at that moment, in that second. This prayer reviews 1,500 years of somebody else's actions, choices, and words. Those ac-

185

tions, their choices, their words had shaped the tangible, daily experiences of Nehemiah and those with him.

Fair? No. Fact? Yes.

Is there any doubt? Sin is worse than we think.

Another reason sin is worse than we think is that *we share in the culpability of others' sin.* As hard as it is to admit that we live with the consequences of others' sin, to admit *culpability* in the sins of others is vastly more difficult to swallow! We have breathed the air of individuality so long that we are convinced that our private lives are no one's business but our own. We've been told we are an island unto ourselves. What you do is your concern and has no relationship to my life.

This passage in Nehemiah, however, is one of those infuriating "we" prayers. You'll find other great examples in Ezra 9 and Daniel 9. You'll discover the same thing there as you do here—confessions of sin that use "we," "us," and "our" instead of "them," "they," and "theirs." Nehemiah and those of his day realized there is a solidarity about the people of God.

A review of a millennium and a half of sin yielded this: "*We* did wrong" (v. 33). How? "Our kings, our leaders, our priests and our fathers did not follow your law" (v. 34)! They didn't; we didn't. They did; we did. Their fault is our fault. *We* have sinned!

We have a pronoun problem. We can't bring ourselves to say "we" if it involves anything more than a potluck dinner or church softball game. Even then it is "their casserole" or "their poor hitting" that brings the whole thing down. If Harrison Ford and Stephen Spielberg ever make another "Indiana Jones" movie I'd like to suggest a title: *Indiana Jones and the Lost Pronoun.* What a treasure it would be to recover a Biblical understanding of sin!

What happens inside you when you learn of another person's sin? Make it someone you know: What's your internal, emotional reaction? Do you say, "What an idiot!" Or do you cry out in anguish not only for them, but also for us? Do you distance yourself from them—physically, emotionally, socially or verbally? Have you ever stopped to pray, "God forgive *us. We* have sinned"?

Sin is worse than we think. Because it is, *confession must go deeper than we think.*

The prayer of the leaders in Nehemiah's day teaches us what true confession is. For one thing, it reminds us that true confession is more far-reaching than we think. When they started confessing sin in verse 16, they began with the sin of refusing to enter the Promised Land when God guided them there. They were confessing a 1,000-year-old sin!

When it came time to get serious about confessing sin, where did they start? How far back did they go? Yesterday? Last week? A year ago? A generation in the past? No, they went back 1,000 years. We quickly realize that Biblical confession is more far-reaching than we imagine.

> *S*IN — *WITH ALL ITS CONSEQUENCES AND OUR CULPABILITY — IS WORSE THAN WE THINK. T*HAT IS WHY CONFESSION MUST GO DEEPER THAN WE THINK.*

I spent a little time in our local cemetery this week. At first I just sat and prayed. Then I began thinking about the graves that surrounded me. I found headstones that are over 150 years old. I started trying to imagine what life was like 150 years ago. Incredibly different, I'm sure. I thought about what those people's lives must have been like, what they did, who they were. I was struck by how completely distant I feel from all that was their lives. After all, that was 150 years ago! Who they were, what they did, what they thought, what they believed seems so completely removed from the way my daily life unfolds.

But then again, it was *only* 150 years ago. When Nehemiah and his people began to pray and confess their sins, they started 1,000 years prior to their time!

True confession is more personal than we imagine—far more personal. Again, note the pronouns. The confession begins with what "they" had done (vv. 16–18, 26, 28–30). We are comfortable with that. In fact, in a twisted, carnal sort of way, it is a bit of a relief, isn't it?

"*They* did it. The bozos! It's those old guys. It's the people way back then. How stupid could they be? It's *them*!"

That much we can stomach. But, as we've already noted, the pronouns quickly change to "we," "our," and "us"!

> Now therefore, O our God, the great, mighty and awesome God, who keeps his covenant of love, do not let all this hardship seem trifling in your eyes—the hardship that has come upon *us*, upon *our* kings and leaders, upon *our* priests and prophets, upon *our* fathers and all your people, from the days of the kings of Assyria until today. In all that has happened to *us*, you have been just; you have acted faithfully, while *we* did wrong. *Our* kings, *our* leaders, *our* priests and *our* fathers did not follow your law; they did not pay attention to your commands or the warnings you gave them. (vv. 32–34)

"*They* did it. It's true. But *we* are their children. Somehow in the mystery of God's ways we share in what they've done!" You don't hear much of that these days. When you do, take note. The Spirit is stirring the coals and revival is bursting into flame.

True confession is also more corporate than we are comfortable with. The text assigns this prayer to a handful of leaders (vv. 4–5), but surely one of them took the lead in voicing the words. Here he is, representing all of the leaders, who represent all of the people; one voice representing many voices, speaking on behalf of them all. They were all praying, but one was speaking audibly, saying, "*We* did wrong" (v. 33).

Over the years as a pastor I've given opportunity for folks to lift their voices in prayers of corporate confession. I normally open the way with a phrase like, "As God moves your heart, lift your voice and confess any sin we are guilty of." The quietest moments in the history of those churches is when I give such an invitation. For personal sins I encourage people to silently, privately confess them to God. For corporate sins I invite public confession.

Confession needs to go as wide as the circle of sin. If you think a dirty thought and no one knows but you and God, confess it to Him. Accept His forgiveness. Ask to be filled anew with the Spirit. Move on in faith. If you must confess to yelling at your children, then confess it—to God first, but also to them. If you won't confess it to your kids, you haven't really confessed it to God. If you bring disrepute upon your church family, then you need to seek the forgiveness of the entire church family. It is this kind of confession we meet here. Surely we are not so arrogant as to think that our lives are perfect before God and we have nothing to confess before Him.

They were confessing "our" sins, not "my" sins. This wasn't one of those misguided meetings in which people are manipulated emotionally until they go to a microphone and share things that ought never be spoken in public.

A pastor once spoke about a man who stood during public confession and made known to the entire church his sin of adultery. His wife learned of it at the same time everyone else did. I dare say his confession was not motivated by genuine repentance, but by cowardice before his wife. He trusted she wouldn't kill him in front of all those witnesses! That is not the kind of confession God honors by sending revival.

For personal sins we need to go to God and those we've injured. If we aren't breaking free of sin's grip we may need to go to one trusted, mature Christian of the same gender and enlist his or her prayer support. But for sins that we share commonly we need to confess corporately. That is what Joe Wright was doing before the Kansas Senate.

True confession is also more of a deliberate choice than we care to admit. It is not a matter of feeling. You may not *feel* like you have anything to repent of. You may not *feel* particularly responsible for the sin of the people of God. That does not relieve you of the *responsibility* to confess those sins.

Follow the chronology of events that are before us in these middle chapters of Nehemiah. It is a study that will highlight the volitional nature of confession.

October 2: The wall around Jerusalem is completed (Neh. 6:15).

October 8: The people ask Ezra to preach the Word of God to them (Neh. 8:2). In response to God's Word the people begin to weep because, having now heard clearly what God's standard is, they realize how far short they have fallen. Ezra and the other leaders, however, check the calendar and realize that this day is the Feast of Trumpets—ordained by God to be a day of rejoicing, not weeping. So they command the people to put their emotions on hold and to do what the Scriptures command them to do. The people dutifully obey.

October 9: The leaders return for further instructions from the Scriptures and discover that the next event on the calendar is the Feast of Tabernacles (Neh. 8:13–15). This was celebrated from the 15th through the 21st of the seventh month (Lev. 23:37–43), so that gave the people approximately two weeks to prepare for the event.

October 22–28: The Feast of Tabernacles is obediently observed by the people under the direction of their leaders (Neh. 8:16–18a).

October 29: A solemn assembly is held, according to the Scriptural regulations (Neh. 8:18b; cf. Lev. 23:39).

October 31: After a one day interval, a convocation is held for the confession of the sin they were first convicted of almost a month before (Neh. 8:2; 9:1). After obediently doing what God's Word clearly taught them, they return to deal with what they knew must be cared for before they could experience the reviving work of the Holy Spirit in their midst.

This is not to say we can put off confession. It is to note that confession is not an emotion. It may well be accompanied by emotion, but it is not primarily an emotion. Confession is a choice. If God is who the Scriptures say He is and I am who they describe me to be in the light of His holiness, then I must agree with God and confess that distance and name it as sin.

Finally, note that true *confession is more God-centered than we understand*. Some have made confession an introspective exercise in which we block out everything, contemplate our navel and dredge up bad thoughts about ourselves. To be truly repentant we think we must repeat the mantra "Bad! Bad! Bad!" repeatedly until we convince ourselves. But that is not true confession. It's really self-worship in disguise; after all, who are you focusing on when you do that? True confession begins with God and is centered upon Him.

> *TRUE CONFESSION IS A CHOICE, NOT AN EMOTION. IT BEGINS WITH GOD AND IS CENTERED ON HIM, NOT US.*

Look at the pronouns. You will find that pronouns for God are used twenty-six times before you meet a single one referring to humans in this confession. In fact, pronouns for God are used a total of eighty-five times in this one prayer! In contrast pronouns referring to humans are used only thirty-three times. Do you see their focus? They had set God in His glory and greatness before themselves. They had God's revelation, actions, character and attributes before them. He was the origin, center and focus of all their thoughts, words and responses.

Trace these pronouns and you'll find that there is a beautiful alternative weave to their prayer: God (vv. 6–15), human (vv. 16–17a), God (v. 17b), human (v. 18), God (vv. 19–25), human (v. 26), God (v. 27), human (v. 28a), God (vv. 28b–30a), human (v. 30b), God (v. 30c–31)!

True confession does not come by introspection but by revelation. Focus on God first, then the truth about yourself will become clear. True confession does not come from sitting around contemplating how bad you are. That only serves to feed the sick, twisted self-centeredness that has led to our problems in the first place. Confession, rather, is setting God in His rightful place and honestly admitting what we see in the light of who He is.

A fresh work of God's grace in our midst must pass through true confession because sin is worse than we think and because confession goes deeper than we think. But it is also essential because the consequences are more serious than we think. Several simple principles about the consequences of unconfessed sin are revealed at the close of this prayer:

> Even while they were in their kingdom, enjoying your great goodness to them in the spacious and fertile land you gave them, they did not serve you or turn from their evil ways.
>
> But see, we are slaves today, slaves in the land you gave our forefathers so they could eat its fruit and the other good things it produces. (vv. 35–36)

Note the words, "they did not serve you . . . we are slaves today, slaves in the land you gave our forefathers." It is a reminder that if you don't serve God, you will serve something else. When we do not go God's way, we do not end up free. Refusal to serve the King of kings does not make us autonomous, but enslaved. We have been created to serve God. It's in our spiritual DNA. Bob Dylan was right: "You're gonna have to serve somebody."[2]

I don't know if he knew it, but he was agreeing with the Scottish theologian P. T. Forsyth who said, "The first duty of every soul is not to find its freedom, but to choose its master." God promises that we will one day reign with Christ (2 Tim. 2:12; Rev. 20:4, 6). But understand this: No one will rule *with* Christ who has not been ruled *by* Christ!

We are also taught that if we aren't good stewards of the gifts God gives, He will give discipline instead. Did you see another repetition in those closing lines?

> Even while they were in their kingdom, enjoying your great goodness to them in the spacious and fertile land you *gave* them, they did not serve you or turn from their evil ways.
>
> But see, we are slaves today, slaves in the land you *gave* our forefathers so they could eat its fruit and the other good things it produces. Because of our sins, its abundant harvest goes to the kings you have *placed over us.* They rule over our bodies and our cattle as they please. We are in great distress. (vv. 35–37)

God is a giver. He gave the Israelites His "great goodness" and "the land." But He also gave them something else because of their response to these first gifts. The word translated "placed over us" in verse 37 is the same one translated "gave" in verses 35 and 36. God gave them His "great goodness" (v. 35) and "the land" of promise (v. 36), but because they did not act as wise stewards of these divine gifts, He gave them pagan "kings" to "rule over [their] bodies and [their] cattle" and the result was "great distress" (v. 37). In other words, God gave them discipline because they did not recognize the source of their bounty nor did they employ it for His purposes and the advancement of His glory.

God is a giver. "For God so loved the world that he gave . . ." (John 3:16). He has showered us with innumerable gifts. He "richly provides us with everything for our enjoyment" (1 Tim. 6:17). "Every good and perfect gift is from above, coming down from the Father of the heavenly lights" (James 1:17). God has showered us with good things. If we do not respond in glad obedience and employ His gifts in His service, He will give us something else—the gift of discipline.

One final principle about the consequences of sin is set before us: *If you try to build your own kingdom instead of God's kingdom, you will end up living in someone else's kingdom.* Note that telling phrase in verse 35: "while they were in their kingdom." With just two words in Hebrew (six in English), Nehemiah captured 1,000 years of Israelite history! And what a summary it is.

Whose kingdom did God choose the Israelites to set up? God's. But after 1,000 years of dealing with them, whose kingdom had they built? Their own. How sad.

What became of their kingdom? "Because of our sins, its abundant harvest goes to the kings you have placed over us" (v. 37). They built their kingdom instead of God's. All He gave they gathered to themselves. In the end it went to someone else's kingdom. And so did they.

Is it possible that the kingdom we were supposed to establish, we haven't? Could it be that we've misappropriated the blessings of God to establish our own kingdom? We've wanted to rule our own lives. We want life on *our* terms. We want our own little corner of the world, where we sit enthroned and everyone and everything answers to us.

Is it possible that, all religious jargon and activity aside, we are not building God's kingdom but our own? Is that why we are so frustrated in our attempt to hold on to what we've got? Is God redistributing the gifts He originally placed in our hands and sending them to others in order to discipline us?

True confession is the pathway to a fresh work of God in our midst. That is a fact because sin is worse than we think and because confession goes deeper than we think and because the consequences are more serious than we think.

Think of it this way: If true confession opens the pathway to a fresh work of God's grace in our midst, what does a lack of true confession, or even an incomplete confession, produce? It keeps us locked in the cell of our own strength. It tightens the bonds of that which rules us. It perpetuates the frustrating experiences of life as we come to know it.

Do we want revival in our midst? Do we really want a fresh work of God's Spirit in our midst? The answer is found not in what we say but in how we pray.

Reaching Toward Revival

1. Why is confession of sin an unavoidable step toward revival?

2. How has the Biblical understanding of sin been distorted in our day? And how does it hold revival at bay?

3. How can God consider us culpable for sins committed by others?

4. What guidelines should govern the public confession of sin?

5. What steps should we take to restore true, Biblical confession to its proper place?

6. If we continue to view the confession of sin as we now do, what will be the outcome?

7. What does our struggle with confession of sin reveal about the reality of our hearts?

12

I the Undersigned

Hereby . . .

A re you committed? It's a tough question, isn't it? Your answer really depends on who's asking and what you believe they mean by their inquiry.

It's a serious question if your boss asks, "Are committed to this business or not?" It's a very different question, however, if your spouse looks you in the eye and asks, "Are you committed to this marriage?" Both queries are serious. Both regard commitment. Yet they relate to two very different matters and the stakes are much higher in one than the other.

One morning a chicken and a pig were trying to decide what to have for breakfast. The chicken suggested, "Let's have bacon and eggs!" The pig replied, "That's easy for you to suggest. For you it requires only a minor contribution, but for me it means total commitment!"

Are you committed? It depends on who's asking and what the issues are. One Sunday, a pastor delivered a sermon in which he kept asking, "Who wants to go to heaven?" At first only a few "Amens" could be heard, but as he continued, repeatedly stopping to ask, "Who wants to go to heaven?" the congregation became more demonstrative with their affirmations, shouting "Amen" and "Hallelujah!" and raising their hands. One mother noticed that her young son seemed not to share in the general eagerness, so she leaned over and asked him, "Don't you want to go to heaven when you die?" "Oh, when you die!" he replied. "I thought they were gathering a bus load to leave right away!"

Are you committed? It all depends on who's asking and what the issues are.

A REAL MESS RESULTS WHEN GOD'S PEOPLE DIFFER IN THEIR DEFINITION OF COMMITMENT TO GOD.

In Nehemiah 10 we see the mess that results when God's people differ in their definition of commitment to God. It still happens today. Two people marry, filled with dreams of a life spent together serving God. But it ends in disappointment, largely because they assumed they were in agreement about what it means to serve God. Homes, churches and ministries end up being less than what God wants them to be because the people who make them up define commitment differently.

The first seven chapters of Nehemiah focus on restoring Jerusalem's physical security through a rebuilt wall around the city. Not until chapter 8 is the real priority discovered—God's people being restored, refreshed and revived in their walk with God. A fresh work of reviving grace begins when God's people put His Word in its proper place in their midst collectively and in their hearts individually (Neh. 8). That reviving work advances when they own up to what the light of that Word reveals, leading them to genuine confession of sin (Neh. 9).

What is life to be like after the Amen? When God's Spirit stirs up His people afresh, it results in a recommitment to God and His purposes (Neh. 10). But what does commitment mean—really? In the details?

Notice the commitments made in the midst of the revival of Nehemiah's day. "In view of all this [the things just prayed

I the Undersigned Hereby . . .

through in 9:5–37], we are making a binding agreement, putting it in writing, and our leaders, our Levites and our priests are affixing their seals to it" (9:38). God lifted up His written Word (ch. 8), the people confessed the sin that became obvious in its light (ch. 9), and then affirmed their recommitment to God by signing their names to a covenant of obedience.

> Those who sealed it were: Nehemiah the governor [and] . . . the priests. The Levites . . . The leaders of the people . . . [and] The rest of the people—priests, Levites, gatekeepers, singers, temple servants and all who separated themselves from the neighboring peoples for the sake of the Law of God, together with their wives and all their sons and daughters who were able to understand—all these now join their brothers the nobles, and bind themselves with a curse and an oath to follow the Law of God given through Moses the servant of God and to obey carefully all the commands, regulations and decrees of the LORD our Lord. (Neh. 10:1, 8–9, 14, 28–29)

Eighty-four specific names appear here—names of those willing to go on record as recommitting themselves to living God's way. That included twenty-two priests, seventeen Levites, and forty-four other "leaders of the people." Others not specifically listed followed their leaders and put their names in black and white as followers of God (vv. 28*ff.*).

Something about signing your name makes you think more seriously about what you're committing to, doesn't it? Just the other night one of my children came and said, "Dad, would you please sign this?" What do you think my first response was? "What is it I'm agreeing to?" They were not trying to pull the wool over my eyes on anything, but I did what any person would do . . . examine what I'm committing to. Signing your name makes it just a little more real, doesn't it?

When I agree to provide premarital counseling for a couple, I make several commitments to them and I expect them to make certain commitments to God in response. I've always listed clearly what those expectations are and discussed them thoroughly with each couple before we began the counseling in earnest. Sometimes couples look over these mutual commitments and decide to look for another pastor to marry them, but most of the time they smile and agree to them.

Over the years I've discovered that, while most couples freely give their consent, some do not think through all that these commitments mean. To some a smile, a nod and even their word mean little other than keeping the pastor happy so they can get from me what they want. They are not *ultimately* committed to what they *say* they are committed to.

For that reason I now do something different when I begin premarital counseling. After reviewing our mutual commitments, I ask, "Are you committed to these things?" When they smile and nod, I say, "Good," and hand them another piece of paper that has the exact same commitments listed, except it includes a spot at the bottom for the date and their signatures. I ask, "Please sign that, as a covenant between the three of us that you will be committed to these things."

It is sometimes a bit humorous to watch their countenance change at the thought of putting their commitments in black and white. There's just something about signing your name.

God is reminding us that *true revival evidences itself in obedience to God's Word.*

Do you believe the Bible? What would you tell me if we stood face to face and I asked that question? What would your countenance tell me? The tone of your voice? To what degree to you believe it? At what cost? If I drew up a covenant detailing what the Bible says and outlining a personal commitment to shape life by its commands, prohibitions and principles, would you sign it? Would you sign it if a copy with your signature was sent to your spouse, co-workers, relatives and neighbors?

Your decision to sign would likely depend on the specifics of those covenant commitments. So what exactly were Nehemiah and his friends committing to? The remainder of Nehemiah 10 outlines three key areas of obedience that evidence a genuine, Spirit-led revival.

Marriage and Family

First, true revival evidences itself in my obedience to God's Word in my *marriage and family*. What did the "rest of the people . . . along with their wives and all their sons and daughters" join their leaders in? "All these now join their brothers the nobles, and bind themselves with a curse and an oath to follow the Law of God given through Moses the servant of God and to obey carefully all the commands, regulations and decrees of the LORD our Lord" (v. 29).

They committed, not simply as individuals, but also as families, to obey God (v. 28). Every member of a family "who [was] able to understand" stood with his or her parents and declared allegiance to God and His Word. (This did not include infants or small children who could not reflectively think through the issues.) The fresh work of God's Spirit in their lives drew out a thoughtful commitment that weighed the issues, knew the costs, and understood the implications.

Not only did they commit to obey God in their *existing* families but in their *future* families. They were specific in this commitment: "We promise not to give our daughters in marriage to the peoples around us or take their daughters for our sons" (v. 30).

The issue was the spiritual purity of marriage. The concern was not racial or ethnic, but spiritual. They were to establish homes that were united in commitment to God. They were to be absolutely, unreservedly committed to Yahweh, to the purity of worship, to raising up a nation that would glorify Him, through which the Messiah would come to save the world. And their commitment to obedience in marriage and family was a key part of the larger overall redemptive plan of God as they built this nation through which Messiah would come.

Their new commitments were not the result of bigoted, narrow-minded, self-righteous thinking. They were evidence that they understood their place in God's plan. It was an acknowledgment that the whole of God's plan is affected by what I do within my marriage and family. They could not take absolute commitment to Yahweh and mingle it with tempered allegiance to some other god.

Any supposed recommitment to God that does not radically affect the home, marriage and family is a sham. Observers often wonder why the spiritual temperature of the American church is so low. We need look no further than our homes. As has already been noted, statistics now reveal that if you label yourself as an evangelical Christian you are more likely to get divorced than if you call yourself an atheist.

In golf, a "mulligan" is a bad shot that you do over. The evangelical message has become little more than a "mulligan" religion. Like a golfer with a bad tee shot saying "That's a mulligan," too many Christians in a difficult marriage call for a redo. The dedication we declare so passionately on Sunday mornings seems unable to endure even the ride home together in the car.

I want to ask some simple questions:

To men I ask, Are you leading your home spiritually? No excuses. Just answer the question. If you have children at home, did you pray each day this week with your children? Saying "Thanks for the food" at the dinner table doesn't count. Are you and your wife praying together? For one another? For your family? Are you nurturing your wife?

To women I ask, What objective acts have you taken this past week to demonstrate that you respect your husband? How many times this week did you seek forgiveness from someone in your family? In the past 72 hours, how have you honored your parents?

The wall you erect will only be as solid as the internal integrity of the individual bricks you use. The most basic building block of any church is the family. Even those who are single— whether by calling and choice, or by calamity or conditions— come from families, or at least from a fragmented affiliation of relationships that served in the place of a family.

Churches are generally as healthy as the families who make them up. If experiencing the fullness of God's will for our lives is the goal, we cannot downplay the importance of obeying God's Word in the matter of marriage and family. A divorce is not a temporary bump in the road. It is the relational and emotional equivalent of having your arm ripped from your torso. It will have lasting effects that ripple through generations to come.

We can never collectively experience a fresh move of God's Spirit among us until we each make a recommitment to obeying God in our marriages and families. When we as marriage partners, parents, children, and siblings again allow God to govern and guide our lives according to the Scriptures, there will be no way to contain the revival of God's Spirit in our midst. Do you think that any group of people going by any name and using any means that could consistently demonstrate the ability to make families and marriages work would fail to have their doors barraged by people wanting to get in on the action?

> *I*F WE RECOMMIT TO OBEYING GOD IN OUR MARRIAGES AND FAMILIES, THERE WILL BE NO WAY TO CONTAIN THE REVIVAL OF GOD'S SPIRIT IN OUR MIDST.

The one who says he is fully committed to Christ and yet is not consistently obeying God in his family relationships is deceived. The only one oblivious to the deception is him. No one is fooled but the fool.

It is our specific, personal obedience that triggers the flow of the waters of His grace. It is obedience that lifts our sails to catch the wind of the Spirit and allows us to move in the stream of His blessing.

Perhaps you are desperately trying to honor Christ in your marriage and home but are finding no cooperation from your spouse, parents or children. Know that God sees and honors your obedience even if your relationships don't bear the full mark of His presence because of the sin of others.

Maybe you claim the Name of Christ, but you have not fully integrated Him into your family relationships. If you continue down that path, it will hinder you from ever enjoying the fullness of His presence and power in your life. Why should He sully His divine presence by manifesting it where He is not welcomed? Why should He expend His divine power on that which has been barred from His influence?

Specific, personal recommitment to obeying God in our marriages and families begins a fresh work of God's grace among His people. Where such obedience is withheld we languish, trying feverishly to hold life together with the glue and tape of gimmicks, gadgets and will power.

Business and Career

You will also find that true revival evidences itself in obedience to God's Word in your *business and career*. "When the neighboring peoples bring merchandise or grain to sell on the Sabbath, we will not buy from them on the Sabbath or on any holy day. Every seventh year we will forgo working the land and will cancel all debts" (v. 31).

Getting ahead in business is not easy, particularly if you are trying to honor God. All kinds of competing demands war upon you daily. Three of these demands are outlined here.

1. God's Word Versus Personal Expediency

There is the battle of *the authority of God's Word versus my personal expediency*. What tips the scale in the multitude of business and career-affecting decisions you face each day? What moves you to decide as you do when a great deal can be had for just a little compromise in ethics? In Nehemiah's day the non-Israelite "neighboring peoples" played a large role in the economic stability of the region. These were people who had come to live in the land of promise while the Jews were gone in exile. They were in Judah and Jerusalem when the Jews came back from Babylon to repopulate the land. They occupied homes, ran businesses, traded goods, made money. They had no allegiance to God, but they lived in God's land, which was now beginning to be filled again with God's people who were trying to live out God's ways. Can you feel the tensions rising? These non-Israelite merchants came to town daily, including the Sabbath, with their wagons full of goods to sell. This was Wal-Mart on wheels.

The Israelites recommitted to obey God. Eventually Saturday—the Jewish Sabbath—rolled around. It was to be a day dedicated to God, a day of rest and worship. But these pagan merchants didn't pledge any allegiance to God. "Perhaps the allegiance of the Jews could be bought," they thought. So they rolled into town with their wares. There they were—it was convenient. Because they were in the habit of compromising the Sabbath, a good many families probably were not prepared for the radical rest it called for. "I'm just going to get us a bite to eat," they could easily justify.

Do you see the issue? Who gets the final word? The Sabbath and how it applies to Christians today is too complex to adequately cover here. We need to see the larger issue: Is God's Word the operating authority in my business and commercial transactions? Or am I ruled by personal expediency?

2. God's Word Versus Business Technique

A second battle relates to *trust in God's Word versus trust in business technique*. In their renewed commitment to obey God the people promised, "Every seventh year we will forgo working the land."

The Law of Moses prescribed that every seventh year the land was to lay fallow; no crops were to be planted. It was to be a time of renewal for the land and a time of trust for the people. God promised to bring such a crop during the sixth year that enough would be had to last through the seventh. Obedience became a matter of trust. Could God be trusted to keep His word?

Think of the pressures such an arrangement brought. In the sixth year, as the harvest proved larger than normal, each family had to maintain a limit on their standard of living so that they would have enough to survive on throughout the seventh year. Obedience required self-discipline. It is a great deal harder to say "no" to that second helping when it's sitting in front of you than when it doesn't exist! If you weren't disciplined in the sixth year when you had plenty, in the seventh year you would feel compelled to plant a crop. Baby has to eat! Even if you *were* disciplined in the sixth year, you might easily say to yourself, "Think how much farther ahead I could be if I plant again in the seventh year!"

Today, fewer and fewer of us make a living by working the land, but you can easily apply this your work world. Trust and self-discipline are necessary regardless of your field of labor.

> *C*AN I TRUST AND OBEY GOD'S WORD, EVEN WHEN IT DOESN'T MAKE "GOOD BUSINESS SENSE"?

Again, I'm not talking about the specific Mosaic laws. I'm highlighting a tension we all live with. Will I trust what God's Word says and apply it to my specific business context? Can God be trusted to keep His word even when it does not make "good business sense"?

3. Community Good Versus Personal Advancement

A third battle line is drawn over *the community's good versus my personal advancement*. The people exuberantly promised, "Every seventh year we . . . will cancel all debts." The purpose of canceling all debt every seventh year was to prevent widespread poverty among God's people (Deut. 15:1–5). It was built on the principle that no man is truly rich who became so at his neighbor's expense. Personal business decisions will bear fruit among the whole community.

Can you imagine a businessman saying, "Every seventh year I forgive all debts that are still on the books"? Why? Because he's a nice guy? No, because he cares about God and about the whole of the community experiencing the life God wants them to have. This was an issue between the good of the community and the unscrupulous growth of one's personal bank account.

God cuts short any outpouring of His Spirit that is not allowed to reach the workplaces of His people. Specific, personal recommitment to obeying God in business and career ushers in a greater measure of God's work in His people. If we obey God only when it is socially convenient, however, we strangle the flow of God's grace, not just in ourselves, but in the whole of the community to which we belong.

Worship and Stewardship

The third area in which true revival evidences itself is in my obedience to God's Word in my *worship and stewardship*. Note the depth of the Jew's commitment:

> We assume the responsibility for carrying out the commands to give a third of a shekel each year for the service of the house of our God: for the bread set out on the table; for the regular grain offerings and burnt offerings; for the offerings on the Sabbaths, New Moon festivals and appointed feasts; for the holy offerings; for sin offerings to make atonement for Israel; and for all the duties of the house of our God.
>
> We—the priests, the Levites and the people—have cast lots to determine when each of our families is to bring to the house of our God at set times each year a contribution of wood to burn on the altar of the LORD our God, as it is written in the Law.
>
> We also assume responsibility for bringing to the house of the LORD each year the firstfruits of our crops and of every fruit tree.
>
> As it is also written in the Law, we will bring the firstborn of our sons and of our cattle, of our herds and of our flocks to the house of our God, to the priests ministering there.
>
> Moreover, we will bring to the storerooms of the house of our God, to the priests, the first of our ground meal, of our grain offerings, of the fruit of all our trees and of our new wine and oil. And we will bring a tithe of our crops to the Levites, for it is the Levites who collect the tithes in all the towns where we work. A priest descended from Aaron is to accompany the Levites when they receive the tithes, and the Levites

are to bring a tenth of the tithes up to the house of our God, to the storerooms of the treasury. The people of Israel, including the Levites, are to bring their contributions of grain, new wine and oil to the storerooms where the articles for the sanctuary are kept and where the ministering priests, the gatekeepers and the singers stay.

We will not neglect the house of our God. (vv. 32–39)

For the purpose of applying this truth to our lives, cut through the Old Covenant language and regulations and see this for what it is: a commitment to their place of worship and the people who serve and worship there. They made these commitments to ensure that the worship of the living God could continue and thrive in their midst. They were committed to personally making sure that the ministry of worship and those charged with leading it would not fail for lack of resources.

Four specific commitments to giving are outlined here. While they related to the old, Jewish order of worship, they instruct us in evaluating our own appropriate response to God's grace in the New Covenant.

1. They committed to paying the temple tax (vv. 32–33). Annually during the census those twenty years of age and above were to contribute toward the ongoing ministry of the house of God (see Exod. 30:11–16). This helped to make certain that the ministries of the temple could continue unencumbered.
2. They committed to the wood offering (v. 34). God had prescribed that a fire was to burn continually on the brazen altar (Lev. 6:12–13). That required a good deal of wood. So the people willingly gave to make certain the fire in their midst never died down.
3. They brought their firstfruit offerings (vv. 35–37a). God had made clear that His people were to return to Him the first and best portion of what He materially blessed them with (Exod. 23:19; 34:26; Prov. 3:9).

4. Finally, they recommitted to tithing (vv. 37b–39). The word *tithe* means "a tenth." The Israelites were to bring one-tenth of what they produced to God each year. This provided for the needs of the Levites who led worship at the temple (Lev. 27:30–34).

What does this mean for us who are a part of the Church, not the physical nation of Israel? This was about corporate worship and about their stewardship as an act of worship to God. This was a commitment to their place of worship and to the people who serve and worship there. They were committed to making certain that the worship of the living God could continue and thrive among them by their giving. They were committed to personally making certain that the ministry of worship and those who were charged with leading it were cared for. This was a commitment to practice *stewardship over all the material things that God had entrusted to them*.

Questions still abound: How much does God want *me* to give? Is tithing meant as a guide for believers today?

Sometimes the search for authoritative answers to such good questions can end up distracting us from the actual act of worship and obedience through giving. Let me ask one simple question that may help: How much did Jesus, who labored as a common carpenter, give? What were His giving practices? For a believer who wants to know the life of Jesus within, this is the real question. Note J. Oswald Sanders' excellent answer:

> Judaism was an expensive religion, and as a devout Jew who fulfilled the whole Law, our Lord was meticulous in fulfilling its financial obligations. What would He pay into the Temple treasury from what He earned as a carpenter?
>
> A Jew was first required to give one-tenth to God. Then at harvest time, the farmer must give the firstfruits to God, and that consisted of one-sixth of his increase. Then every three years a second tenth was given for the poor—social security tax. In addition were the special offerings of cleansing and consecration. That means that his total contributions to religion were nearer a fifth of his income than a tenth—and that

does not include voluntary support to the local synagogue. . . . So here we have our answer to how much of His income Jesus gave to God.

If we object that the Jews were under law and we Christians are under grace, and that for us the law of the tithe has been abrogated, another question arises. Will a Christian who is experiencing intimacy with his Lord wish to take advantage of grace so that he can give less to God's work than the less privileged Jew who knew nothing of Calvary's sacrifice and the inestimable blessings it has brought? . . . Jesus gave tithes and offerings. Is the servant greater than his Lord?[1]

Are you doing what Jesus would do if He were physically living in your place and entrusted with the resources that have been placed in your hands? If you are, God is already beginning to give you greater measures of the life of His Spirit. If you are not, no words you say about your walk with God can speak louder than your lack of obedience to God in your worship and stewardship. That may seem harsh, but true revival always evidences itself in obedience to God.

Are you absolutely, unreservedly, and without question committed to obey God whatever His Book may say about your life, circumstances and choices? Show me a person like that and I will show you a life experiencing personal revival—all resistance removed, all hindrances and obstacles knocked down, all objections laid aside. All that remains is joyful, yielded, consistent obedience offered up in the moment-by-moment fresh empowering of God's own Spirit living in and flowing through that life. That is revival. God will not fail to pour out His Spirit in floods of grace upon such a life.

Show me a church where people are willing to say, "Count me in. I'm committed to making sure that in *my marriage and family*, God will be honored. I'm committed in *my business and career* to honor God. And I'm going to honor God by giving to make sure *my local place of worship and its leadership* not only survive, but thrive." Show me a such a church and I will show you a church alive with the presence of God.

Let us close with the same question with which we began: *Are you committed?*

It depends on who's asking. This time it's God, and the topic is your marriage and family, your business and career, your worship and stewardship.

What's your answer?

Reaching Toward Revival

1. What is the ultimate proof of genuine revival?

   _____

   _____

2. How can leaders in a local church lead the way in a fresh commitment to obeying God?

   _____

   _____

3. What changes would take place in our family lives if true revival visited us?

   _____

   _____

4. Are changes in our marriages and family life a precursor to revival or the outcome of revival? What difference does our answer make?

   _____

   _____

5. Describe some of the challenges that come when you seek to bring your career and business under the authority of God's Word.

   _____

   _____

6. What would be different in your business or workplace next week if revival touched your life this weekend?

   _____

   _____

7. Describe the spending and giving practices of a person living in revival.

   _____

   _____

Part 4

The Perpetuation of Revival

They tell me a revival is only temporary;
so is a bath, but it does you good.
—Billy Sunday

A revival out of balance is soon a revival out of power.
—Richard Owen Roberts

What lasting results should be expected from a legitimate move of God? What strengths linger? What vulnerabilities remain? What is the lasting legacy of revival? Is there anything we can do to perpetuate the effects of a fresh move of God's Spirit? These are only a few of the questions we must wrestle with when we are sovereignly graced to be a part of revival.

13

To Obscurity — and Beyond!

B uzz Lightyear cracks me up. He is the self-important co-star of the animated children's movie *Toy Story*. Buzz is convinced that the prefix "co-" should never be added to the word "star." Buzz believes himself to be an intergalactic superhero with amazing powers, including flight. In actual fact he is no more than a collection of plastic, metal and rubber.

The bulk of the film is spent educating Buzz to the fact that he is just a toy. The laser on his arm is nothing but a little light bulb behind red plastic. It doesn't do anything in particular, but Buzz doesn't know that. Everyone else knows he is just a toy, but not Buzz. His philosophy of life and persona are wrapped up in a singular expression that he uses every time he thinks he's about to take flight. He thrusts his fist forward, and with great bravado and the deep resonance of a television pitchman, he declares, "To infinity—and beyond!"

Buzz is convinced that he is worthwhile only if he is extraordinary. He thinks his worth is found in how he compares to the others around him. Eventually, however, Buzz realizes he is just a toy. He is ordinary—and so he becomes depressed.

Nehemiah 11 contains the names of a lot of real heroes. There's no one named Buzz, but there are some named Joed, Uzzi, and Zabdi.

Who?

215

That's exactly the point. You don't know them. Their names are obscure and almost unpronounceable. They didn't do what they did for fame or recognition. They served in quiet ways that made an impact disproportionate to their earthly recognition. In fact, what they did changed the course of world history. Not one of them would have been named *Time* magazine's "Person of the Year." Their copy of *Time* probably even got delivered to the wrong address! These were ordinary folks who served an extraordinary Master and found delight in allowing the spotlight to fall on Him.

To borrow Buzz's phrase, but to infuse it with a different spirit, their motto might well have been "To obscurity—and beyond!"

Keep the flow of Nehemiah's book in mind. The first seven chapters describe the preparation for revival. Chapters eight through ten describe the experience of genuine revival. Now chapters eleven through thirteen describe the results that flow from revival. We find here how revival continues to evidence itself after its onset.

Sacrificers

One of the first results of a fresh move of God's Spirit is a resurgence of faithful, but often obscure, servants. *Revived believers willingly embrace obscurity to advance God's will.* Believers revived by God's Spirit gladly cry, "To obscurity and beyond—if it will further God's purposes and promote His praise!"

> ONE MAJOR SIGN OF REVIVAL: BELIEVERS WHO ARE SACRIFICERS—WHO WILLINGLY EMBRACE OBSCURITY TO ADVANCE GOD'S WILL.

What kind of people are they? They are people willing to be sacrificers. Sacrificers were needed because they had a problem.

A problem! How could they have a problem? They had completed their God-given task of rebuilding the wall around the city in miraculous time (Neh. 1–7) and they had experienced a supernatural moving of God's Spirit in their midst (Neh. 8–10). How could they have a problem?

Doing God's will and experiencing revival does not instantly remove all challenges. Their challenge has already been hinted at. "Now the city was large and spacious, but there were few people living in it, and the houses had not yet been rebuilt" (Neh. 7:4). They had a nice wall, but relatively few wanted to live within it. The city, you see, had been destroyed by the Babylonian armies long before. The rubble remained in ruins for decades. Jerusalem was desolate, wind-swept and vacuous, with comparatively few people living there. Without a wall to protect it, few wanted to reside there.

Now the wall was rebuilt, but not many were jumping to relocate from the homes they'd already established in outlying areas. If God's purposes were going to go forward that city needed to be repopulated. We should not be surprised, then, that as Nehemiah 11 opens a repopulation plan is afoot.

"Now the leaders of the people settled in Jerusalem" (v. 1a). That apparently means that the leaders were uprooting from wherever it was they had previously settled in Judah and were now relocating their homes and families to Jerusalem. ". . . and the rest of the people cast lots to bring one out of every ten to live in Jerusalem, the holy city, while the remaining nine were to stay in their own towns" (v. 1b). About ten percent of the remaining populace was drafted to similarly relocate their families, businesses, and interests to the capital city. But not even that was sufficient to get the city off the ground again. "The people commended all the men who *volunteered* to live in Jerusalem" (v. 2). Still others chose of their own accord to do as their leaders and draftees were doing.

Whether they be leaders, draftees or volunteers they were all making huge sacrifices. There was only one reason for those sacrifices—the advancement of God's purposes. They were called to be a holy nation through which the Messiah would come to the world. To be a nation they needed a capital. For that city to be a capital it needed residents. They viewed history as headed somewhere. They saw God as sovereign and doing something significant in their day. They wanted their lives to count for something bigger than themselves. They concluded, "If this is going to happen, then I've got to move into the city."

Think of the sacrifice that such a move likely entailed. Many of these people had likely returned under either Zerubbabel or Ezra, more than a decade earlier. They had built or rebuilt homes, established businesses or planted fields, made friends, cultivated neighborhoods. Now they were going to uproot, leave all of that behind and start over. They were not unlike twenty-first century families—if possible they wanted to live out away from the hustle and bustle and raise their children where they had some space.

They were designated as "able men" (v. 6). One translation (NEB) calls them "men of substance." These were courageous folk who led their families and lived their lives with conviction and purpose. They all, leaders and people alike, made sacrifices. They did so for one great purpose—to advance God's will—but they did so from a variety of motives. Some, as leaders, sacrificed out of duty and responsibility (v. 1a). Others sacrificed out of a right understanding of authority and submission (v. 1b). Still others did so out of raw enthusiasm and desire (v. 2).

Let's try to give this a contemporary spin. Imagine that this Sunday when you go to your local church something unusual takes place. First the pastor stands up and announces that after much prayer it has been decided that your church is called of God to begin a new congregation in a community thirty miles away. He also announces that seventy-five percent of the leaders in the church will be selling their homes and moving to the designated town to take the lead in this outreach. He calls them to come stand with him in a symbol of commitment. Then the leading lay-man of your church joins the pastor up front and says, "In this hat we've placed slips of paper that each have the name of one of our church households written on them. We are going to randomly se-lect names, reading them off, until we have named ten percent of the remaining members." Then he adds, "Please come forward and join the leaders when your name is called." And that's not all —once these folks have gone forward the leaders issue an altar call, asking all the remaining members to consider if God is also calling them to sell their homes, quit their jobs, uproot their families, put their kids in new schools, and start all over in new neighborhoods. "Come forward as a sign of your commitment if God is calling you!"

Would you go?

Leaders

Revived people are sacrificers. That's not all they are, however. Revived people are also willing to be leaders. Nehemiah certainly took the lead in encouraging people to embrace God's purposes and relocate to Jerusalem, but he was not alone. The leaders of the people led the way in this disruptive but necessary change of location (v. 1). There were priests (vv. 10–14) who took the lead in worship. Among them was "Seraiah . . . supervisor in the house of God" (v. 11). And there were Levites who took the lead in caring for the temple and the details necessary for the priests to lead in worship there (vv. 15–18). Among them "Ziha and Gispha were in charge of" the temple servants (v. 21). Uzzi was the "chief officer of the Levites in Jerusalem as well" (v. 22).

A skeptic may ask, "They took the lead. Isn't that a sign that they didn't want to embrace the obscurity of service—that they wanted to be in the spotlight as leaders?"

Perhaps, but the stage they chose was pretty small, and the spotlight pretty dim. Whenever a person steps into leadership he is sacrificing something else in order to lead God's people. What could these folks have done with the time they were investing in God's ministry? What if they put the energy expended on God's purposes into

> *A* PERSON WHO STEPS INTO LEADERSHIP MAKES A SACRIFICE IN ORDER TO LEAD *GOD'S PEOPLE.*

something else? When you see people willingly taking the lead in ministry, recognize that they are probably forgoing some other area of high recognition in order to see God's purposes advanced. They are embracing obscurity for the glory of God!

Followers

Revived people are not only leaders but also followers. Obviously not everyone can be a leader. When everyone is a leader it's called anarchy! "In those days Israel had no king; everyone did as he saw fit" (Judges 17:6; 21:25).

No, there must be those who willingly accept their place in the crowd, their role among the masses, and serve as one of the labor force. As the Spirit of God stirred up the hearts of people in Nehemiah's day to embrace God's purposes again there were many who followed His will and His leadership gladly. "The people commended all the men who volunteered" (v. 2). There were many willing to be known simply as "the rest of the Israelites" (v. 20). Their names were not in marquee lights, but, if it helped get God's work done, they willingly served. Note the humility of two men in particular. "Judah the son of Hassenuah was second in command of the city" (v. 9, NASB) and a man named Bakbukiah was "second among his associates" (v. 17).

It's hard to be happy being second. Someone once asked Arthur Fiedler, legendary conductor of the Boston Pops, what the most difficult instrument in the orchestra is to play. His reply: "Second fiddle." If you find a person willingly embracing obscurity to get God's work done, you'll find a person controlled by the Holy Spirit. George Duncan has said it right:

Think for a moment how often we come across those whose worth is seldom recognized by men, but I am sure will never be overlooked by God, and will certainly not go unrewarded. Many are prepared to recognize the prominent part played by Simon Peter among the disciples, but forget that if there had not been an Andrew who "brought him to Jesus" there would never have been a Peter! The church universal gives thanks to God for Paul, the greatest Christian who ever lived, but forget that if there had not been a Barnabas there might never have been a Paul![1]

As Duncan goes on to point out, not many recognize the name Albert McMakin. Yet it was McMakin who invited a sixteen-year-old boy named Billy Graham to an evangelistic service where he placed his faith in Christ. "So before there could be a Billy there had to be an Albert!"[2]

Defenders

Where God revives His people with a fresh outpouring of His Spirit, there will also be defenders. Among the obscure and unfamiliar names making up much of this eleventh chapter of Nehemiah are many whose ministry as defenders of the Lord's cause were essential. Some are designated as "valiant warriors" (v. 14, NASB). The term is one used to describe military personnel —in this case, those trained to defend the temple area. The phrase lays emphasis on their physical prowess and fighting skill. There were also 172 "gatekeepers" (v. 19). They too served as security guards at the temple gates. They made certain that the physical place where God dwelt in that day was kept pure and holy, befitting the worship of God.

Certainly our application would be different today. God dwelt in their midst in a physical temple where the outward manifestation of their worship was made through animal sacrifices, burning incense, and grain offerings. God now dwells in His people—they are His temple individually (1 Cor. 6:19) and collectively (1 Cor. 3:16).

While the application is different it does us well to ask, "Who protects us? Who guards God's people today? Who guards God's presence in our midst?" If your church enjoys a relative harmony in loving, sharing, giving and reciprocal fellowship, how do you think that happened? Have you assumed that no threats have come? Perhaps you can think of a time or two when the unity of the body was threatened, but would you

221

believe there were probably many more times than you ever imagined? While you were busy living your life, loving your family, working your job, showing up for your fellowship groups, Sunday school classes and Bible studies, and coming together for times of worship, there has been a group of leaders protecting the flock.

These individuals have taken time out of their lives to resolve conflict, confront error, deal with rebellion and address anything else that would serve to quietly and faithfully protect you and those in your church family. It's probable that you don't know about most of that. And that's okay, as long as you don't take for granted that someone is doing it so that you'll never have to know.

Trustees

Revived people are also willing to serve as trustees. Nehemiah lists those "who had charge of the outside work of the house of God" (v. 16). The temple had been rebuilt. Now it needed to be cared for. There was gold to be polished, floors to be cleaned, an exterior to be repaired, supplies to be brought in.

Any local assembly of believers today needs those willing to care for the physical facilities the Lord has entrusted to them for furthering His purposes. It takes nothing less than the Spirit of God to enable a person to gladly embrace the obscurity of such a ministry for God's glory.

How about your church? Chances are the grass is mowed in the summer, and in the winter the parking lot is plowed and the sidewalks shoveled. Enter the restrooms. Someone has scrubbed the toilets, washed the mirrors, and restocked the paper products. Light bulbs have been replaced, windows cleaned, carpets vacuumed, walls painted, flowerbeds weeded, shrubs trimmed. Someone has been active while you've been consumed with the rest of life. When God revives His people He raises up those who are willing to be servants.

Pray-ers

When God revives His people He also brings forward those who are willing to be pray-ers. Nehemiah made certain to mention "Mattaniah . . . the director who led in thanksgiving and prayer" (v. 17). Here was a man who led God's people, not simply in prayer but by prayer. He made certain that the people not only prayed about everything but did everything *by prayer*. God's people need those who are ever provoking them toward God in prayer. We need those raised up among us to remind us just how dependent we are on God and just how blessed we are by Him. God has sent them among us to move us to united prayer.

> *I*N THE OBSCURITY OF THE PRAYER CLOSET WE FIND A *"HIDDEN"* FORM OF LEADERSHIP. *Y*OU WON'T BECOME FAMOUS AS A PRAYER WARRIOR.

You don't become famous as a prayer warrior. You spend much of your time in the obscurity of your prayer closet (Matt. 6:6). As a leader in prayer, your leadership is only seen by those who participate in the prayer ministries of your church—and even then their eyes are closed most of the time!

In His book *Serving God*, Ben Patterson tells of visiting a church in the Minneapolis area where he observed a simple cardboard box with a picture on it. The sign next to the box read: "Tim Lindloom's Prayer Ministry." The picture showed a young man in a wheelchair and wearing a helmet. It appeared he suffered from cerebral palsy. The box had a small slit in the top that allowed people to insert personal prayer requests. There was only one other thing. The sign said, "I only ask that you let me know what happens." Patterson writes,

> What work could this young man possibly do with his limitations? He could patiently endure, and he could pray—especially pray. The only hints he might have that he was getting something done was to hear what had happened from those for whom he prayed—a special fellowship, and a special reward.[3]

Organizers

Among those who experience the fresh work of God's grace in revival there are also people willing to be organizers. The Jews now had a rebuilt temple. They were taking up again the worship of God as prescribed through Moses. Priests were responsible to serve at the temple on a rotating basis for six months at a time. By New Testament times it was possible that as a priest your rotation might come around only once in a lifetime. Someone had to make certain that these servants were trained and could undertake their ministry in holiness and with efficiency. Someone had to make certain that the right priests were contacted at the right time, that they showed up on time, were in their places, and were properly prepared in spirit as well as mind and body. Who did that? Two men named Ziha and Gishpa (v. 21).

Do you think the ushers at your church simply pop up like mushrooms, out of nowhere? How do you think they learned to "ush"? Who got that army of Sunday school teachers and helpers in place, on time, and prepared? How do the mailings and phone calls and memos get to the right people at the right time? Where do those servants in the nursery come from?

Someone is willingly serving the Lord by doing so—and often without reward or recognition. It's only the Spirit of God that can move a person to undertake such a ministry and sustain them in their service with joy!

Worship Leaders

When people are revived by God there are also those who are willing to be worship leaders. Wade through the strange-sounding names and find what they did for the glory of God: "The chief officer of the Levites in Jerusalem was Uzzi son of Bani, the son of Hashabiah, the son of Mattaniah, the son of Mica. Uzzi was one of Asaph's descendants, who were the singers responsible for the service of the house of God" (v. 22).

Uzzi was "one of Asaph's descendants." Asaph was the one appointed by David to lead the singers in the praise of God (1

Chron. 16:7; 25:1). In fact, twelve of the psalms in our Bible bear this clan's signature. They were worship leaders.

In any age there must be leaders in worship. They believe it is their calling to so mold their hearts as worshipers before God that they are then able to stand before people and move their hearts toward God as well. They aren't just leaders; they're worshipers. They have learned to worship in private so that they can stand before the people and say, "Come with me and look at the beauty of our God." That's a special ministry that the Spirit gives to them.

I'm guessing that not many reading these lines have any idea of the number of hours and the amount of energy that goes into preparing the worship services at their local churches. At our church numerous people give many hours every week for the express purpose of preparing a worship experience that allows the rest of us to freely focus our hearts on God and freely express our love and adoration to Him in song. Next time you feel bad about how early you have to get up to go to worship, consider what time the musicians and worship leaders had to get up in order to beat you there, practice, and make final preparations for your worship experience that day.

Facilitators

Finally, notice that when God revives His people some are going to be willing to be facilitators. "Pethahiah . . . was the king's agent in all affairs relating to the people" (v. 24). What is that all about?

The kings of Persia gave great liberties to their captive peoples when it came to their religion. They wanted all the prayers they could get, so they encouraged the people to worship whatever god they wished. But they did not give them total freedom in these matters. Apparently the king of Persia wanted to keep tabs on what was happening in Jerusalem so he selected Pethahiah and told him to keep him posted. It was his job to make certain communication lines between Susa and Jerusalem remained open. Pethahiah facilitated things by making sure communication with authorities was clear, accurate and kept God's work going forward.

Any church in America has a good deal of paperwork that is required by the government. Someone needs to work with state and local authorities for buildings to be built and ministries to be conducted. Reading, understanding and responding wisely to official letters, forms and requests requires deciphering some difficult language and bringing clarity to some tough issues. Who does that? Someone who gladly serves to the glory of God by the Spirit of God so that the people of God can carry out the ministry of God.

There are others who facilitate making sure the gears of the organizational machinery within a local church continue to run smoothly. Someone makes certain the schedule is clear and free of conflicting events. Someone schedules the use of the facilities. Someone prepares for each event and cleans up after it's over, so the next ministry group can use the space. Someone makes certain the men's ministry doesn't schedule an event to take all the men away on the same day the women plan an outing. All that and much more takes place because someone has met the Lord in a fresh way and is glad to express his worship to Him through being a facilitator of God's work.

Perhaps it seems silly to ask this question so far into a book on revival, but I'm still going to ask: *What does revival look like?* There might be a variety of signs that God is visiting His people with a fresh outpouring of His Spirit. There is one sure evidence, however. *Revived people willingly embrace obscurity to advance God's will.*

It is a reminder that a church with few servants has little of the Holy Spirit's presence and work. It reminds each of us personally that if we're not serving somewhere and somehow, then we're not revived. If you are, on the other hand, joyfully embracing some obscure place of ministry in order to advance God's purposes, He delights in you. Your investment in that which will last forever brings a greater measure of His Spirit invested in you.

Reaching Toward Revival

1. Describe the dynamic relationship between revival and sacrifice.

   _____

   _____

2. How would revival affect the annual business meeting of a local church?

   _____

   _____

3. How might the care of a church's building be an indicator of revival or its absence among its people?

   _____

   _____

4. What happens to a church's prayer life when they are touched by revival?

   _____

   _____

5. Why are people gifted in organization essential to long-term revival?

   _____

   _____

6. How would revival affect the corporate worship of God's people?

   _____

   _____

7. In what way is God asking you to embrace obscurity in order to advance His purposes?

   _____

   _____

14

Joy in the Lord

We have so much. How can we have so little joy? We have entertainment options galore, but we have little joy. We have amusements of every stripe and variety, but little joy. We have options and opportunities that previous generations could not even dream of, but we have little joy.

We are the richest society in the world—indeed, in history! Yet we are poverty stricken when it comes to joy. Technological advancements are exploding at an exponential rate, but the joy in our hearts recedes year by year. We have a flood of comforts, but a drought of joy.

How can this be? *How can this be!?*

The church in North America appears to be little better off in this regard than her non-Christian neighbors. We have doctrine, denominations, style, pizzaz, old songs, new songs, instruments, programs, seminars, media, personality, marketing technique, organization, PowerPoint, the Internet . . . and then some! The one thing we have too little of is joy.

What, may we ask, is joy? What is it exactly?

That's hard to say for certain. It helps to clarify what joy is not. Joy is not what you feel, it's what you know. Joy is not what happens to you, it's how you see what happens to you. Joy is not what you do, it's who you are. Joy is not what you think, but what you're convinced of. Joy is not something that is worked up; it is something that bubbles up. Joy is not determined by your circumstances, but by your convictions. Joy is not a thing to be obtained, but a flow of life to be entered into.

Where do I get ahold of joy? How can I experience it?

Nehemiah 12 gives us some guidance in this. As the book draws to a close we discover the results of true revival. One result is multiplication of servants of God (Neh. 11). Here we find a second result—renewed joy in the Lord. Joy is the theme of Nehemiah 12; it is found six times at the heart of the chapter (v. 27, "joyfully"; vv. 43–44, "rejoicing . . . joy . . . rejoiced . . . rejoicing . . . pleased" [same Hebrew root word]).

When the wall had been completed (Neh. 1–7) and the revival began (Neh. 8–10), Nehemiah reminded the people not to be overcome with grief "for the joy of the LORD is your strength" (8:10). Chew on that a moment—"the joy of the LORD is your strength." If our strength in life is tied directly to the level of our joy in the Lord, it's little wonder many of us feel as we do! Is it any shock that we struggle as we do?

Our trouble is that we approach the matter backward. We want strength without the necessity of first pursuing joy. We seldom obtain power that way. We posture, position, maneuver, wrestle, fight and exhaust ourselves—often in vain. Yet when we begin with reestablishing our hearts before God in joy, we find the power we need.

This chapter contains a description of the dedication of the newly rebuilt wall around Jerusalem. That wall and their completion of it provided the physical, outward occasion for the release of their newly reborn joy in the Lord. Amid all the festivities let's not lose sight of things, however. The Jews had fresh joy not because they rebuilt the wall, but because they met God in a fresh way. The completion of the project could provide satisfaction, but only God could provide joy.

Human accomplishment, even remarkable human accomplishment, cannot ultimately deliver joy to the human heart. There may be a fleeting sensation that feels like joy, but it is a cheap substitute for the real thing and may even become an idol set up in place of the Lord, who enabled us to complete the project. The Jews found joy through the outpouring of God's Spirit, the One who used the building of the wall to prepare them for revival.

It reminds us that ultimately joy grows out of being right with God. It comes not by self-improvement but divine grace. It bubbles up within, not because of what we've achieved but because God has come upon us anew.

> *J*OY GROWS OUT OF BEING RIGHT WITH GOD. IT COMES NOT BY SELF-IMPROVEMENT BUT DIVINE GRACE.

Nehemiah prepared the people for the dedication of the wall by calling together all the Levites scattered around the region. They "were brought to Jerusalem to celebrate *joyfully* the dedication" of the wall (v. 27). Singers were also assembled (vv. 28–29). As they prepared to carry out the ceremony of dedication, what was the first thing they did to make sure it was "joyfully" celebrated? "When the priests and Levites had *purified* themselves ceremonially, they *purified* the people, the gates and the wall" (v. 30).

There is no joy without purity. Joy comes before purity not only in the dictionary but also in the flow of life. You may experience pleasure without purity, but never joy.

Question: Is God more interested in your holiness or your happiness? I used to think that God had more interest in my holiness than my happiness. I've changed my mind. Now I know He cares intimately about both.[1] But which, may I ask, comes first? Happiness flows from holiness! I can only experience true joy as I live in a right relationship to God through Christ. As you draw near to God in faith that Jesus is the Lamb of God who takes away the sin of the world, as you place the weight of your hope upon His unique and only sacrifice on the cross and His resurrection from the dead, joy is conceived in the womb of your soul.

Notice that Nehemiah called them together to be "purified . . . *ceremonially*" (v. 30). The Mosaic regulations detailed the specifics of just what would make one clean or unclean in God's presence under the old covenant. One's uncleanness was dealt with through various sacrifices and rituals also prescribed by God through Moses. All these were a mere foreshadowing of Christ's ultimate and perfect sacrifice to end all sacrifices (Heb. 9:26; 10:1–12). But in any age the first step toward a new life of joy is found in an open, unhindered relationship with God. The obstacles to the flow of God's joy in the lives of the priests, Levites, and people needed to be removed. Are there such obstructions within you?

We live on this side of the cross. We reside, gratefully, under the new covenant, not the old. The old covenant served to reveal the sin that keeps us from enjoying the kind of intimacy with God that He desires and we need. The Law prescribed rituals, ceremonies, and sacrifices that were to be carried out in faith that the obstructing sin would be covered before God. No Old Testament sacrifice completely removed sin (Heb. 10:4). They only covered it, waiting for the one sacrifice that would completely remove our sin from before God.

> [Christ] has entered that great, perfect sanctuary in heaven, not made by human hands and not part of this created world. Once for all time he took blood into that Most Holy Place, but not the blood of goats and calves. He took his own blood, and with it he secured our salvation forever.
>
> Under the old system, the blood of goats and bulls and the ashes of a young cow could cleanse people's bodies from ritual defilement. Just think how much more the blood of Christ will purify our hearts from deeds that lead to death so that we can worship the living God. (Heb. 9:11–14, NLT)

Nehemiah and his contemporaries knew nothing of Christ personally. His death and resurrection were still obscured from their sight before the sun of revelation would burn off the fog of divine mystery. The wonder that God would become flesh and bear their sin-debt away was not yet completely clear to them. Yet they found unspeakable joy even in the shadow of these Old Testament provisions.

How could the unenlightened Jew of Nehemiah's time have more joy than many Christians today, who bask in the full sunshine of the redemptive work of Christ? Is it possible that those who did not know the indwelling of the resurrected Christ in their hearts could actually have a higher level of joy than many of us who live on this side of the cross?

What has happened to us? Peter speaks of the one who "is nearsighted and blind, and has forgotten that he has been cleansed from his past sins" (2 Pet. 1:9). Joy and Calvary are never far apart. A look at the one requires bringing the other into our field of view as well. Is this part of the answer to our lack of joy? It was for good reason that Jesus taught, "He who has been forgiven little loves little" (Luke 7:47).

Joy also grows out of remembering what God has done in the past and connecting it with what He is doing in the present. The first twenty-six verses of Nehemiah 12 comprise another list of the nearly unpronounceable names common to this book. It's natural to ask, What is this? Why is it here?

The names you find here are of "the priests and Levites who returned with Zerubbabel" (v. 1).

Yawn! In today's remote-control world, the average reader flips to Psalm 23 or John 3:16 to feast on truth that seems more relevant.

But don't rush off too quickly or you'll miss dessert. Remember who Zerubbabel was? There had been three groups of exiles who returned to Jerusalem and Judah. The first came under the leadership of Zerubbabel, while later others came back with Ezra and then, of course, with Nehemiah. Nehemiah 12:1–26 lists the official twenty-four divisions of Israel's priests as they came up with Zerubbabel about a century prior to the dedication of the wall.

Again the objection, *Who cares? So what?!*

If nothing else, these verses remind us that true joy is not found merely in something new, novel or different. One day in our lives provides us with more new stuff, novel experiences, and fresh knowledge than our grandparents experienced in a decade. But honestly ask yourself, are you more joyful than they were?

As Christians, we cannot escape the fact that our identity is bound up with what happened in time and space in the past. God became a man. He lived here. He died. He rose from the dead. It is historical, verifiable, objective, and can be dated in the annals of history. Our entire existence, now and forever, is bound up in what happened at that hinge of history in the Person of Jesus Christ.

It means, however, even more than that. We are the product of centuries and generations of believers who have gone before us. Paul and Peter and John have all affected our lives. So have people like Hus, Luther, Calvin, Knox, Whitefield, Wesley and Edwards. If you think that we can just be who we are today and the actions of the dusty relics of history do not matter, you are wrong. The past has implications for everything from our music to how we do missions!

However, we need to focus not only on what God has done in the past but also what He has done around us in the present. Beginning in verse 27, Nehemiah and his contemporaries begin their elaborate dedication ceremony for the wall.

Don't miss the significance of these events. What may appear to us as a dry history lesson was proof to them that all this God-talk was not merely rhetoric. They realized that the God of the past was now acting in the present. This was nothing short of a miracle! Despite the death threats, drought, famine, internal strife, external pressure, and staggering odds stacked against them, they had by God's grace rebuilt the wall around Jerusalem! The God they had heard about in the stories told by their grandparents around the fire was now active in their midst. The God they'd read about in the Scriptures was more than a legend, myth or epic —He was present in their midst. There was simply no other way to explain what had taken place. The result? Joy—an overflowing, ever-springing, bubbling flow of joy from deep within!

If our Christianity is nothing more than a history lesson, it won't produce much joy. But if somehow we find the God of the past at work in our present, everything changes. But joy also springs from what God has done in me personally. We read that they were "rejoicing because *God had given* them great joy" (v. 43). This was not worked up. It wasn't whipped up by crowd control and emotional manipulation. It was *given* to them. There was no prescription to take. No buttons to push. No techniques to master. No mantra to ape. Joy is received, not produced. What they now experienced flowing up from the depths of their hearts was a dynamic move of the eternal, sovereign God—not only in their midst but in each of their lives. As they responded obediently to His grace, God opened the floodgates and sent a fresh surge of cleansing, holy, ecstatic joy cascading through their lives.

*T*HE GOD OF THE PAST IS AT WORK IN THE PRESENT—AND HE IS AT WORK IN US. WHEN WE DISCOVER THAT, JOY FLOWS.

Joy is given when we discover that the God of the past is at work in the present and that He is at work in us. Stand back. Grab a towel. When we discover that, joy flows.

We also discover that joy grows out of renewal, not rescue. Joy comes not because my circumstances have changed but because I have. We'll verify this from the text, but first let's set the stage so we can see it for what it is. Watch the Polaroid image of the event slowly come into full, crisp color.

"I had the leaders of Judah go up on top of the wall. I also assigned two large choirs to give thanks. One was to proceed on top of the wall to the right, toward the Dung Gate" (v. 31). Get the picture? Nehemiah, all the community leaders and massive choirs begin a procession along the top of the wall they'd rebuilt around Jerusalem. Remember, excavations have shown that the wall was some eight feet thick. This is the same wall that Tobiah had said a fox would cause to crumble if it tripped along the top (Neh. 4:3). Do you suppose they scanned the thronging crowds for Tobiah's face now?

Nehemiah probably provides his description from a vantage point on the west, facing east. So as the one group of leaders and choir members proceed to the right (v. 31), they were probably marching along the south side of the city. Behind the choir "Hoshaiah and half the leaders of Judah followed them, along with Azariah, Ezra, Meshullam . . ." and a host of others (vv. 32*ff.*). Among them were "some priests with trumpets" and even more folks following behind them (vv. 35–36). Some of those played other "musical instruments" (v. 36). At the head of the entire procession circling to the south was Ezra, the man through whom the Word of God was restored to the people (v. 36).

So, headed south and working their way east you have Ezra in the lead, a great choir singing praises and giving thanksgiving to God, priests marching in holy array, people playing on all manner of instruments, and the whole bunch of them lifting joyful noise to God!

This is only half the story, however.

> The second choir proceeded in the opposite direction. I [Nehemiah] followed them on top of the wall, together with half the people—past the Tower of the Ovens to the Broad Wall, over the Gate of Ephraim, the Jeshanah Gate, the Fish Gate, the Tower of Hananel and the Tower of the Hundred, as far as the Sheep Gate. At the Gate of the Guard they stopped. (vv. 38–39)

Take a deep breath. Take in the drama of the scene. This mass of people have in drill-team precision marched around the perimeter of the city on top of the wall, celebrating, singing thanksgiving with trumpets blasting and harps and lyres and instruments accompanying. The city and surrounding populace have turned out and are taking it all in. This is a grand celebration! But it's not the end. "The two choirs that gave thanks then took their places in the house of God; so did I [Nehemiah], together with half the officials" (v. 40).

When they had circumnavigated the city, each and every one of them "took their stand in the house of God" (NASB). When the two groups marching in opposite directions met at the eastern edge of the city, they climbed down the stairs, marched into the temple, planted their feet and declared their allegiance to God.

Nehemiah, the officials, the priests (by name), the choirs— all of them—"offered great sacrifices, rejoicing because God

had given them great joy. The women and children also rejoiced. The sound of rejoicing in Jerusalem could be heard far
away" (v. 43).

Great scene! But what does that have to do with my asser-
tion that joy grows out of renewal, not rescue?

We've noted that there were two "large choirs" marching in
opposite directions along the wall and meeting up at the east
side of town and marching together into the temple (vv. 31, 38,
40). Instead of "two choirs" as the English translation has ren-
dered it, the Hebrew text literally calls them "two thanksgiv-
ings." That is an odd way to describe a choir, isn't it? They were
two mass groups of people appointed to offer thanks to God.

Think of it! What they were called upon to do became so
much a part of who they were that the best way to describe them
is by their ministry. They not only offered thanksgiving, they together became the essence of thanksgiving! Derek Kidner says
that it is "almost as though these choirs were the embodiment of
what they sang."[2]

They were appointed to give thanks to God, but it became
more than a song, a duty, a ritual; it became *them*. *They* became
the thanksgiving! They could be and do nothing else if indeed
this God had done in their lives all the things Nehemiah records.
This was not simply two groups of skilled musicians singing
about thanksgiving to God, but a group of people so amazed at
the goodness of God that they were knit together as one in a living expression of gratitude. *They* became secondary, *He* became
primary. Their sole existence became giving thanks to this God
who had acted on their behalf.

What do you call that? Let's call it revival.

How does someone arrive at that kind of gratitude to God?
By being rescued out of bad circumstances? That wouldn't hurt,
but it's not the primary way gratitude grows within us.

Consider Nehemiah and his people. Their circumstances were
less than ideal. They experienced exile (1:3), desolation (1:3),
poverty (5:1–19), famine (5:3), prejudice (4:2), mockery (4:1–5),
threats of violence (4:6–23; 6:1–4), economic oppression (5:4*ff.*),

political blackmail (6:5–9), and religious manipulation (6:10–14). Now the wall was built, but little else had changed. They may have been suffering drought and crop failure, or at least the lingering effects of it. Their enemies still surrounded them and remained a serious threat. Most of the people still lived in poverty, their homes half-demolished and yet to be rebuilt. Many families were in the throes of being uprooted from their homes and relocating to Jerusalem.

Almost nothing had changed *around* them, but almost everything had changed *within* them. Almost none of their circumstances had changed, but their view of those circumstances was radically altered. *They* were different, not their circumstances.

How did this internal change take place? God had worked in their midst by His Spirit. He had begun a revival within them. They had sought God, preparing their hearts and lives through brokenness, repentance, and prayer. And God had extended Himself to them.

> *REVIVAL CHANGES US, NOT OUR CIRCUMSTANCES. JOY IS NOT FOUND IN A NEW SITUATION BUT IN A NEW SELF.*

Joy is not found in a new situation but in a new self. We cannot expect to find joy waiting for us on the other side of a new job, a new home, a new car or a new location. Joy comes because we are changed by the renewing work of God's Spirit in revival, not because of a new set of circumstances.

Joy grows out of being right with God, having eyes to see the renewing work of His Holy Spirit in our lives. Joy grows *out of* these things, but it grows *into* several important things as well. What is the purpose of joy? What is its goal? For one thing, joy grows into a sacrifice of worship.

Look again at that key verse: "And on that day *they offered great sacrifices*, rejoicing because God had given them great joy" (v. 43).

What's wrong with that sentence? It sounds strange to our twenty-first century, American Christian ears. The problem is that the words sacrifice and joy are mentioned in the same sentence. To most people in our culture, the mention of sacrifice and joy in the same breath makes no sense at all. We believe that joy is found not in giving but in getting. Joy, we think, is about accumulating, not sacrificing.

We are wrong. Could this be the reason we know so little of joy? When joy is released into a person's life, one of the first places it shows up is in the sacrifice of their worship. For Nehemiah and his contemporaries, this included the animal sacrifices and other details found in Leviticus.

As we know from the New Testament, Jesus is the one sacrifice to end all sacrifices. When He offered Himself as our sin-bearer He provided the one sacrifice for sin. His sacrifice can never be supplemented or improved and it need never be repeated. It need only be trusted.

That does not mean, however, that there is no place for sacrifice in our worship. The New Testament calls for several key sacrifices from those who enjoy the grace of God through Christ:

> You also, like living stones, are being built into a spiritual house to be a holy priesthood, offering spiritual sacrifices acceptable to God through Jesus Christ. (1 Pet. 2:5)

> If I am being poured out like a drink offering on the sacrifice and service coming from your faith, I am glad and rejoice with all of you. (Phil 2:17)

> Through Jesus, therefore, let us continually offer to God a sacrifice of praise—the fruit of lips that confess his name. And do not forget to do good and to share with others, for with such sacrifices God is pleased. (Heb. 13:15–16)

> Therefore, I urge you, brothers, in view of God's mercy, to offer your bodies as living sacrifices, holy and pleasing to God—this is your spiritual act of worship. (Rom. 12:1)

Notice the basic principle—if it doesn't cost you something, it's not worship. If it doesn't hurt, there is no joy behind it.

What does it cost you to live for Christ? I challenge you to begin evaluating your worship by that question. A natural outburst of uncontainable joy is released by doing or giving that which under any other circumstances would be painful to do or to give. J. Oswald Sanders was correct: "Sacrifice is the ecstasy of giving the best we have to the One whom we love the most."[3] Listen to the testimony of David Livingstone who gave his life opening the continent of Africa to the gospel:

> For my own part, I have never ceased to rejoice that God has appointed me to such an office. People talk of the sacrifice I have made in spending so much of my life in Africa. Can that be called a sacrifice which is simply paid back as a small part of a great debt owing to our God, which we can never repay? Is that a sacrifice which brings its own blest reward in healthful activity, the consciousness of doing good, peace of mind, and a bright hope of a glorious destiny hereafter? Away with the word in such a view, and with such a thought! It is emphatically no sacrifice. Say rather it is a privilege. Anxiety, sickness, suffering, or danger, now and then, with a foregoing of the common conveniences and charities of this life, may make us pause, and cause the spirit to waver, and the soul to sink; but let this only be for a moment. All these are nothing when compared with the glory which shall be revealed in and for us. *I never made a sacrifice.*[4]

Joy begins when there is a fresh inward movement of the Holy Spirit into our hearts. Joy then grows upward in a movement of sacrificial worship. It also grows into an outward movement of significant witness. Note that key verse again: "And on that day they offered great sacrifices, rejoicing because God had given them great joy. The women and children also rejoiced. *The sound of rejoicing in Jerusalem could be heard far away*" (v. 43).

What does it say was heard far away?

Look again.

Was it the music heard from a distance? The shouts of triumph? Amens? Hallelujahs? No. What was heard far away was the "sound of rejoicing"—or more literally, "the joy."

We've heard music, but have we ever heard the sound of joy? We have heard testimonies, prayers and sermons, but what does joy sound like? We've heard "Amen," but joy? What does joy sound like . . . exactly? I'm not sure. But when you hear it, I think you'll recognize it.

I've got a feeling that if we experienced true joy in our relationship with God, the world would rush the doors of our churches and we couldn't lock them out. H. L. Mencken once described a Puritan as "a person with a haunting fear that someone, somewhere is happy."[5] Mencken was wrong, of course, but a great many people look at Christians today as just that kind of people. Allow yourself to ponder this: What would happen if we let God give us true joy?

Let me say it again. Joy is not what you feel, it's what you know. Joy is not what happens to you, it's how you see what happens to you. Joy is not what you do, it's who you are. Joy is not what you think, but what you're convinced of. Joy is not something that is worked up; it is something that bubbles up. Joy is not determined by your circumstances, but by your convictions. Joy is not a thing to be obtained, but a flow of life to be entered into.

When you've got the genuine article, the circumstances of your life won't be able to drown it out and your feelings won't be able to block it. Joy is your soul's shout of exhilaration within you as it finds God drawing near in grace and love and mercy and kindness. Joy is your will's glad response of surrender and obedience as God stakes His claim upon your life. Joy is your mind's glad struggle to comprehend the wonder of who God is and the miracle of what He's doing in your life. Joy is your heart's fresh leaping after having been resuscitated from the long night of sin's death.

Joy is . . . well, I can't fully describe it, but I don't want to live without it. And please understand—the reticence is all on your side. God is longing to pour out His life within you. What are you waiting for?

1. Take some moments to write out a definition of joy.

   _____

   _____

2. How would you counsel a person seeking increased joy?

   _____

   _____

3. What is the relationship between joy and purity?

   _____

   _____

4. How is present joy tied to the past faithfulness of God?

   _____

   _____

5. What must change for you to be truly joyful?

   _____

   _____

6. How can sacrifice and joy be interdependent?

   _____

   _____

7. What would a fresh inflow of joy do for our witness to the unbelieving world?

   _____

   _____

15

A Creeping Compromise

I n the final analysis, what does revival really achieve? Is there any lasting benefit to our search for revival? What was the long-term result of the revival in Nehemiah's day?

The final three chapters of Nehemiah describe for us the results of revival. Revival produces a renewed desire to serve God (Neh. 11). It also produces a renewed joy in God (Neh. 12). Is that it? The final chapter of Nehemiah's memoirs reveals to us a third outcome. In this case it is not a necessary one but unfortunately a frequent one—compromise.

How does genuine revival give way to compromise? Time and inattention, usually. It is not unlike the state of the church in America. We began with a great move of God in people's hearts to establish a nation where we would be free to worship God. That vision carried us as a nation for many years, but as prosperity and relative ease set in, so did compromise. It is a pattern that is predictable on the individual level as well. God moves in a life. The person puts his or her trust in Jesus Christ. They are made new. They are filled with fervor for the Lord. But time passes and other affairs demand attention. Inattention to the things of God is barely noticeable amid the rush of prosperity and the ease of modern life. Before anyone notices, compromise has slipped under the sheets and seduced us away from God.

That is the sad picture we find as the book of Nehemiah

closes. As the book opened we discovered that when God wants to do a new thing among His people He generally finds one willing heart and breaks it. From that brokenness is born the revival that will spread from that one life to countless others. That was some twelve years before the events we find here in Nehemiah 13. In fact, all the events we've recounted in the first twelve chapters of Nehemiah took place over a decade prior to what we encounter here. Nehemiah had come, led the rebuilding of the city and the revival among the people, and then returned to his duties as a servant of the king of Persia just as he had originally promised he would do (Neh. 2:6). The events of Nehemiah 1–12 were probably compressed into that first year of Nehemiah's residence in Jerusalem. At some point he returned to Susa, the Persian capital, and again served the king. Eventually he received permission to return to Jerusalem (Neh. 13:6–7). What he found upon his return was both disappointing and infuriating.

The steps of obedience the people had committed themselves to during the height of the revival (Neh. 10) had long since been forgotten. The sins they had signed on the dotted line never to commit again had crept back into their lifestyles and had become their undoing. Sadly, the revival that had so boldly imprinted itself across their lives a decade earlier now faded into the washed-out colors of compromised religion.

We are reminded that no revival can guarantee its own continuance. The event of revival must become the life of obedience or the move of God means little. Say what you like at the altar, but it's what you do with your life after the service is over that proves the reality of your commitment. No revival can guarantee its own continuance. Only consistent, daily obedience can save us from the cancer of compromise.

No revival can guarantee its own continuance. The event of revival must become the life of obedience.

Take a few moments with me to discover the key areas where compromise most often appears.

For one, we must constantly guard against compromise in our *relationships*.

> On that day[1] the Book of Moses was read aloud in the hearing of the people and there it was found written that no Ammonite or Moabite should ever be admitted into the assembly of God, because they had not met the Israelites with food and water but had hired Balaam to call a curse down on them. (Our God, however, turned the curse into a blessing.) When the people heard this law, they excluded from Israel all who were of foreign descent. (vv. 1–3)

Compromise in relationships had long been a problem for God's people, as these historical reminders indicate. But just how does this signal a compromise in relationships? As they read God's Word "in the book of Moses" they probably happened upon Deuteronomy 23:3–6. There they were instructed that "no Ammonite or Moabite should ever be admitted into the assembly of God" (Neh. 13:1). Why? Because during the days of Balaam they had tried to seduce the people of God into compromise. They were a people bent on luring the people of God into compromise.

Now admittedly, this goes against the trend in our pluralistic society. "What do you mean, they can't worship with us? How narrow-minded and arrogant! Indeed, how hateful!" You can hear the objections even now: "We just all need to be more open! After all, we all worship the same God!"

No, we don't! The Ammonites worshiped a god called Molech, and a primary component of their worship was child sacrifice (Lev. 18:21; 2 Kings 23:10, 13). Similarly, the Moabites worshiped a god called Chemosh, and they too did so through the offering of their children in live sacrifice (Num. 21:29; 2 Kings 3:27). These were people who sacrificed their children in grisly, horrifying rituals to pagan deities!

Yet even there the grace of God reigned. If a Moabite or Ammonite came in repentance and faith in the one true God, he or she would be welcomed as any other follower of God. This we know from Scripture, for Ruth—through whose line would eventually come King David and ultimately the Christ—was from Moab. When she humbled herself and sought God, she was not only welcomed in the assembly as one of God's people but she became part of His redemptive purposes in the world. So this was not about ethnic exclusion, but about rampant compromise.

We face many of the same pressures today as the claims of pluralism are pressed upon us by a secular society. Compromise is venerated as the supreme virtue!

In their relationships the Jews had compromised God's Word, as well as God's holiness. Now Nehemiah recounts a specific example of such relational failure in his day.

> Before this, Eliashib the priest had been put in charge of the storerooms of the house of our God. He was closely associated with Tobiah, and he had provided him with a large room formerly used to store the grain offerings and incense and temple articles, and also the tithes of grain, new wine and oil prescribed for the Levites, singers and gatekeepers, as well as the contributions for the priests.
>
> But while all this was going on, I was not in Jerusalem, for in the thirty-second year of Artaxerxes king of Babylon I had returned to the king. Some time later I asked his permission and came back to Jerusalem. Here I learned about the evil thing Eliashib had done in providing Tobiah a room in the courts of the house of God. I was greatly displeased and threw all Tobiah's household goods out of the room. I gave orders to purify the rooms, and then I put back into them the equipment of the house of God, with the grain offerings and the incense. (vv. 4–9)

Tobiah had been one of Nehemiah's chief opponents throughout his ministry. Tobiah had opposed Nehemiah's ministry and despised his leadership (2:19). He had mocked the efforts of the people to do God's will (4:3). He joined with others to bring physical violence against the people (4:7–8) and then even plotted Nehemiah's assassination (6:1–4). And just as the Ammonites and Moabites of old had done through Balaam (Num. 22:1–11), Tobiah had hired a false prophet to utter a curse against Nehemiah (6:12).

Can you guess where Tobiah was from? Ammon. Throughout the book he is known as "Tobiah the Ammonite" (2:19). And look where he's been allowed to set up shop in Nehemiah's absence: smack in the middle of God's temple (13:4–5)!

What do you call such blatant compromise? Nehemiah chose the word "evil" (v. 7). Isn't it strange how that word is so hated in our society? For a brief moment following the terrorist attacks of September 11, 2001, the word "evil" was used by everyone from presidents to secular news media. But before long we retreated from its use; it seems far too narrow and self-righteous a word for informed, clear-headed people such as ourselves to use.

> WHAT WORD WOULD YOU USE TO DESCRIBE BLATANT COMPROMISE? NEHEMIAH CHOSE THE WORD "EVIL."

Yet here it is, on the lips of God's man for the hour. "This is evil!" And where is this evil found? In the house of God—the very place where God's presence was to dwell and they were to worship Him! Right there at the heart of everything that was set apart to God, evil had found a toehold.

We are to be, as Jesus was, a friend of sinners. We are to intentionally pursue those without Christ with open arms that we might win them to faith in Him. We are to build relationships with people, show them the love of Christ, and tell them of the hope of Christ. But when it comes to the truth of who God is, the truth of how we can know Him through Jesus Christ, the truth about what it means to worship Him, there can be no compromise.

We must, as did Nehemiah, address such compromise with a holy disgust. Nehemiah records, "I was greatly displeased" (v. 8a). That is an unfortunate translation that guts the original words of their power. More literally it means "It was very evil to me." Nehemiah was not "displeased" as if the whole matter were merely some kind of personal inconvenience. This was an affront to the holiness of God! When was the last time you were disgusted, not because something inconvenienced you personally but because it attacked the holiness of God? I wonder, could God trust His emotions to us?

Nehemiah also addressed the compromise of relationships with a holy housecleaning. He "threw all of Tobiah's household goods out of the room" (v. 8b). Can't you picture that! You can hear the murmurs rumbling through the streets, "Nehemiah's back! And he found out where Tobiah's been living." People began gathering in the temple courtyard, then moved into the temple and near the hallway and the room where Tobiah had been given a place. As the people drew closer they heard a muttering, angry voice: "Ahhhh! Tobiah, this Ammonite, I can't believe this!" Articles of clothing, furniture and personal belongings were flying out the door and slamming against the cold, stone surfaces of the hallway.

Then Nehemiah reports, "I gave orders to purify the rooms" (v. 9a). They spiritually fumigated the place. He had it ceremonially cleansed and rededicated to the purposes to which God set it apart in the first place. It was a room to hold all the grain offerings that people brought as worship to God to support those who served God. It was the place where they kept holy utensils that were for use in the worship of God.

Remember, on this side of the cross and empty tomb the temple is not a building, it's not a physical place where God alone dwells. In the New Testament era God dwells in His people. The body, mind, and life of every believer in Jesus Christ is the temple of the living God. We together collectively are also the dwelling of God. What would such a holy housecleaning look like in our "temple"?

The holy disgust and holy housecleaning were followed by a holy recommitment. Nehemiah returned to the rooms "the equipment of the house of God, with the grain offerings and the incense" (v. 9b). Is there any place among your relationships where you have violated the purposes of God for those relationships? Do you need to reestablish them as God's own possession, recommitting to honoring Him there?

Compromise does not confine itself to our relationships; it is often also found in our *stewardship*.

> I also learned that the portions assigned to the Levites had not been given to them, and that all the Levites and singers responsible for the service had gone back to their own fields. So I rebuked the officials and asked them, "Why is the house of God neglected?" Then I called them together and stationed them at their posts.
>
> All Judah brought the tithes of grain, new wine and oil into the storerooms. I put Shelemiah the priest, Zadok the scribe, and a Levite named Pedaiah in charge of the storerooms and made Hanan son of Zaccur, the son of Mattaniah, their assistant, because these men were considered trustworthy. They were made responsible for distributing the supplies to their brothers. (vv. 10–13)

Over time the people of God had quit giving. They ceased to believe that all they possessed was from God and to demonstrate that belief through returning a portion of their goods to God as He outlined in the Scriptures. In so doing they again compromised God's Word in order to fit their preferences. The books of Exodus, Leviticus and Deuteronomy all taught them that they were to give these offerings to God. They were to see that they owned nothing but were stewards of much. They were to reflect this understanding in their giving.

Under the Old Testament law they were to give ten percent of their income, what we call a tithe. On top of that they were to give another ten percent for special celebrations in Jerusalem (Deut. 12:5–6, 11, 18). Every three years God prescribed that another ten percent was to be given to care for the poor, a kind of a social security net for strangers, widows, orphans and others who were in need (Deut. 14:28–29). So in any given year God had told them to give approximately twenty-three percent of their income to Him. We must remember that in the Mosaic law God was not only establishing a worshiping community but a government for a nation.

We must be careful in our application of the old covenant instructions to life under the new covenant. Yet in the New Testament we are told to give proportionately (1 Cor. 16:2). It's not commanded that we tithe, but we are to give proportionately as God has blessed us. So, everyone wants to know, what's the proportion? God wants us to carefully consider what it meant to live under the old covenant and then what it means to live under the privileges and blessings of the new covenant in Christ, and then decide what the proportion should be. If, however, a worshiping Jew was to begin with ten percent, where should we begin? If we understand anything about the privileged place we have been given in the plan of God, how can we do less than one who lived under the old covenant?

Their failure in stewardship was not careless accounting or real-world mathematics. It was a compromise of God's Word which lead to a compromise of God's worship. Nehemiah had to ask, "Why is the house of God neglected?" (v. 11).

> *N*EHEMIAH SAID THE HOUSE OF GOD WAS "NEGLECTED." IT IS THE SAME WORD USED FOR APOSTASY.

The "house of God" was where they worshiped. They went to the temple to worship God. They "neglected" that place of worship. The word translated "neglected" is the one used to describe spiritual apostasy. By continuing to go to the temple to worship while they failed to appropriately include their money in that worship, God said they were turning their backs on Him. Their bodies were in the pews, but their hearts had long since left the sanctuary!

This also marked a compromise of their previous promise. In the height of the revival over a decade before they had signed a covenant saying that they would support the worship of God and its ministers (Neh. 10:32–39). They had promised, "We will not neglect the house of our God" (Neh. 10:39)! But over time they found something they loved more than they loved God. With the passage of years they found themselves more committed to a certain lifestyle than they were to God. Promises are easy to make at the altar during a revival, but are far more difficult to keep in our homes, our workplaces and our schools over the years.

To counteract the compromise Nehemiah demanded that the people return to what was right. They were to shun what seemed expedient and return to what was commanded. The right thing to do was to reestablish the regular worship of God. So Nehemiah put the worship leaders back in place and told them to get busy. He recalled the priests, Levites and temple servants (remember, they had left to make a living and support their families after God's people quit giving). No doubt some of the people objected, saying, "Okay, Nehemiah, you're right. We didn't keep our promise. But we can't just bring all the temple workers back. People aren't giving! We have no cash flow. We need to do an impact study. We need to set up a budget. We need to . . ."

No, what they needed to do was the right thing. They needed to start worshiping God and they needed the servants of God to lead them in doing that.

Once they reestablished the worship of God, look what happened: "All Judah brought the tithes of grain, new wine and oil into the storerooms." You do what's right, then call on the people of God to support it. And then make certain the resources are cared for with integrity and honesty (v. 13).

If compromise shows up in our relationships and stewardship, it's little wonder that it also shows up in our *business practices*.

> In those days I saw men in Judah treading winepresses on the Sabbath and bringing in grain and loading it on donkeys, together with wine, grapes, figs and all other kinds of loads. And they were bringing all this into Jerusalem on the Sabbath.

Therefore I warned them against selling food on that day. Men from Tyre who lived in Jerusalem were bringing in fish and all kinds of merchandise and selling them in Jerusalem on the Sabbath to the people of Judah. I rebuked the nobles of Judah and said to them, "What is this wicked thing you are doing—desecrating the Sabbath day? Didn't your forefathers do the same things, so that our God brought all this calamity upon us and upon this city? Now you are stirring up more wrath against Israel by desecrating the Sabbath."

When evening shadows fell on the gates of Jerusalem before the Sabbath, I ordered the doors to be shut and not opened until the Sabbath was over. I stationed some of my own men at the gates so that no load could be brought in on the Sabbath day. Once or twice the merchants and sellers of all kinds of goods spent the night outside Jerusalem. But I warned them and said, "Why do you spend the night by the wall? If you do this again, I will lay hands on you." From that time on they no longer came on the Sabbath. Then I commanded the Levites to purify themselves and go and guard the gates in order to keep the Sabbath day holy. (vv. 15–22)

They were compromising God's day by doing business on the Sabbath.

The Jewish Sabbath was and is Saturday. No amount of interpretational gymnastics will make it to be Sunday. The Church began early to worship on Sunday, the day Jesus was risen from the dead. Sunday became the day of Christian worship. The New Testament does not reiterate the specific Sabbath command to us, but it does, I believe, reaffirm the Sabbath principle to us. We need some time that belongs just to God. Every day is His day, but we need to set aside some time to concentrate on Him alone —as proof that we know He is Master of it all. Jesus declared that the Sabbath was created for the benefit of man (Mark 2:27). It should be a day of worship and service to God, as well as a day of refreshing and renewal—physically, emotionally, spiritually and mentally. To what extent any or all of the Old Testament stipulations of the Sabbath still apply this side of the cross is a matter beyond the scope of our present study. What is clear is that some things belong only to God. And for these people *that* had ceased to be true because of compromise in their business practices. Business became more important than their relationship to God and their obedience to His Word.

That is a pressure that you likely feel every day as you make your living and conduct yourself in the workplace.

Nehemiah called their failure "this wicked thing" (v. 17). The word means to defile, desecrate or pollute something. The sewage of covetousness had seeped into the pristine waters of what was to belong only to God. It is evil to take what belongs to God and use it for our own ends. Beyond our rationalizations our actions remain an attack on the holiness and uniqueness of God in our lives.

When it comes to business decisions, how do you determine what's off limits? What's too far? Where do you draw the line?

Nehemiah verbally rebuked those who had compromised (vv. 15, 17) and pressed home the far-ranging impact of such actions (v. 18). Then, with firm resolve, he called them to transform their business world. Note the powerful imperatives: "I ordered" (v. 19), "I stationed" (v. 19), "I warned" (v. 21), "I commanded" (v. 22). He warned "I will lay hands on you" (v. 21)!

Once we've compromised ourselves in our relationships, worship, and businesses, it's a safe bet *marriage* has been compromised as well:

> Moreover, in those days I saw men of Judah who had married women from Ashdod, Ammon and Moab. Half of their children spoke the language of Ashdod or the language of one of the other peoples, and did not know how to speak the language of Judah. (vv. 23–24)

A casual reader might ask, "So?" The answer surely lies partially in the fact that they were intermarrying with pagans who went as far as child sacrifice in their worship. But there is something even more than this here.

What language were the Scriptures written in? Hebrew. What language were their offspring now losing track of because it wasn't being spoken in their homes by their pagan mothers? The same.

Beyond all the spiritual implications of wedding paganism with the worship of the one true God, they were running the risk of cutting off the next generation from the revelation of God. They were setting their children up to receive truth only by hearsay and rumor. "God-talk" was becoming merely something only grandpa talked about. The Jewish faith was in danger of degenerating into a folk religion, passed on by mere oral tradition, not written revelation.

These coming generations were the ones through whom the Messiah was to come. Their failure in the present threatened to jeopardize God's redemptive program in the future.

> *I*F WE DO NOT HONOR *G*OD IN OUR MARRIAGES AND HOMES, WHAT WILL BECOME OF THE NEXT GENERATION?

If we do not honor God in our marriages and homes, taking sacrificial steps to see that the purposes and priorities of Christ are honored, what will become of the next generation? It may not be because they are unable to put their hands on an English Bible but because they won't ever pick one up after they hear our claims and watch our actions.

Nehemiah called such compromise "this terrible wickedness" and declared that such marital choices amounted to "being unfaithful to our God" (v. 27).

The New Testament tells us that marriage is to be a reflection of Jesus Christ and His relationship to the Church. You may object that you didn't volunteer to take on that responsibility, but you weren't asked your opinion. Marriage is God's invention—it is His gift to us. And if it is designed to reflect the relationship of Jesus Christ to the Church, there is a lot more at stake in decisions made about and within marriage than simply one's own pleasure, opinions, wishes and desires. Scripture says, "Marriage should be honored by all, and the marriage bed kept pure, for God will judge the adulterer and all the sexually immoral" (Heb. 13:4).

Our marriages are a matter of holiness. Sounds strange, doesn't it? It is about far more than happiness, companionship, love, and joy . . . it is a matter of holiness.

Don't miss Nehemiah's passion for holiness in marriage:

> I rebuked them and called curses down on them. I beat some of the men and pulled out their hair. I made them take an oath in God's name and said: "You are not to give your daughters in marriage to their sons, nor are you to take their daughters in marriage for your sons or for yourselves" (v. 25)

Shouldn't past experience teach us that messing with marriage doesn't pay? "Was it not because of marriages like these that Solomon king of Israel sinned? Among the many nations there was no king like him. He was loved by his God, and God made him king over all Israel, but even he was led into sin by foreign women" (v. 26).

Observe Nehemiah's ruthless obedience to God. "One of the sons of Joiada son of Eliashib the high priest was son-in-law to Sanballat the Horonite [one of Nehemiah's key enemies]. And I drove him away from me" (v. 28).

Don't you wonder what that looked like? Don't you wonder what people thought as Nehemiah ran down the streets, cursing and screaming at this guy? They'd already seen Nehemiah beat people and yank their beards out, and now he was chasing this guy right out the city gates and yelling, *"DON'T YOU EVER COME BACK!"*

That's strange to our ears! We don't want to duplicate these actions, but we do want to duplicate that sense of ruthless obedience. We want to apply it inwardly, not outwardly . . . and to ourselves first.

The appropriate response to the text is to turn inward and ask, "How ruthless am I toward myself when it comes to guarding my obedience to Christ?"

We play with sin. We toy with it. We tiptoe around its edges. We get a thrill out of seeing how close we can come. "It's okay. I haven't technically sinned. The Bible doesn't specifically say that you can't . . ."

"Put to death, therefore, whatever belongs to your earthly nature: sexual immorality, impurity, lust, evil desires and greed, which is idolatry" (Col. 3:5). Put it to death! Get the picture? It's ruthless, unrelenting, absolute! *Put it to death!* Don't play with it! That which we ought to slay, we've made our playmate. We need ruthless obedience to the will of God that grows out of a passion for holiness.

As this marvelous chronicle of revival draws to a close God reminds us that no revival can guarantee its own continuance. Only regular, daily obedience can save us from the cancer of compromise.

Don't you wish Nehemiah's story could have ended better?

Take courage. We are left with a glimmer of hope. It comes in the form of a simple, repeated prayer that is found every time compromise is identified and dealt with. Hear Nehemiah's heart: "Remember me for this, O my God" (v. 14). "Remember me for this also, O my God, and show mercy to me according to your great love" (v. 22). "Remember me with favor, O my God" (v. 31).

These are not wishes for a forgetful God to do better in the future. To "remember" means to act on someone's behalf by answering prayer, granting grace, bestowing strength or bringing deliverance. It is an expression of dependence. It is a window revealing a heart of active obedience, undergirded by and dependent upon the God who hears our prayers, sees our actions, knows our hearts, and who alone can grant the ability to rise above the cancer of compromise that nips at the heels of every servant of God.

That is our hope. *He* is our hope!

Have you noticed? We are right back at the place where revival began—humble brokenness. Once again, as in the beginning, when God wants to begin a new work of grace, He looks for one heart and breaks it.

Now again, after our drift and failure, God wants to bring us revival out of the rubble of our lives, marriages and churches. As in the beginning, He doesn't start by discarding the broken but by seeking them out. He is sifting through the rubble of broken relationships, addictive habits, hidden sins and divided churches, looking for people who are broken. They are the foundation stones of the altar upon which He will rekindle a blaze of revival. Broken people are God's most cherished resource in revival. Arthur Wallis well said, "Brokenness is not revival; it is a vital and indispensable step toward it."

In the end we find Nehemiah exactly where we found him in the beginning—broken before God. Does that discourage you? It shouldn't. Brokenness is not a sign of hopelessness but the breaking through of the brightest ray of hope! There was all the hope in the world that they could yet be what God wanted them to be . . . precisely because Nehemiah was still broken before the Lord.

There are some things that cannot be created but can only be broken into existence. Living in vital union with the living God through His Son Jesus Christ is one of them.

Reaching Toward Revival

1. Why is compromise held up as a virtue in our society? Why then does God warn us so passionately against it?

_____

_____

2. What responses are appropriate in our personal lives when we identify compromise? In our lives collectively?

_____

_____

3. Why does compromise so consistently evidence itself in our stewardship?

_____

_____

4. What pressures in your business life make compromise attractive right now?

_____

_____

5. Is compromise inevitable? Why?

_____

_____

6. Why must revival be tied to brokenness from first to last?

_____

_____

7. How is brokenness a ray of hope in the darkness of compromise?

_____

_____

Endnotes

Preface

1. Available online at www.barna.org.

Chapter 1: Becoming a Person of Influence

1. Eugene H. Peterson, *Run With The Horses* (Downers Grove, IL: Inter-Varsity, 1983), 25.
2. Ibid.

Chapter 2: Make It or Break It

1. Available online at www.stardestroyer.net/Creationism/Morality/CrimeAndDivorce.shtml
2. Available online at www.barna.org.
3. Charles Arn, *ASCG Journal of Church Growth*, Autumn 1996.
4. Available online at www.barna.org.
5. Ibid.
6. Derek Kidner, *Ezra and Nehemiah* (Downer's Grove, IL: InterVarsity, 1979), 79.
7. Edwin M. Yamauchi, "Nehemiah" in *The Expositor's Bible Commentary* (Grand Rapids, MI: Zondervan, 1988), 4:680.
8. Arthur Wallis, *In the Day of Thy Power* (Fort Washington, PA: CLC Publications, 1990), 111.

Chapter 4: I Don't Even Know Where to Begin!

1. Derek Kidner, *Ezra and Nehemiah* (Downers Grove, IL: InterVarsity, 1979), 83.

Chapter 5: Big Job, Little Time

1. Edwin M. Yamauchi, "Ezra-Nehemiah" in *The Expositor's Bible Commentary* (Grand Rapids, MI: Zondervan, 1988), 4:692.
2. Mervin Breneman, *Ezra, Nehemiah, Esther* (Nashville: Broadman and Holman, 1993), 184.
3. Quoted online at www.hopeglendora.org/pastor2309.html
4. Gene Getz, "Nehemiah" in *The Bible Knowledge Commentary* (Wheaton, IL: Victor Books, 1985), 1:678.

Chapter 6: When Opposition Mounts

1. Derek Kidner, *Ezra and Nehemiah* (Downers Grove, IL: InterVarsity, 1979), 90.
2. Edwin M. Yamauchi, "Ezra-Nehemiah" in *The Expositor's Bible Commentary* (Grand Rapids, MI: Zondervan, 1988), 4:703–704.
3. Ibid., 4:704.
4. S. D. Gordon, *Quiet Talks on Prayer* (Old Tappan, NJ: Fleming H. Revell, n.d.), 16.
5. A. W. Tozer, *The Knowledge of the Holy* (San Francisco: Harper and Row, 1961), 1.

Chapter 7: Flawed Foundations

1. Available online at www.rzim.org/publications/essay_arttext.php?id=13
2. Mervin Breneman, *Ezra, Nehemiah, Esther* (Nashville: Broadman and Holman, 1993), 202.
3. Edwin M. Yamauchi, "Ezra-Nehemiah" in *The Expositor's Bible Commentary* (Grand Rapids, MI: Zondervan, 1988), 4:711.
4. Erwin Lutzer, *Your Eternal Reward* (Chicago: Moody, 1998), 80.

Chapter 8: A Bull's-Eye on Your Back

1. Edward G. Dobson, Speed B. Leas, and Marshall Shelley, *Mastering Conflict and Controversy* (Portland, OR: Multnomah, 1992), 175.
2. Kenneth C. Haugk, *Antagonists in the Church* (Minneapolis: Augsburg, 1988), 20–21.
3. Amy Carmichael, *Mountain Breezes* (Fort Washington, PA: CLC Publications, 1999), 173.
4. J. Oswald Sanders, *Spiritual Leadership* (Chicago: Moody, 1967), 112.
5. Larry J. Michael, "Responding to Personal Attacks," available online at www.churchcentral.com/nw/template/Article.html/id/16051.
6. Derek Kidner, *Ezra and Nehemiah* (Downers Grove, IL: InterVarsity, 1979), 100.
7. Winston Churchill, speech to the House of Commons, May 13, 1940.

Chapter 9: We've Got It All—But Something's Missing

1. Message delivered to The Christian and Missionary Alliance General Council, Columbus, Ohio, May 2001.

Chapter 10: The Power of God's Word

1. David L. Larsen, *The Company of the Preachers* (Grand Rapids, MI: Kregel Publications, 1998), 376.
2. John Piper, *Desiring God* (Sisters, OR: Multnomah, 1986), 65–66.

Chapter 11: It's My Fault!

1. In the New International Version.
2. "Gotta Serve Somebody," by Bob Dylan, 1979, Special Rider Music, Columbia Records.

Chapter 12: I The Undersigned Hereby . . .

1. J. Oswald Sanders, *Enjoying Intimacy With God* (Grand Rapids, MI: Discovery House, 2000), 137–138.

Chapter 13: To Obscurity—and Beyond!

1. George Duncan, *Marks of Christian Maturity* (London: Marshall Pickering, 1986), 145–146.
2. Ibid.
3. Ben Patterson, *Serving God: The Grand Essentials of Work and Worship* (Downers Grove, IL: InterVarsity, 1994), 76.

Chapter 14: Joy in the Lord

1. John Piper, *Desiring God: Meditations of a Christian Hedonist* (Sisters, OR: Multnomah, 1986) and *The Pleasures of God: Meditations on God's Delight in Being God* (Sisters, OR: Multnomah, 2000).
2. Derek Kidner, *Ezra and Nehemiah* (Downers Grove, IL: InterVarsity, 1979), 126.
3. J. Oswald Sanders, *Enjoying Intimacy With God* (Grand Rapids, MI: Discovery House, 2000), 139.
4. Quoted in John Piper, *Desiring God: Meditations of a Christian Hedonist* (Sisters, OR: Multnomah, 1986), 201–202 (emphasis added).
5. Quoted in Philip Yancey, *What's So Amazing About Grace?* (Grand Rapids, MI: Zondervan, 1997), 29.

Chapter 15: A Creeping Compromise

1. "On that day" refers not to the day on which the events of Nehemiah 12 transpired but to the time when Nehemiah had returned to Jerusalem after a period of time in Persia. The phrase points forward to the day described in the ensuing verses, not backward to the day already described in the previous chapter.

This book was produced by CLC Publications. We hope it has been life-changing and has given you a fresh experience of God through the work of the Holy Spirit. CLC Publications is an outreach of CLC International, a global literature mission with work in over 50 countries. If you would like to know more about us or are interested in opportunities to serve with a faith mission, we invite you to contact us at:

CLC Ministries International
P.O. Box 1449
Fort Washington, PA 19034

Phone: (215) 542-1242
E-mail: clcmail@clcusa.org
www.clcusa.org

DO YOU LOVE GOOD CHRISTIAN BOOKS?
Do you have a heart for worldwide missions?

You can receive a free subscription to:

Floodtide

CLC's magazine on global literature missions

Order by e-mail at:
floodtide@clcusa.org

or fill in the coupon below and mail to:

CLC Ministries International
P.O. Box 1449
Fort Washington, PA 19034

FREE FLOODTIDE SUBSCRIPTION!

Name _____

Address _____

City, State, Zip_____

READ THE REMARKABLE STORY OF
the founding of
CLC INTERNATIONAL

"Any who doubt that Elijah's God still lives ought to read of the money supplied when needed, the stores and houses provided, and the appearance of personnel in answer to prayer."
—Moody Monthly

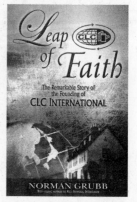

Is it possible that the printing press, the editor's desk, the Christian bookstore and the mail-order department can glow with the fast-moving drama of an "Acts of the Apostles"?

Find out, as you are carried from two people in an upstairs bookroom to a worldwide chain of Christian bookcenters and publishing, multiplied by only a "shoestring" of faith and committed, though unlikely, lives.

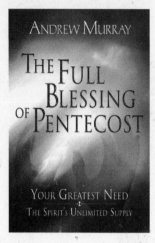

The Full Blessing of Pentecost

Andrew Murray

We believe it—
we preach it—
we strive for it—
BUT . . .

. . . still for many, the kind of free-flowing life in the fullness of the Spirit is more of a dream than a reality.

Andrew Murray skillfully identifies the defects in faith that prevent the life-giving flow, and guides us to the Spirit's full blessing.

"Only as we understand that believing in Him means a yielding up of the whole heart and life and will, to let Him live and rule within us, can we confidently count upon receiving all that we need of the Holy Spirit's power and presence," Murray says. "When Christ becomes to us all that God has made Him to be, then the Holy Spirit can flow from Him and do His blessed work of leading us back to know Him better, and to believe in Him more completely."

Let **The Full Blessing of Pentecost** lead you to the well of living water you've been longing for.

ISBN 0-87508-785-X

Continuous Revival

Norman Grubb

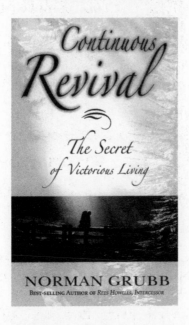

You can be a channel of revival!

Revival is within reach of everyday people and can be experienced in your heart, home, and church. Follow the author and witness the effect on his life of the brokenness and ongoing personal revival he found through his exposure to the Revival Movement in Rwanda, Africa, in 1950.

Learn the working secret which brought continuous revival to thousands over a period of sixteen years. Not mere theory, but personal experience!

Read this book and let the Reviver do His work in you.

Mass Market ISBN 0-87508-352-8

The Awakening in Wales

Jessie Penn-Lewis

A clear and unvarnished record of the facts concerning the remarkable outpouring of God's Spirit in Wales at the time of the 1903–1905 revival, showing the central place given to the cross of Christ in that divine visitation.

Mass Market ISBN 0-87508-937-2

Enjoy Your Journey

Dr. Alyn E. Waller

Join Pastor Alyn Waller as he follows in the footsteps of Moses and the children of Israel, in the journey of growth we all must take—an exodus from sin and selfishness to the promised land of a deeper relationship with God. Learn how to move ahead with purpose—how to *enjoy your journey*.

Hardcover ISBN 0-87508-824-4